·Successful Catering·

THIRD EDITION

Successful

Catering

THIRD EDITION

Bernard Splaver

EDITED BY

William N. Reynolds

Michael Roman

JOHN WILEY & SONS, INC.

New York   Chichester   Weinheim   Brisbane   Singapore   Toronto

98 99 10

Library of Congress Cataloging-in-Publication Data

Splaver, Bernard R.
   Successful catering / Bernard Splaver; edited by William N. Reynolds and
Michael Roman.—3rd ed.
       p.   cm.
   Includes index.
   ISBN 0-471-28925-6
   1. Caterers and catering. I. Reynolds, William N. II. Roman, Michael. III.
Title.
TX921.S64   1991
642'.4—dc20
                                                        90-43547
                                                          CIP

Dedication

To today's caterers, who accept the challenge
of providing outstanding food and service for their client's
most important and cherished celebrations.

Contents

Foreword

The key to successful catering in today's market is actually a combination of many important components. In addition to basic business skills and a strong culinary background, caterers must have a knowledge of wines and spirits and table service, a keen desire to please the people they serve, and the organizational ability to master the complexities of the business.

Bill Reynolds and Michael Roman bring a combined 48 years of experience as hospitality professionals and educators to the revision of Bernard Splaver's classic work on catering. The book addresses the myriad considerations facing today's caterer, from menu development, current health and sanitation requirements, and the need for precise timing, whether working on or off premises, to choosing appropriate equipment, understanding traditions and customs of entertaining and proper serving techniques, and developing a feel for style.

Mr. Reynolds and Mr. Roman have responded to the many changes in the hospitality industry, particularly in the fast-growing catering segment, that have occurred since *Successful Catering* was first published. Like its predecessor, this edition provides sound guidelines for all types of catering, while adding pertinent information to keep today's caterers up-to-date and prepared to meet the challenges of the future.

Ferdinand E. Metz
President, The Culinary Institute of America

Acknowledgments

The co-editors gratefully express their appreciation to the following people, who helped us update this book:

Lyde Buchtenkirch-Biscardi   Rabbi Dr. Joshua Shuchatowitz
John Canner   Brian Smith
John Grubell   Lorna Smith
Carol McDonald   Rich Vergili
Rose Occhialino   Mac Winker
Bernice Phillips

and to the many helpful and supportive members of the staff and faculty of The Culinary Institute of America.

Chapter 10 was edited by Rabbi Dr. Joshua Shuchatowitz, President of Planning Resources, Inc., and a recognized authority on planning kosher events and implementing kosher food operations. He is a noted author, university lecturer, and consultant for kosher food service, and was formerly Director of Management Services for the Orthodox Union, the world's largest kosher supervision service.

He has worked with hotels, caterers, party planners, and organizations nationwide in executing every phase of strictly kosher events where culinary creativity and presentation are matched only by the highest kashruth standards.

Rabbi Shuchatowitz received his ordination from Yeshiva University and also holds advanced degrees in Judaica and a Ph.D. in the sciences.

·1·

Getting Started

Going into business for yourself is not a move to be taken lightly. Going into the business of catering is a total commitment to the art of providing outstanding food, beverages, and service to clients for social and business events. The highly specialized skills and level of professionalism needed in a catering business are unlike those required in any other form of foodservice.

To be successful you need a mastery of the three main elements of catering:

1. Selling your services successfully in a competitive marketplace.
2. Producing outstanding food and beverages profitably.
3. Presenting and serving your food safely and with style.

In this demanding business, most caterers quickly learn that their reputations and business futures depend greatly on the quality of their last performance. It is precisely these initial "performances" that will make or break your new business, since your success will depend largely on how your first clients, and their guests, view your work. If you do an outstanding job, then your business will grow because some guests at the event will hire you later to cater their own affairs. By doing great catering from the start you will be demonstrating your abilities to possibly hundreds of people who haven't yet heard of your company. In other words, a caterer's performance is one of the best forms of business advertising—word of mouth.

Catering cannot be considered a hobby; it is a business as real as any other professional endeavor. Great responsibility is placed on the shoulders of caterers, but personal and financial rewards await those who promise and deliver outstanding service.

Two important factors to be considered if you are contemplating entering this business are your personal qualifications and skills, and the type and number of caterers already in your area. It would be foolhardy to incur the expense of

FACTS ABOUT PROFIT POTENTIAL

- Profit margins in catering operations relate to the size of the business and how well the sales and production personnel are managed.
- A $100,000 operation should achieve a 15 to 30 percent bottom line profit before taxes. An $800,000 operation should achieve a 10 to 20 percent bottom line profit before taxes.
- A restaurant doing a million dollars in sales can earn an additional $200,000 in the first year if it adds a catering operation.
- Because of word of mouth and referrals, most caterers double their first year's gross sales in the next year, then it slows down.
- Building accounts rather than sales is the secret of increased profitability.
- Increased volume is not always a monetary advantage.

SOURCE: The National Institute for Off-Premises Catering, Chicago, IL.

establishing a commissary—a place where food is prepared, stored, and delivered—or equipping a kitchen without making a thorough and objective analysis of the community's need for your services. Otherwise, you could end up making a worthless investment of time and money.

EVALUATING YOUR QUALIFICATIONS

A self-evaluation can help you determine if you are qualified and sufficiently prepared to meet the heavy demands of the catering business. These questions are not meant to scare or dishearten you, but rather to make you aware of the business realities.

1. *Basic Foundation*

    Do you have a basic knowledge of food and beverages?

    Do you know how to get full value from the food you purchase or prepare?

    Do you have direct and alternative sources of supplies?

    Can you attractively display your foods so as to distinguish your work from other caterers?

    Are you knowledgeable and up to date about your community's regulations and laws regarding catering?

2. *Service*

    Are you familiar with various styles and forms of serving foods?

    Are you familiar with the serving of alcoholic beverages?

    Will you be able to hire and direct a team of serving staff?

    Will you be able to hire additional part-time staff to get you through the busy seasons?

    Can you serve a sit-down dinner to small or large groups of people while keeping the food hot?

    How knowledgeable and adept are you with American, French and Russian table service?

    Can you produce a clambake, barbecue, or picnic for 500 or more people?

3. *Food Preparation*

    Can you personally cook the foods you wish to feature?

    Will you need to rely on other professionals to cook for you? If so, could you replace any of these professionals if needed?

    Are you familiar with all the food products available to the foodservice industry?

    Can you prepare a budget, classical, or expensive buffet?

4. *Creative Talent*

    What aesthetic and artistic abilities do you possess?

Can you arrange and garnish foods attractively for full-service or self-service buffets or plated dinners?

Can you drape tables and make linens and skirting look special?

Do you understand the correct use of colors?

Can you arrange flowers?

Can you make fruit, vegetable, tallow, or ice carvings?

5. *Business Abilities*

Do you have a basic understanding of business accounting and mathematics?

Do you know how to check invoices, figure discounts, determine the proper food cost, set prices, compute correct food amounts, and track profits and losses?

Can you calculate wages, taxes, inventories, and reconcile bank statements?

Will you be able to determine the correct number of servers needed for each event and maintain control of your cost/profit ratio?

6. *Employee Relations*

Will you be able to establish and maintain good working relations with your employees while maintaining authority and control?

Can you keep your friendships with your staff separate from your need to control and manage?

7. *Equipment*

Are you familiar with foodservice equipment and its operation and maintenance?

Can you make simple repairs such as replace a worn compressor belt or washer, unplug a clogged drain, or fix a frayed electrical cord?

Do you know the proper safety precautions when working with electric and gas cooking equipment?

8. *Salesmanship*

Are you a confident person in front of groups?

Are you good with people?

Will you be able to become a servant to other people's wishes, fantasies, and wants?

Can you live by the concept that the customer is always right?

9. *Social Awareness*

Do you understand the principles of social and corporate protocol and etiquette?

Will you be able to advise your clients on how to plan major events such as weddings, cocktail parties, bar mitzvahs, and grand openings?

Could you sensitively make the arrangements for a reception following a funeral?

Do you have a general understanding of the social customs of the religious and ethnic groups in your market area?

Do you understand the dietary restrictions of some people because of religious or medical reasons?

Do you have a comprehensive library of books on cooking, food presentation, and table settings that will help you present your ideas?

10. *Emotional Stamina*

Are you by nature a level-headed individual?

Can you recognize crises and take charge of emergency situations?

Could you handle a sudden guest illness, guest misbehavior, the collapse of a dining table, or food spill? How well could you help a guest who is choking, extinguish a fire, or treat a burn?

11. *Physical Stamina*

Will you be able to handle the physical demands and time commitment required in catering?

Can you move furniture, carry tables up stairs, and lift heavy objects and still keep smiling?

Can you work 60 to 80 hours each week?

Will your family or personal life be negatively affected?

Are you able to renew your energy quickly?

Do you have a sense of humor?
12. *Financial Resources*

Do you have the money necessary to enter catering?

Can you build or rent a kitchen?

Do you have enough money to sustain yourself until you start making a profit?

Can you pay for your insurance and licensing?

Will you be able to pay employment taxes or sales taxes on schedule?

ANALYZING THE CATERING POTENTIAL IN YOUR COMMUNITY

After evaluating your personal qualifications, the next step is to survey the catering potential in the area you wish to service. A careful analysis will help you develop insights into your potential customer base as well as knowledge of the market's economy. Data can be gathered from several sources.

Check with the local Bureau of Vital Statistics or Bureau of Records for the number of marriages, births, and deaths in your community. This can indicate the number of weddings, baby showers, and funerals that you might be able to cater. Talk with the Better Business Bureau and ask what the trend has been in your area's economic growth.

Visit the offices of your area's clubs, churches, and temples and ask how many catered events in the last year have taken place in their function rooms. Check with fraternal organizations such as the American Legion, Veterans of Foreign Wars, Knights of Columbus, Masonic Lodges, and Elks for the same information. (Look in the Yellow Pages under Clubs and Associations for additional sources.)

Local Chambers of Commerce will gladly furnish valuable statistical data to help you forecast your area's business potential. Consult with the nearest office of the Small Business Administration and make an appointment with a member of the Service Corps of Retired Executives (SCORE). This service is free and available throughout the nation.

SELECTING THE TYPE OF CATERING YOU WISH TO OFFER

After appraising your personal qualifications and the catering potential within your market area, you must next decide what type of catering you will offer—whether you wish to do on-premises catering or off-premises catering, or perhaps a little of each.

On-Premises Catering

In on-premises catering, all the food preparation and serving is done in a facility that is owned, leased, or rented by the caterer. This type of catering is often referred to as "banquet" or "hall" catering. On-premises catering is dominated by the hotel and motel industry along with the thousands of free-standing privately owned banquet halls.

On-premises catering is a difficult and competitive business that requires excellent selling skills to convince potential clients why they should pick you over another.

Off-Premises Catering

In off-premises catering, the food is prepared in a licensed commissary, transported to a location selected by the client, and served often without the support of an available kitchen. Off-premises catering can be very difficult since many of the sites clients select—such as open fields, building lobbies, museums, warehouses, public streets, and tents—were never designed to be places for serving a large number of guests.

Many of these locations are very attractive places to hold parties or special events, but they invariably lack sufficient electrical power, water, or working space. These conditions can challenge a caterer's creativity and practical ability to provide a memorable and impressive occasion for the client while ensuring that all food and service safety standards are met.

Advantages and Disadvantages

It is not uncommon for on-premises caterers to eventually offer off-premises services, or for off-premises caterers to seek a permanent location. These two businesses, however, are totally different and each has unique advantages and disadvantages.

For example, on-premises caterers have a complete kitchen just steps away from the guests, whereas caterers cooking in off-premises locations are usually faced with a make-do situation. On the other hand, the off-premises caterers can service as many events as they can manage on a particular day since they are not limited to catering in one location, whereas the activities of on-premises caterers are governed by the space they have available. Additionally, because of space and location constraints, on-premises caterers are usually limited to traditional buffet and plate-service catering, whereas off-premises caterers can do outdoor events such as picnics, barbecues and fairs.

ESTABLISHING YOUR BUSINESS

Once you have found your niche and you've selected the type of catering you wish to offer, it becomes necessary to get the word out that you are open for business. This brings up a very important question . . . Who are you? What is the name of your company?

Selecting a Name

The name of your business can be an important selling tool. It can describe your services, as in "The Picnic People" or "The Movable Feast"; it can describe your food, such as "Country Classic Fine Foods" or "Glorious Food"; or it may simply represent the personal touch of your own name—for example, "Jones' Home Cooking" or "Catering by Claudette." Sensational names like "More Than a Mouthful" or "The Full Belli Deli Caterers" can also be successful in forming a lasting impression in the prospective client's mind. Whether you choose a name that describes your services, your food, your image, or a name that is simply your own, it is an important way to identify who you are to your clients.

Getting Your Name Out

Civic, fraternal, social, corporate, and religious organizations usually have program committees or chairpersons who are responsible for planning interesting presentations for their meetings, often as fund-raisers or to increase attendance. To get yourself known, you might arrange to appear at one of these meetings and demonstrate some interesting cooking techniques or cuisines, or discuss the "ins and outs" of catering. As an additional inducement, you could offer to prepare complimentary appetizers for those who attend.

Get business cards printed and distribute them to everyone you know and meet. Remind your friends and relatives that you are now in the catering business.

Place simple ads in community newspapers; these need not be expensive. Inquire about the rates for placing an ad in the Yellow Pages. Print a flier that describes your services, and distribute it everywhere.

Other Resources

Contact local business people who provide services related to social functions. Bridal shops, florists, photographers, orchestras, and printers may be willing to supply leads for prospective customers. This, of course, is a two-way street; you must be prepared to reciprocate by providing them with leads.

Call other caterers or party rental dealers to ask if there are organizations for caterers or other foodservice professionals in your area. Check with junior colleges and other educational sources to see if they offer classes on catering or courses on food preparation, sanitation, and styles of service.

Read the society pages of newspapers for engagement announcements. Then write a note of best wishes and congratulations to the young lady or call her. Describe your facilities and offer your expert help with her future plans. Stress that there is no obligation attached to a consultation. Be sincere in your offer of help; regardless of whether or not it is accepted, you will gain immeasurable goodwill.

From newspapers you can also learn about upcoming plans for testimonials, special luncheons, reunions, bowling banquets, fraternity gatherings, or fund-raising affairs. Since many of these articles deal with future events, plans may not be finalized and the options are wide open. It could be advantageous to contact the person mentioned in the news item and promote your services.

If your local newspaper has a food editor, try to arrange an interview to discuss your special abilities. You might submit a favorite recipe or even become the subject of a feature story.

Community Involvement

Society affiliations, participation in civic affairs, serving on committees, involvement in popular causes, and even limited and nonpartisan political activities can be valuable in generating reciprocal benefits. An association with Red Cross or Civil Defense to offer your expertise in times of emergency will serve a twofold purpose—it will fulfill the obligation of a sincere, concerned cit-izen and will result in favorable publicity that could enhance your image.

Learn a lesson from the large multinational companies that insist their local representatives become civically involved so as to keep their name projected favorably.

Above all, talk with people who can help you, such as the food editors of newspapers or the event coordinators for your city or state governments. Look in the Yellow Pages under receptions, convention planning, fund-raising services, function rooms, and party planning services and call them all—what have you got to lose? Remember, all of the great caterers were once small and struggling. To be successful requires hard work, great timing, support from other people, and a little luck.

GETTING THE RIGHT GUIDANCE

The operation of any business, including catering, involves the rights of buyers and sellers, landlords and tenants, creditors and debtors, and employers and employees. The laws of doing business are many, complicated, and continually changing. Therefore, unless you are thoroughly familiar with the ins and outs of running a business, you may need a specialist to guide you. A wise move before starting is to seek the advice of a lawyer, accountant, insurance agent, and business consultant, preferably ones who have already assisted other caterers or foodservice operators with their businesses.

Legal Considerations

When to Use a Lawyer
A lawyer provides four basic services—checking, advising, guiding, and representing. Legal services should not be sought only for emergencies. Emergencies can be avoided if legal counsel is consulted in the first place.

Legal services are particularly desirable in business organization, property acquisition, money borrowing, tax planning, employer-employee relations, litigation, credit problems, and securing the proper licenses and permits from regulatory bodies and other government agencies.

A lawyer can advise as to whether the business should be formed under sole ownership or as a partnership or corporation. For example, under sole proprietorship, losses incurred in the start-up years could be used to offset other income. As the business grows and profits increase, the owner could decide to incorporate, or to obtain a tax advantage by selling shares in the business to the public. At the same time, this would reduce any personal liability for possible business losses. As management responsibilities increase, a partnership could ease the personal load. Legal contracts would then be drawn as to the responsibilities of each partner and the sharing of profits. Consult your attorney regarding federal and state laws on wages, employees' hours, workmen's compensation, unemployment compensation, and any applicable fair employment legislation.

Zoning

Your physical plant, whether an on-premises or off-premises catering facility, is subject to proper clearances from the local zoning board. Since local requirements and the classifications assigned to catering establishments differ, have your attorney look into these ordinances.

Local ordinances may impose restrictions on where you can locate your business. They may also require provisions for employee and guest parking, or restrict truck storage and/or truck parking. They may prohibit any sort of business activity on Sundays or holidays, or prohibit truck traffic within specified hours (say, between 11 PM and 7 AM), thus severely restricting delivery or loading. This could be a crippling blow to your schedule.

Garbage collection may also be covered by local ordinances. For example, if outside garbage collection areas are prohibited, you may have to develop an alternate plan, probably refrigerating your garbage. These ordinances should not be taken lightly nor circumvented. Even if the local authority is lax, there is certain to be a civic or ecological group that will bring pressure to have these ordinances enforced. Your attorney should instruct you thoroughly regarding all ordinances so that you can comply with them. Failure to do so can impair your reputation and lead to expensive litigation.

Licensing

After meeting zoning specifications, you must then secure the necessary licenses, particularly the license of your local board of health. A board of health license is mandatory. Without it, you will not be permitted to operate or offer your services to the public. Local boards vary as to how they classify a catering business. Your establishment might be considered a commissary, a restaurant, or a food-processing plant. However, determining the proper type of license to apply for should be a carefully considered decision and one made with an eye to the future. Select a license that will permit flexibility, allow for business growth, and provide broader privileges, such as retailing. This will allow prepared food to be sold for off-premises consumption, or baked merchandise to be sold either at the wholesale or retail level. Some states require a special license if milk or other dairy products are kept on the premises, either for on-premises consumption or for the preparation of food. The small additional fee incurred at the outset is well worth the expense—it can eliminate the time-consuming red tape and even greater cost of applying for a different or auxiliary license at a later date.

During the same period, you will be contacted by other municipal officials to make certain that you meet additional requirements.

Consequently, fire, building, plumbing, and electrical inspectors will visit to check required safety precautions. It is not necessary to contact these inspectors as they will be notified by the zoning board.

Accounting

It is also essential to hire an accountant. In addition to obtaining your state sales tax and Internal Revenue identification numbers, the accountant can set up, organize, and properly maintain your financial records, making certain that they fully comply with all government regulations and laws, and can pass regular and unannounced inspections by local, state, or federal auditors.

Although the services of a professional accountant (as well as an attorney) are usually expensive, they are a wise investment. The accountant who is expert in business/financial matters will ensure that you take advantage of all tax and business deductions to which you are entitled and thus avoid paying unnecessary taxes.

In addition to completing all necessary tax forms or helping you with them, an accountant will immediately recognize the danger signals of overrides or underrides on all expenditures, and help you institute the necessary controls to keep them within the prescribed ratios.

Essential Insurance

Some insurance coverage is essential; other types are desirable, but optional. There are also coverages for employee benefits. Check all your requirements with an insurance agent. For detailed insurance information, contact your local Small Business Administration office and ask for Small Marketer Aid #148.

First, you must recognize the risks to which you will be exposed. Follow the guides for buying insurance economically and seek professional advice. Used correctly, it can contribute to your success by reducing the uncertainties under

which you operate. Insurance premiums are the price paid for freedom from worry about economic losses from conditions outside your control. Insurance can improve your bank credit since it keeps your business going when an insured peril interrupts operation. The potential benefits of a good insurance program should not be overlooked.

There are five kinds of essential insurance: fire, liability, automobile, workers' compensation, and products insurance.

Fire Insurance

Basic fire insurance can be extended to cover additional perils, such as windstorm, hail, smoke, explosion, vandalism, and malicious mischief, at a small additional cost. Comprehensive coverage on all policies is suggested as it includes all-risk contracts that offer the broadest available coverage for the money. Special protection, other than a standard fire insurance policy, is needed to cover the loss by fire of accounts, bills, currency, deeds, evidence of sales, money, and securities.

Liability Insurance

Due to the abnormally high settlements made by juries in liability cases, it is advisable to secure the maximum your business will permit. Most liability policies, in addition to covering bodily injuries, now cover personal injuries such as libel and slander, if these are specifically insured. Note that because off-premises caterers always work in other people's property and in their care, they may be held responsible for fire and general liability unless the caterer's policy specifically mentions that they are covered by fire legal liability insurance.

Automobile Insurance

Five or more automobiles under one ownership, operated as a fleet for business purposes, can generally be insured under a low-cost fleet policy.

This covers both material damage to your vehicle and liability to others for property damage or personal injury. The higher the deductibles, which are available in any amount, the greater reduction there can be on premiums.

Most states require liability insurance or proof of financial responsibility. You may also be able to purchase uninsured motorist protection to cover your own bodily injury claims from someone who has no insurance, even if your state does not have "no fault" insurance. Personal property stored in an automobile and not attached to it (merchandise being delivered) is not covered under an automobile policy.

Be aware that when an employee uses his or her own car on your behalf, you could be legally liable, even if you don't own a car or truck yourself.

Workers' Compensation Insurance

Common law requires that an employer: (1) provide employees a safe place to work, (2) hire competent fellow employees, (3) provide safe tools, and (4) warn employees of an existing danger. If the employer fails to provide the above, under both common law and workers' compensation laws, he is liable for damage suits brought by an employee. Not all employees are covered by workers' compensation laws; the laws vary from state to state.

Products Insurance

Do not attempt to operate your business unless you are fully covered by products insurance. This will protect you if, for instance, a foreign object is found in your food or contaminated foods processed by you cause illness. Also, if a foreign object is found in foods processed by someone else, but served by you, you could still be sued. However, if you are covered by products insurance, your insurance carrier will protect you and perhaps take action against the manufacturer of the product.

Optional Coverages

Although not absolutely essential, coverages such as business interruption insurance, crime insurance, glass insurance, and rent insurance can add greatly to the security of your business.

Business interruption insurance covers fixed expenses that would continue if a fire, for example, shut down your business. These expenses include salaries to key employees, taxes, interest, and utilities, as well as lost profits. This type of policy can also provide payments for costs incurred in reopening your business after a fire or other insured peril. Moreover, it can indemnify you if your business is suspended because of failure or interruption of the supply of power, light, heat, gas, or water furnished by a public utility company.

Crime insurance policies will pay only if there are visible marks of forced entry. These policies will also pay for loss of property or equipment due to force or violence on or off the premises. This insurance is particularly important for off-premises caterers.

Employee Benefit Coverages

Insurance coverages can be used to provide health insurance, group life insurance, group health insurance, disability insurance, and retirement insurance.

Emphasis has been made on insurance in this chapter because of the reality of the many risks connected with social catering. Wishful thinking or an "It can't happen to me" attitude won't lessen or remove the possibility that a ruinous misfortune may strike. Before purchasing any insurance, decide what perils to insure against and how much loss you might suffer from each. Cover your largest loss exposure first. Use as high a deductible as you can afford. Seek professional help and review your insurance program periodically to prevent duplication. Investigate package plans that might give you adequate protection at a more reasonable rate.

·2·

On-Premises Catering

In the future, many areas will be running out of good locations to hold the increasing numbers of catered events, prompting caterers to build or rent new on-premises facilities to accommodate the demand. Even restaurants and hotels, which have banquet rooms, are experiencing the need for more rentable party space. Now, more than ever, is the time to offer the public new places to hold their events. Even during a sluggish economy, there are always clients for weddings, bar mitzvahs, Christmas parties, and other special events.

On-premises catering is also a good way for restaurants to make use of those resources, such as building maintenance, lighting and heat, and staff, that must be maintained even during the "down" seasons. Slow periods can be taken advantage of by promoting events other than social functions, such as business seminars and corporate meetings.

PROMOTING ON-PREMISES CATERING AS AN ADDITIONAL SERVICE

There are many ways to inform people of your catering services. To start, you might attach clip-ons to the regular daily menus explaining that your facility is available for wedding breakfasts, bridge parties, sales meetings, service and fraternal club banquets, and so forth. "Tents" (miniature "signboards" folded into a triangle, making a standup A-frame) at each table can elaborate on your on-premises catering or cite special prices. You can also have professionally lettered placards made and posted in prominent positions. If space is at a premium, remove signs installed by cigarette and beverage salesmen and put up your own signs advertising your services.

If you use floor stanchions to control traffic while guests wait to be seated, use them as a message board to display pictures of your buffet presentations or of a fully set guest table for a catered party. A handsomely decorated wedding or birthday cake (with dummy layers) placed in a visible location can be worth a hundred words.

Another possibility is to have an extra panel made for your outdoor sign. The message should contain strong, positive adjectives or a descriptive phrase, not just the single word "catering." Examples include Distinctive On-Premises Catering, Unexcelled Catering Facilities, Attractive Rates for Catering, Celebrate Your Next Happy Occasion with Us, or Ask About Special Rates.

FREE-STANDING BANQUET HALLS

Because the initial costs of building or renting and equipping a facility can be steep, most on-premises caterers were successful off-premises caterers before they expanded their services and moved into their own banquet halls. A banquet-hall caterer can offer the same services as a restaurant and hotel catering department. In addition to a commissary or kitchen, the facilities must include at least one large, tastefully decorated, air-conditioned room, often containing a stage or raised dais, with perhaps several smaller rooms suitable for bridal showers, club and business luncheons, and other such functions.

FUNCTION ROOM FURNITURE

The equipment used for public functions held in hotels, restaurants, banquet halls, and clubs is known collectively as function room furniture. As these operations are host to business functions and community and social events, the furniture must be structurally sound to withstand

mishandling and abuse, and at the same time be aesthetically pleasing.

Function room furniture should meet the following criteria:

Strength and durability. The use of household-grade furniture in a commercial establishment is foolhardy and can lead to disastrous incidents. Furnishings should be rugged enough to withstand transport from one area to another, and be sturdy enough to be pushed, rolled, set up, knocked down, stacked, and stored without damage. The roughest handling should still leave the equipment relatively unscathed and totally functional.

Ease of handling. The equipment must be easy to move and arrange, and not be too heavy or bulky to handle. It should require only a few people to load and unload it on transport dollies and trucks.

Ease of storing. The equipment should fit in available storage areas and through standard openings without the furniture having to be dismantled. Chairs should stack high, one on the other, without marring or toppling. Tables should have underframes wide enough to totally enclose folded legs, so that when stacked, dangerous slide-offs will be avoided. (The wishbone-style leg offers the most comfortable knee and foot room. See Figure 2-1.)

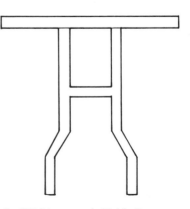

Figure 2-1. Wishbone-style Table Leg.

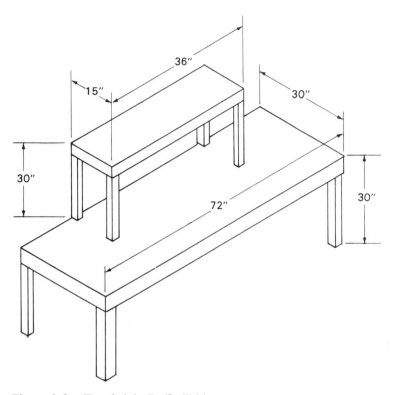

Figure 2-2. Two-height Buffet Table.

Flexibility. Try to purchase furniture that can serve two or more purposes. For example, a schoolroom table placed atop a standard oblong table can create an elevated buffet setup (see Figure 2-2); center column and heavy base café tables can be used as cocktail tables or converted into dinner tables by adding a large round top, or serve as an extender for an oblong table by adding a square top.

Tables

Folding tables come in many sizes and shapes. Round tables may be 24 to 108 inches in diameter; oblong tables may be 15 to 30 inches in width and up to 10 feet in length. Larger tables are available on special order, but they are bulky to handle and manipulate.

The 12- to 15-inch-wide oblongs are called schoolroom tables, with two widths equaling a standard 30-inch table. They are suited to crowded meeting halls (although they are not convenient for meal service) and make excellent display tables at merchandise shows and fairs (see Figure 2-3).

Folding tables come with various shaped tops: oblong, round, serpentine, oval, quarter-round, half-round, and trapezoid (see Figures 2-4 and 2-5). Serpentine tables are shaped like arcs, which make them part of a circle. Butted in reverse, they make an S-shaped setup. Serpentines, which can be used to form round, half round, S-shaped, and horseshoe groupings, make graceful buffet and headtable setups. Used in conjunction with oblong tables, they round off a rectangular buffet into half-round projections.

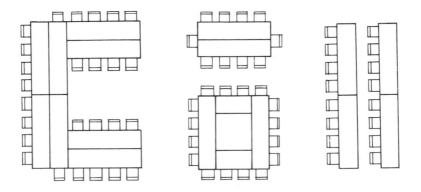

Figure 2-3. Suggested Configurations of Schoolroom Tables.

A quarter-round table makes a rounded corner for two tables placed at right angles; half-round tables can be used to round out rectangular ends (see Figures 2-4 and 2-5). This unit makes a particularly effective raised center for buffet or spotlighted presentations.

There is a folding trapezoidal table that makes a solid hexagonal table when two are placed together on the longer sides. Many other variations and effective combinations are also possible.

Regardless of the type of table purchased, make certain that the locking devices are strong, simple to use, and reliable. The simpler the mechanism, the less likelihood of human error when locking it.

Stack and Folding Chairs

Stack chairs, whether they are framed in aluminum, steel, chrome, or iron, are easier to handle than folding chairs and can be set up more easily, with less noise, and in less time. Because they don't fold, you don't have to worry about infirmly locked legs that can buckle. The seats and backs can be upholstered more comfort- ably than can folding chairs. Good stack chairs have "wall-saver" legs that extend beyond the back, thus preventing them from marring the walls.

For formal and luxurious dining areas, you can select more massive-looking chairs, and have the arms, backs, and seats upholstered in more expensive materials to create a more luxurious ambience.

Folding Platforms

Folding platforms are available in many sizes and styles to suit numerous needs. Some are equipped with two sets of folding legs to vary the height. These platforms can be used to elevate banquet tables, set up in tiers for distinguished guests, or used as runways for fashion shows or as elevated platforms for musical groups. (Reliable manufacturers furnish liability insurance with each sale.)

Portable Dance Floors

Portable dance floors offer several advantages over permanent installations. They do not require an initial permanent and expensive installation, nor do they require zip-out sections of rugs to make them functional. Portables can be set in any room-area arrangement and therefore do not restrict guest setups.

Modular Units

Modular units offer a myriad of possibilities for unusual and effective food presentation. Their use is limited only by one's sense of innovation. The units, which are from 30 inches to 72 inches long, can be interlocked to form a continuous display or used independently as serving islands in various parts of the dining area. They can be rolled directly to guest tables to create a special and intimate dining atmosphere.

Modulars are well constructed and are available covered in grained mica, leather, metal, or tufted fabrics. With a maneuverability that makes them equally valuable for the on- and off-premises caterer, they are comparatively light and can be rolled on or off trucks using portable ramps or mechanical tailgates.

Particularly useful for beef carving, modular units can be equipped with infrared lamps that keep food at the proper temperature and lend warmth and beauty to the dining environment. Mechanically, they retain heat or cold at the degree programmed. Built-in, interchangeable, and sized hot wells retain constant heat without the use of liquids or solid fuels. Units with a cooling system are also available for use as salad bars; built-in and surface-spaced units only require filling, eliminating the need for decorative showpieces, thus saving labor. Crushed ice displays retain their volume and effectiveness even in the hottest and most humid weather, which makes these units practical for displaying chilled fruits and frozen desserts.

Modular units do come with a few drawbacks, however. Because they are so self-contained, they offer few opportunities to express decorative ingenuity. (This can be a plus factor, however, if you lack the skilled help to create the display.) Displays must be contained within square or rectangular areas, and the display height is limited because of mandatory sneeze or dust guards. There isn't sufficient space for spectacular carvings of ice or tallow, or special fruit displays. Because of these restrictions, flower arrangements must be arranged separately or placed on tables alongside. (Free-standing buffet tables, on the other hand, have

Figure 2-4. Suggested Configurations Using Schoolroom, Serpentine, Round, Trapezoid, Quarter-round, and Half-round Tables.

practically no size restrictions and flowers can be integrated with carvings to create spectacular arrangements.)

Trays of all sizes and shapes with masterful decorations can be set on stands of varying heights, creating interest and attractiveness. Many distinctive table configurations can be achieved (see Figures 2-3, 2-4, and 2-5) that are impossible with modulars.

Some models are available with frame bottoms that allow for personalized draping. Skirting and theme drapings, ready-made or not, accent and add beauty to the presentations. The units can be effectively combined with free-standing tables to form functional and aesthetic groupings.

Service Stands

Service stands or stations are essential in every fixed dining area. Located close to serving areas, the storage and service unit eliminates the need for service personnel to make frequent trips to

Figure 2-5. Suggested Table Configurations for Unique and Effective Buffet Table Layouts.

the kitchen for supplies. Supplying and maintaining the stand should be assigned to one person in each station. Stocked items differ depending on the menu and style of service; however, typical supplies include:

Condiments such as salt, pepper, mustard, horseradish, Tabasco, sugar, and artificial sweeteners stored in clean, filled containers.
Lemon wedges, coffee, cream, tea bags, and tea pots
Extra silverware, china, and glassware
Coffee warmer
Clean ash trays and matches if smoking is allowed
Sponges and towels
Extra linen (tablecloths and napkins)

·3·

Off-Premises Catering

Off-premises catering presents a greater challenge than on-premises operations. Expected to provide flawless foodservice in locations that were never meant to handle catered events, such as museums, parks, warehouses, and backyards, the caterer is confronted with numerous problems to be overcome, both technical and aesthetic.

These locations most often do not have proper electrical power and sufficient water supply, nor do they have adequate kitchens, if any at all, or coolers to keep foods safely chilled before and after serving. In addition, caterers usually have little privacy while working, and their actions are constantly on display. In short, trying to do a commendable job in off-premises catering is like trying to walk through a mine field wearing snowshoes!

So, why should you do it? Well, many caterers don't because of the great difficulties involved in working with foods away from their own premises. Others, however, accept the challenges in exchange for greater flexibility and the opportu-

nity to work in many unusual and unique locations. The experience can make your company stronger, your staff will learn to handle just about everything that can go wrong (see box on page 18), and you can earn a significant amount of money.

Off-premises catering is purchased for both private and corporate functions for either social or business reasons. Although some corporate catering is social in nature, with the corporation or business sponsoring the off-site event, most corporate accounts are for delivered meals, usually lunches, which are either self-service or served with minimal assistance. In any case, the caterer assumes total responsibility for supplying the food, equipment, and personnel crucial to the successful functioning of an affair. The caterer relieves the client of all responsibilities, other than making menu decisions and buying the alcoholic beverages. (In most states, a caterer cannot sell liquor.) See Chapter 11 for a further discussion of this topic.

WHAT CAN GO WRONG WILL . . .

- A staff member assigned for an event doesn't show up or is late.
- The client ordered for 300 guests and 500 arrive.
- The tent you are working in falls down during the first course.
- You burn your food and need to travel thirty miles to your commissary to get more.
- A policeman pulls the delivery truck over and finds your driver has an expired license, delaying your food delivery.
- While packing two different orders, the entrée for one event is accidentally put into the box for the other party.

SOCIAL CATERING

Many private functions are catered in the client's home, which offers a special warmness. The pace is usually more leisurely, the surroundings more comfortable, the opportunity for conversation greater, and the atmosphere perhaps more elegant than dining in a public area. Moreover, the clients who host their own parties at home have the pleasure of doing something special for their friends—always a gratifying experience for the partygiver. Of course, not every client's home is adequate for large private functions such as weddings or bar mitzvahs; some popular alternatives are church and temple halls and social or civic organizations' facilities. Wherever your clients choose to entertain their guests, they will expect you, the caterer, to make it work.

Pre-event Site Inspection

Social catering parties should never be negotiated blindly. You must visit the home or hall in advance to familiarize yourself with the kitchen facilities, most often limited, and to study the layout of the dining areas. In each kitchen you must ensure that there will be space to cook, spread out your equipment, store supplies, and scrape and wash dishes. Another essential aspect of this visit is to check how convenient it will be to load and unload, which, if not convenient, can be extremely time-consuming. It is also necessary to find out how much parking is available for equipment delivery and staff.

If the function is being held at a private residence, take more than a superficial glance at the home furnishings. They could be fragile and delicate and incapable of withstanding the demands of numerous guests. The dining room table may not be sturdy enough to hold the quantities of proposed food and tableware. The furnishings may be so luxurious that possible damage to them by your staff or the guests could be devastatingly expensive to repair or to replace. If the furnishings are bulky or too heavy to move, bringing in supplementary seating or tables may be impossible.

You must also be aware that standard quantity preparation, serving, and holding equipment, such as used in your commissary, *is not appropriate or properly sized* for home service. Home stoves generally will not accommodate large, commercial-size pots, which could damage stove surfaces. Nor will large pans fit into most home ovens. You must supply your own properly sized pans, of good quality and impeccable condition. Guests, who cannot be gracefully restricted, will visit your area either out of curiosity, to compliment you, or to discuss a party of their own, and your cooking equipment will not escape their scrutiny.

The checklist at the right is a sample questionnaire to bring with you during the pre-event visit. The more thorough you are, the more professional you will appear, and the better edge you will have over your competition. The pre-event visit can help to close the sale if you present your questions in a way that inspires confidence in the client. In addition you must assess all the factors in the accompanying checklist before finalizing the price, menu, and staff and equipment requirements.

If you are bringing in auxiliary equipment for cooking or heating, make certain that it will be placed in a safe and secure area and will not present a fire hazard. If the units are electric-powered, check that the home wiring and wattage can handle the extra current requirements and not cause any power outages. If an electric disruption does occur, once the energy is restored *check with the host* to see that all appliances, such as the refrigerator, freezer, and laundry equipment, are functioning normally. Some appliances are not self-activated and require that a starter button be pushed.

Menu

The choice of the menu requires studied deliberation. It need not be French haute cuisine, but it must not lack richness in content and presentation. It can offer simple peasant foods or elaborate classical dishes. But whatever is chosen, you must be resourceful and creative to enhance not only the taste but also the meal's visual appeal. Remember, in social catering, the way in which you present the food is as important as the food itself. People eat with their eyes.

Although you may have your own repertoire of food specialties—and this is one of the reasons you were engaged—there is nothing wrong in adding a specialty dish that the client may want you to prepare according to his or her own recipe. Try it out first. If it is good, offer it to the guests, with kudos for the client. This will add to your client's pleasure and enhance your reputation for cooperation. You may also be able to add this dish to your own menu offerings.

Buffet presentations can be made more effective, and even spectacular, by table-top cooking of omelets, crepes, or pasta. The slicing of beef, poultry, or fish, by one of your employees at the buffet table adds a touch of the theatrical,

---

EVENT VISIT CHECKLIST

- Measure all rooms and determine how much work space will be available.
- Measure rooms to determine how many tables, chairs, and people will fit.
- How far is it from the cooking area to the guests?
- Do clients have any equipment you can use?
- Are there stairs or multiple floors?
- Where should the bar and buffet tables be placed?
- How adequate is the kitchen? Do the ovens work? Will your pans fit? Is there enough working area for preparation?
- How many outlets are there? Do they all go to the same circuit breaker?
- How will the delivery be made?
- Will there be enough hot and cold water?
- Where will staff and trucks park?
- Where will the equipment and rentals be stored?
- Who is in charge of the maintenance?
- Who will provide security?
- What colors will coordinate with the decor?
- Where will the staff change? Is there a place for them to take a break?
- What effect will weather have on this location?
- How will you dispose of the garbage?
- What are the phone numbers at the location or do they have a pay phone?
- Is the lighting adequate?

---

and this demonstration may even become a topic of conversation. See Chapter 9 for a complete discussion about preparing and presenting buffets.

In social catering, it is also the caterer's responsibility to encourage the client to plan an event suitable to the occasion and to the time of day. For example, a customer wanting a light cocktail reception on a Saturday night between 7:00 PM and 11:00 PM should be diplomatically advised that since this is the normal dinner hour, guests will be expecting something more substantial than hors d'oeuvres.

Bar Facilities

If there is a fixed bar, you will probably have no alternative but to use it. Otherwise, you have the option of placing the bar where it interferes least with room-to-room traffic. Storage and serving facilities will probably be limited, and the bartender may be working in tight quarters; this burden should be reduced as much as possible to ensure efficient service. For example, your clients should be advised that they need not duplicate the variety of liquors available at the neighborhood bar, nor should they offer an overwhelming array of brands, which will delay decisions and confuse the guests. Limit glassware to a style that can be used for just about everything. An all-purpose wine glass and an on-the-rocks glass will allow you to serve beer, wine, soda, and liquor effectively. Remember, simplicity is the key to providing an efficient and well-stocked bar. Also, always keep a plentiful supply of ice for drinks and chilling wine. (See Chapter 11 for more details.)

Caterers assume and accept vast liability when helping a host select and serve alcoholic beverages. Check with your lawyer to understand your possible liability. Society takes a firm view toward those who drink and drive and to all who have helped to put that person behind the wheel.

Staff Pre-Party Meeting

When catering a large or complex event for a private or corporate function, you may want to hold a short staff meeting at the party site before the festivities begin. This meeting will give you the opportunity to discuss with your entire staff the order in which to serve the menu, task responsibilities, and any other information relevant to the event.

Give each employee specific assignments and areas of responsibility. In addition to these specific duties, every service person should be encouraged never to go to the kitchen empty-handed; they should pick up dirty dishes and glasses as they accumulate.

Make certain that at least one employee is responsible for keeping ashtrays clean. Be sure to inform all personnel that they are to remain in the area where they are to perform their duties; they must not wander around the house to inspect rooms and furnishings.

Decor

There are unlimited opportunities to express your creativity in presentation: statuary, fabrics, plants, baskets, appropriate holiday decorations, and unusual accessories that can be incorporated into table arrangements. At a home party, for example, there is no reason for all the table arrangements to be the same. Your resourcefulness and creativity will add to the guests' appreciation of the setting, particularly those with artistic sensibilities. These decorations can even add a sense of opulence. The art of food presentation is not confined to a plate or platter, but rather begins with creating an environment for the food.

Traffic and Parking

At large parties in suburban or rural settings where many guests are expected, street parking may be necessary. In this case, tell the client to notify the police department about the beginning and ending times for the affair. This will please the police, neighbors, and guests by easing problems of traffic control.

The client should also be made aware that it may be necessary for a police officer to direct the flow of traffic. If a special officer must be assigned to the task, a fee will probably be charged.

Bad Weather Procedures

In rainy weather, provide umbrellas for guests and assign one of your employees the task of escorting them to and from their cars. If there is snow or slush, put a mat in front of the door leading to the house, as well as a container in the entryway for rubbers and boots. You should also provide a broom or a brush so that guests can remove snow from their footwear.

Clothes Racks or Coat-Hanging Areas

If your client requests them, you can provide folding clothes racks at a price that will cover their use, as well as your transportation and set-up costs. However, with the permission of the client, you could also use a specific room where apparel could be hung or simply placed on a bed.

Guests should be responsible for their own garments. If one of your employees takes the guest's coat to the "coat room," then you, the caterer, have given an implied assumption of responsibility. When guests take care of their own coats, you cannot be held for any liability.

Food and Equipment Storage

Food and equipment should be stored where it will not interfere with guest traffic. Store everything in an orderly, systematic manner—food in one area, linens in another, china in yet another. By doing this, you will not have to search through all of your equipment to find what you need.

Food Preparation and Service Area

All personnel, but especially those who work in the kitchen, must wear impeccably clean uniforms and keep their stations clean at all times. Take care to supply plenty of clean side towels and extra uniforms.

The garbage receptacle should be placed inconspicuously and the entire kitchen area kept clean and organized at all times. If curious guests wander into the kitchen to see who you are and how you manage to serve so much food from such a confined area, your operation will look neat and orderly.

It is inadvisable to use your client's garbage disposal. Most home units are not built to withstand heavy-duty use, and the extra strain could do serious damage. Bag your garbage in thick, strong plastic bags that won't tear or spill while being moved. This is not a place to try to save money by purchasing cheap and inferior quality.

Food Display Area

Advise your client to remove fragile crystal, china, and other valuable pieces from food-serving or other areas where guests gather and where crowding could result in an accident. If these pieces cannot be removed, they should at least be pushed out of the way.

If you use your client's dining table, buffet credenza, or other furniture for food display or service, place pads or buffers under trays and chafing dishes to prevent damaging the surface.

If possible, avoid rearranging the furniture. Doing so can change the character of the room that your client may have spent considerable time and effort in creating. In addition, you risk damaging the furniture when moving it.

Toilet Facilities

Inquire as to which toilet facility in the home the client wishes your staff to use. If necessary, inform your client that your staff will need to change into their uniforms at the party site.

Leftovers

When selling full service parties, there should be a definite understanding, preferably as part of the contract, regarding the definition of leftovers and their ultimate disposition. Food that has left the safe temperature zone (see Chapter 6) and that has been plated and offered for service should be thrown out. Foods that have been safely held at the correct temperatures and not served may be left with the client or taken back to your commissary, depending on your prior agreement.

Most clients entertaining at home expect to have at least some leftovers placed in their refrigerators before the caterer leaves. However, leaving excessive amounts of foods that can't be properly stored in their refrigerators or freezers risks the possibility of spoilage and then potential litigation over food poisoning. Be sure to check your community's health codes about regulations pertaining to leftover food.

After-Party Inspection

Following the party, thoroughly clean all areas (see page 31 for a more detailed discussion about cleaning). Check all rooms for glasses, dishes, and any other property that belongs to you. Even though a disposal area may be provided by the client, remove all garbage from the premises so that the client will have sufficient space until the regular collection time.

Before leaving, inspect every area in which you have worked or served. In this way, any damage incurred during the party will be noticed immediately, thus reducing the possibility of a delayed claim or a dispute by either party at a later date. It is also a good practice to ask the client to take a "walk-through" with you in order to verify that everything has been left in the condition it was in before you arrived.

Catering in Rented Facilities

When catering in a hall or large dining room of a club, church, temple, or fraternal organization, do not assume that the kitchen, preparation area, and furnishings are of standard institutional construction and design. You must make a personal inspection of the premises to see the quality and condition of the facilities.

Negotiations for the rental of the facility are generally taken care of by the client, who informs the superintendent or rental agent that a caterer has been hired. However, the rental agent can refuse to lease the premises to any individual or organization using a catering firm with whom the lessor has had previous difficulties. Such refusal is usually based on a caterer's previous disrespect and abuse of the facilities or because of late or nonpayment of accrued fees. Many organizations will only allow caterers with proof of liability insurance or those who have been placed on their approved list.

Some facilities charge one fee for the use of the hall and the kitchen. Other facilities charge the client a rental fee for the hall, and the caterer a separate fee, or per diem rate, for the use of the kitchen and cooking area. You may also have to pay for the use of the dishwashing machine and, perhaps, for the use of refrigerators, freezers, and for garbage removal. Some kitchens permit you—for a fee—to use their pots, pans, and other utensils. They may even allow you to use their dishes, glassware, and silverware. If you do use them, be certain they are returned to their proper place and are in perfect condition and clean. Should you inadvertently take any of these items back with you, immediately notify the manager of the facility and then return them right away. If an item owned by the facility breaks or is damaged, promptly report it and assume responsibility for it.

Following these rules will ensure that you are welcomed to subsequent events at the facility, and may even result in party referrals by the lessor. Tipping the superintendent of the facility up front will encourage cooperation and increase the possibility that all equipment will be available and functioning properly when needed.

Since some dining areas are rented without tables or chairs, your client may expect you to know where to obtain these items. In this case, refer your client directly to the party rental agency. Let the client make arrangements for the delivery, pickup, and payment. Avoid, when possible, transporting tables and chairs; they are bulky and heavy, and take up much needed space in trucks. Furthermore, rental agencies have the special equipment for handling and delivering these items.

Your client may ask you for a floor plan showing where the tables will be located to help them plan the seating arrangements. If a floor plan is not available, you will have to measure the area and make scale templates to plan the table layout (see Chapter 7). Keep a copy of the floor plan for your permanent records because you may work in that facility again. Also, make out a detailed work sheet so that everyone will be aware of party details (see Figure 3-1).

Liquor Arrangements

Some public halls may rent all their facilities except for the bar. If the facility has a liquor license and does not allow liquor to be brought in, you will probably have one of the following options:

- *Cash bar.* Guests pay for liquor and drinks individually.
- *Limited bar.* The client furnishes tickets to guests, and they present a ticket for each drink.
- *Unlimited bar.* Guests order as many drinks as they wish. Payment is subsequently made by the client, based on a predetermined charge.

If the facility does not have a licensed bar and liquor is to be served, you must furnish bartenders and portable bars—the client supplies the liquor. This plan is similar to the arrangements made for catering in a client's home, but since it is on a larger scale, the quarters may be roomier and, therefore, you can serve a greater variety of drinks.

Organization Affairs

Many functions that take place at rented facilities are for organizations that hold affairs on limited budgets. You may not make your deserved profit if you agree to take the account. Don't assume these modest affairs will be of great advertising value in exchange for taking a profit cut. They could, in fact, have the opposite effect.

In order to accommodate an organization's limited budget, you may have to "cut corners," such as reduce portion sizes, eliminate a course, serve simpler and less expensive foods, use fewer serving staff, or substitute paper for linens. If any of these practices are deviations from your standards, your reputation may be harmed. Guests are not concerned about whether or not you are making or losing money on an affair. They are concerned with good service, good food, and a pleasant ambience.

If you decide to go ahead anyway, knowing that your profit will either be reduced or eliminated entirely, do so *without compromising your standards of quality or service.* You will be respected for doing this, and your standards will be maintained.

Many events for organizations and clubs will include a prearranged program or presentation. In addition to good food and service, pay careful attention to the following when catering such a function.

- Coordinate the timing and service of the meal with the client's plans for speeches, entertainment, or ceremonies. Determine in advance at what time, or place, or by what cue, service should cease or continue.
- Do not serve a course while guests are dancing. Food served before guests are ready for it will either cool, get warm, or wilt.
- Caution waiters and other employees not to move place settings from one table to another without permission from the client or committee chairperson.
- While the program is in progress, keep your entire staff still and quiet.
- Make sure water goblets are kept 7/8 full during the meal and are then filled to this level

JOHN DOE CATERERS — HYDE PARK, NEW YORK

DETAILED WORKSHEET (SPECIMEN)
(To be issued to person in charge of affair)

NAME OF CLIENT:	State Historical Association
ADDRESS:	149 Oregon Street, E. Chicago, Illinois
AREA OF PARTY:	First Hungarian Church
ADDRESS:	1595 Sunrise Highway, E. Chicago, Illinois
PERSON(S) IN CHARGE:	Mrs. D. R. Jones Mr. F. G. Hussen
DAY AND DATE:	Saturday, January 18, 1983
TIME:	Reception — 5:00 P.M. Dinner — 6:30 P.M.
NUMBER OF GUESTS:	250 persons
GUARANTEED NUMBER:	245 persons
SPECIAL ARRANGEMENTS:	Use two church bars, but we supply two additional portable bars and supply four bartenders. Association will provide all liquor, carbonated beverages, soft drinks, and ice. Our bartender will inventory all liquor at setup; breakdown. During dinner, our portable bars will be wheeled into the dining room, and each will be attended by one or more of our bartenders. Association member in charge is Mr. F. G. Hussen.
RECEPTION: (One of our persons in charge.)	In reception area, set up two 8-ft. tables (belonging to facility) with equal amounts of Wisconsin and New York cheese, celery sticks, carrot sticks, and cocktail rye slices (as packed) on each. (One waitress will be assigned to each table.) Drape tables in blue and use 5-in. plates, service knives, and cocktail napkins. *PASS BUTLER STYLE*—400 speared cocktail franks, 300 rondelles of lobster, and 300 cocktail meatballs (all as packed).
COAT ROOM:	Attendants to be supplied by church. (We feed.)
PARKING:	Handled by policemen provided by the organization. (We feed them and all other personnel.)
ORCHESTRA:	Provided by the organization. Band leader is Hy Williams; our coordinator is Bob White. (We supply sandwiches only; it is our treat.)
CENTERPIECES:	Floral centerpieces will be provided by the organization. (Guests will not be permitted to take centerpieces, which will be sent to Shriner's Hospital. Orchestra will announce.)
LECTERN:	Tabletop, center head table, two mikes.
HOUSE COUNT:	Before soup course, check with organization's Mr. Hussen. Check program with Mrs. Jones of the organization.
HEAD TABLE:	12 guests, blue table top, gold lame front skirt, gold napkins, 2/3-tier candelabra, blue candles, and dagger ferns across front.

Figure 3-1. Work Plan.

DINING ROOM:	According to floor plan submitted. Organization to set out table cards. (Retain master guest list.)
DINNER:	6:30 P.M. *sharp,* blue cloths, and gold napkins. (Edith and captain left side of dining room; Norman and captain right side of dining room.)
MENU:	Fresh Fruit Cocktail, Supreme, Garniture of Strawberries (Silver coupes).
	In ice: Ripe and Green Olives, Radishes, Celery Hearts, Iced Butter Curls; bread and butter plates at each setting.
	From tureens: Potage Mongole
	Russian service: Chicken Kiev, Escoffier of Vegetables
	Preplated: Wedge of Cheese Cake, pass warm Blueberry Sauce; 12 Petits Fours per table.
	Coffee, self-poured; one pitcher per table, on candle warmer.
	(Following coffee service—one dish mints and nuts per table.)
GENERAL DIRECTIONS:	Wash dishes and glasses as used, two church crew members and two of our regular crew members. (Pay church crew minimum wage and tip at your discretion.)
	Following dessert service, one hour of dancing. All tables must be cleared, leaving only cloths and ashtrays. All dishes and glassware must be washed and truck-packed.
	DISPOSABLE GLASSES TO BE USED AT BAR DURING LAST HOUR OF SERVICE.
	Broom-sweep dining room only, with brushes to be supplied by church.
	Thoroughly wash kitchen floor, clean work tables, stoves, and reefers (refrigerators).
	Check garbage dumpster; make certain no garbage on ground.
	Check with church superintendent to make certain all areas meet with his/her complete satisfaction. Give superintendent gratuity check.

Figure 3-1. (continued)

before the waiters leave at the start of the program.

- Remove all unused glasses, dishes, and unnecessary items from the tables as soon as possible. It is not pleasant for guests to have to sit at a cluttered table.
- Keep ashtrays clean at all times.
- Keep the client's or committee's original guest and seating lists accessible for ready reference.

Renting a Tent

On some occasions, a client may want to hold the party in a tent to take advantage of a large backyard. You should know which companies in your locality specialize in setting up. Pass this information on to your client, and let him or her determine the feasibility of erecting the tent in the desired area and negotiate the price. At the same time, you or your client may want to compare the cost of renting a tent, along with the necessary tables, chairs, dance floors, and platforms, to the price of renting a fully enclosed and equipped air-conditioned facility.

If your client decides to go ahead with the tent, encourage him or her to have it erected on a hard-topped surface or perfectly level grass area. If the surface is uneven, it may be necessary to place shims under table legs to keep them from rocking.

If a tent will be used, you will have many factors to resolve. For example, your preparation or kitchen facilities will probably have to be set up in another tent erected close enough for efficient service but preferably not visible to the guests. Field cooking ranges will probably have to be rented and set up. Ample refrigeration such as a refrigerated truck will have to be rented and positioned so that it is efficient for the "kitchen" but not seen or heard by the guests. Pest control services may be necessary to assure that guests are not plagued by flies and mosquitos. These factors will affect your operating costs considerably and are often not obvious to the client. Remember, once again, your client and guests will expect excellent food and service even under the worst possible physical conditions.

Despite these difficulties, tents do have some advantages. They generally offer more elbow-room for both guests and employees, since people can circulate indoors and out. Tents protect people and food from the sun and inclement weather. And, because events held under tents tend to be gala and festive affairs, your participation will be appreciated and noted.

Packing

Packing List

A packing list is of much more importance to an off-premises caterer than to an on-premises operator, whose equipment is always on hand. Setting up for a party some distance from the commissary and discovering that some essential equipment was short-packed or omitted entirely could cause considerable confusion, embarrassment, and even trauma if time does not allow for sending back to the commissary for the missing items. Purchasing substitutes could be impossible if stores are closed or if substitutes are unsuitable. (An off-premises caterer should always carry enough pocket money for these emergency purchases.)

Making out the list requires a concentrated and methodical approach. Carelessness can cause expensive repercussions.

In preparing a packing list, an effective system is to study each course on the menu and decide exactly what and how much service equipment it requires. Examine each line of the menu in succession and, on a blank sheet of paper, list the equipment required and the amount needed for that service (see Figure 3-2). Skipping around or using preprinted forms can lead to unnecessary detail and confusion.

If a subsequent course uses a dish or piece of equipment previously listed, simply add it to the subtotal. Continue this process until you have gone through every course in the menu and then *recheck for accuracy*. Total the amounts under each heading and transfer the numbers to a packing sheet (see Figure 3-3). Be sure to also include on the packing list all items that will be needed for ancillary services—water and coffee pitchers, creamers, candelabras, cloths, napkins, work tools, ice buckets, baskets, and so forth.

You must always know the number of items packed in each box, rack, or cabinet. Pack full racks of glasses or dishes, even if the amount exceeds the actual number needed. Full racks are safer to transport and are easier to tally when packing for the return trip. Having extras on hand will enable you to serve unexpected extra guests, or compensate for any breakage or damage.

If dishwashing facilities are available, you probably will not need to pack as much equipment as you have tallied. For example, if you are serving a party of 150, you will probably need wine glasses, which are normally packed 6 by 6, or 36 glasses to a rack. Where washing facilities are available, you could safely pack 5 racks of glasses, or 180 glasses, knowing that you can wash the glasses as needed. When dirty glasses are returned, accumulate them until you have enough for one rack, at which time they can be washed and returned to the bar. By the time they are ready to be used again, they will be clean and cool enough to handle. Without dishwashing facilities, you would have to pack at least 10 racks of glasses, or 360 glasses, which would take up more truck space and require additional packing time. This same principle applies to other items. For example, the underliner used in the starter course can be used again, after washing, for the dessert course.

14" ROUND TRAYS (#1)	5" DOILIES (#11)	BUTTER KNIVES (#21)
IIII (4)	(1 BOX)	IIII (4 BAGS)
COCKTAIL NAPKINS (#2)	7" UNDERLINERS (#12)	DESSERT FORKS (#22)
I (1 BOX)	IIII IIII IIII IIII IIII II (27 DZ. OR 324 COUNT)	IIII (4 BAGS)
FRILLED PICKS (#3)	10" PLATES (#13)	REVERE BOWLS (#23)
I (1 BOX)	IIII IIII (10 DZ.)	I (1 BOX)
10" DOILIES (#4)	TEASPOONS (#14)	SERVICE SPOONS (#24)
I (1 BOX)	IIII III (8 BAGS)	I (1 BOX)
HI-BALLS (#5)	FORKS (#15)	COFFEE CUPS (#25)
IIII (4 RACKS)	IIII (4 BAGS)	IIII (5 RACKS)
LO-BALLS (#6)	ALL PURPOSE WINES (#16)	SAUCERS (#26)
II (2 RACKS)	IIII (5 RACKS)	IIII IIII (9 DZ.)
WATER GOBLETS (#7)	TULIP CHAMPAGNES (#17)	BRANDY PONIES (#27)
III (3 RACKS)	III (3 RACKS)	I (1 CASE)
SUPREMES (#8)	DINNER KNIVES (#18)	SALT-PEPPERS (#28)
IIII II (7 RACKS)	IIII (4 BAGS)	2 (2 BOXES)
SUPREME INSETS (#9)	RELISH DISHES (#19)	SUGAR BOWLS (#29)
IIO (IIO)	I (1 BOX)	I (1 BOX)
SUPREME RINGS (#10)	BREAD TRAYS (#20)	CREAMERS (#30)
IIO (IIO)	I (1 BOX)	II (2 BOXES)
		ASH TRAYS (#31)
		I (1 BOX)

Figure 3-2. Menu Service Equipment.

PACKING LIST
(This list is intended only as a guide)

Job no. _____ Supervisor _____ Packed in truck _____

To be packed by, day _____ Date _____ Scheduled by _____

ABC CATERERS, CENTRAL CITY, N. Y.

PACK		RET'D	PACK		RET'D
	Service plates			Serving forks	
120	10″ Dinner plates			Tongs	
324	7″ Plates				
	Bread and butter		3	Water goblets	
	Monkey dishes		4	Hi-balls	
5	Coffee cups		2	Lo-balls	
108	Saucers			Pilsner	
	Bouillon cups		5	All purpose wines	
1	Relish dishes, china			Sherry glasses	
	Silver ___ 1 BOX ___			Manhattans	
	Casseroles, type			Whiskey sours	
	Gravy boats, china			Champagnes, saucer _____	
	Silver _____		3	Tulip	
	Individual salad bowls		1	Cordials	
	Demi tasse combos				
7	Supremes		1	Silver bread trays	
110	Rings for supremes		1	Silver crumbers	
	Insets, glass _____		1	Ash trays	
	Silver ___ 110 ___			Lg. round silver trays	
				Lg. square silver trays	
8	Teaspoons			Lg. oval silver trays	
	Bouillon spoons		4	Med. ovals __14″__ Small ___	
	Salad forks			Russian service trays	
4	Dinner forks				
4	Dessert forks			Stainless bowls _____ size	
	Oyster forks			Stainless pans _____ lg. small	
4	Dinner knives			St. serving ladles	
4	Butter knives			Ice cream scoops, size	
	Demi tasse spoons				

Figure 3-3. Packing List.

PACK		RET'D	PACK		RET'D
1	Chef's tools (1 _____) (2 _____)			Large Mahogany salads	
1	Bar tools			Small Mahogany salads	
1	All purpose tool box		1	Silver water pitchers	
1	First aid kit		1	Silver coffee pitchers	
4	Stainless bar pitchers		2	Silver creamers	
	Gueridons		2	Silver sugar bowls	
	Portable bars _____ 1 _____ 2 _____ 3			Silver candy dishes	
1	Stirrers			Silver coupes	
1	Coasters		1	Revere bowls, size __9"__	
2	Waste baskets — Garbage cans *NONE*		1	Silver ice bowls	
	Garbage liners			Silver compotes	
1	Table numbers		1	Silver coffee urns	
	Portable fry pots			Silver punch bowls	
	Silver chafing dishes		1	Silver candelabra	
	Stainless chafers			Silver ladles	
	Marmite stands and insets			Silver vegetable dishes	
	Rechaud burners				
	Sterno, lg. small				
	Electric extensions		1	Frill picks	
	Westinghouse ovens			Plain picks	
	Gas grills _____ Tank gas		1	Ferns	
1	Skirts, color __BLUE__		1	Smilax	
4	Lace overlay		1	Flowers	
	White cloths, size _____				
	Napkins, color _____ size _____		1	Cocktail napkins __BLUE__ color	
18	Colored cloths __BLUE__ size __96__		1	Doilies __10"__ size __BLUE__ color	
16	Silence cloths			Place mats *ADD 1 BOX 5"*	
	Lace tablecloths			Punch cups	
4	Chef's coats			Styrofoam cups	
10	Aprons, bib _____ half _____			Folding table tops	
12	Side towels			Ice carving pans _____ tongs	
2	Bar jackets _____ Waiters			Ice carving tools _____	
1	Corsage pins			Light wheel _____ foil _____	
1	Stapler			Round tables _____ long _____	
1	Candles __1 DZ.__ color __BLUE__			Serpentine _____	

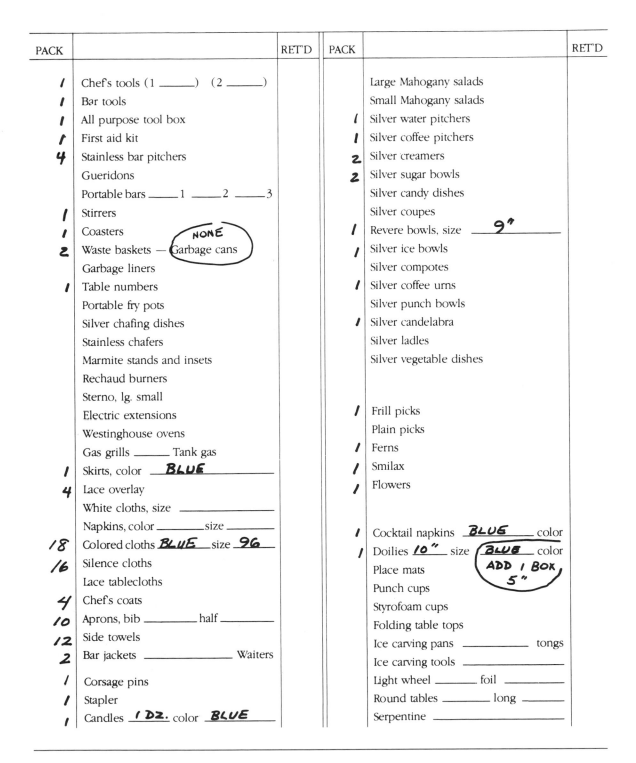

Figure 3-3. (continued)

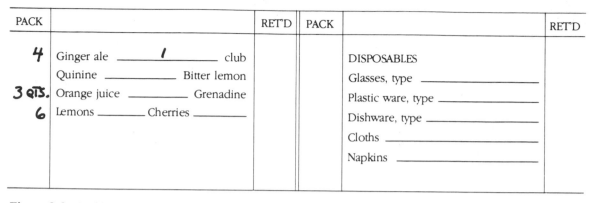

PACK		RET'D		PACK		RET'D
4	Ginger ale _____ *l* _____ club				DISPOSABLES	
	Quinine _____ Bitter lemon				Glasses, type _____	
3 QTS.	Orange juice _____ Grenadine				Plastic ware, type _____	
6	Lemons _____ Cherries _____				Dishware, type _____	
					Cloths _____	
					Napkins _____	

Figure 3-3. Packing List. (continued)

The packing list is also useful as a record of where equipment was previously used. It pinpoints the time and place and, if a particular piece of equipment is missing, it can make the task of getting it back much easier. Make notations on each packing list as to its accuracy, whether any items are missing, the condition of the equipment, and any other pertinent comments. Do not destroy the packing list, but keep it with other permanent records of that particular affair.

Aside from the equipment listed on the packing sheet, you should also consider the following recommendations:

- Each truck should always have a broom, shovel, dustpan, mop, pail with squeegee, and a number of large heavy-duty plastic bags.
- Carry two pairs of work gloves for use in the event of mechanical breakdowns, or for handling garbage cans and other such items.
- A good first aid kit is a wise investment. It should be carried at all times, and include pamphlets explaining what to do in emergencies. Contact your local Red Cross for this literature. (It's advisable that your staff read these pamphlets as part of their training.)

- Your catering tool box should be equipped with at least *two* can openers: an electric and a manual model. (Always include a manual opener since electric power may not always be available at all sites.) Nothing is more frustrating than having to open a can and learning you do not have a usable opener.

Packing the Van or Truck

Trained personnel should be available to pack your vehicles for off-premises catering events. If schedules permit, it is advantageous to have the truck packed with nonperishables at least a day in advance of the party. This will minimize the tension and rush at the last minute, and fewer mistakes in packing will occur.

The employee assigned to packing should be given the menu, in addition to the packing list, so that he or she will be alert to omissions from the list. For example, if the event is a reception with passed-around hors d'oeuvres and cocktail napkins are not listed, the packer should recognize the omission. The packer should also alert the manager when the equipment inventory is low.

The truck must be packed in a sequential manner. The equipment needed first at the destination should be packed last. The items must be securely wedged to prevent shifting or sliding. The weight must be evenly distributed—overloading on either side can cause the truck to overturn when making a sharp turn. Excess weight over the axles can cause tire blowouts or cause the axle or springs to snap.

Heavy containers must not be placed on top of light packages; cardboard containers should not be set directly on the floor of the truck as they could disintegrate if wet.

Food should be the last loaded, and, even if properly insulated or heated, should not remain there longer than necessary.

When loading or unloading, *never* place equipment or packaged food, even temporarily, on a grassy area, especially in the summer. Ants and other insects will magically appear and swarm over the contents.

Plan for Deliveries

All factors involved in the delivery of food and equipment to off-premises jobs are important. When planning a delivery, keep in mind that certain streets may be restricted to commercial traffic during certain hours and that trucks may be prohibited in residential areas. Therefore, you may have to use other routes. You may also have to adjust your delivery pattern for school bus routes and locations where schools, factories, office buildings, stadiums, and other recreational and amusement areas could cause traffic jams.

Be aware of road construction and detours. If uncertain, check with the state police or the local automobile club. Also listen to local radio reports; many give traffic information that could be important, particularly in bad weather. Always allow plenty of time. Give your driver sufficient cash for emergencies, additional gas, and tolls. He should also have enough money to pay for minor repairs and be supplied with the names of reputable service stations with towing facilities along the route. Your driver should always know where you will be and how to get in touch with

you. You might consider installing a mobile phone in your trucks, as well as in your lead car. Short-wave communications may also be of value.

Put a "hide-a-key" in a place known only to you on each vehicle that you own. Keys can get lost or misplaced, so it is a good idea to have a spare.

General Cleanup

Cleanup following any party should be systematic. All glasses and dishes of the same type should be removed at one time from all tables. This speeds handling and packing in the dishwashing area and minimizes the number of packing cases needed at the exit end of the washing table.

Keep forks, knives, teaspoons, and other utensils in individual containers, each having a specific number of utensils, and then label each by contents and number.

When packing silverware, be methodical. With forks, pack all tines in the first row close together and facing the same way; tines in the second row should also all face the same way, but rest on the handles of those in the first row. Repeat this same procedure for the third and fourth rows and do the same thing with spoons.

When packing knives with hollow handles, place the flat side down, one row at a time. Reverse the handles on every other row so that knife blades in one row will rest on knife handles in the row below.

Remove napkins separately and count them before tying in a soiled but dry tablecloth. Leave tablecloths on two tables and, as the other cloths are removed, shake them out onto one of the cloth-covered tables. This will keep the dirt off the floor and enable you to quickly discover any valuables that have been inadvertently left behind. Cloths already shaken out can then be thrown onto the second table, counted, and tied up into the tablecloth.

Keep wet and damp cloths separate, and, after returning to your commissary, spread them out to dry. This will prevent mildew, which is difficult to remove.

Deciding When Not to Take a Party

Professional caterers know when to say no or walk away from an event. Some reasons for rejecting a job are:

- When you can't produce or perform what the client wishes because it can't or shouldn't be done under the current or pending circumstances—for example, when a client insists on setting up a tent on very uneven terrain or wishes to serve light hors d'oeuvres only at a function planned from 6–9 PM.
- When you have too many other parties or have other reasons to doubt your ability to give 100 percent.
- When you have lost control of the situation or the client.
- When financial obligations are not fulfilled.

CORPORATE CATERING

In the 1990s, corporate catering, with its potential for repeat business, will become the most profitable of all types of catering. Corporate clients select caterers on their overall professionalism, versatility, and punctuality. In other words, corporations are very concerned about hiring a caterer who can fulfill a variety of needs, whenever and wherever service is desired. Corporations use caterers for simple cold buffet luncheons, holiday parties, picnics, special event galas, and much more. It is within most caterers' abilities to handle these requests routinely.

Approximately 60 cents out of every dollar spent by a corporation on catering is for self-service or drop-off catering during lunch. The order may very well require three different drop orders, each at a different price range. For example, they may want a $5-per-person box lunch for 25 staff members, a $12-per-person cold buffet for 36 managers in a meeting, and a $26-per-person hot meal for 12 executives during a board meeting. The caterer who can meet those needs has an advantage over other food delivery services that offer only one level of quality or price range.

Distributing a preprinted menu through the mail or in person on a cold call is the best way to sell your services to corporate clients. A well-written preprinted menu, as opposed to a customized one, can increase your sales volume with the least amount of effort. If you have these menus on hand, you will be able to respond quickly should a client inquire about your services. You will have less paperwork and need less office assistance since you will not have to plan and type individualized menus every time. Preprinted menus also make it much easier for your kitchen staff since they will be familiar with the foods being offered. And the client will have an easier time placing an order, with fewer opportunities for misunderstanding. Preprinted menus also make ordering by fax machine easier.

·4·

Catering Personnel

STAFFING BASICS

The quality of your employees makes the difference between success and failure. It is important for every caterer to remember that it is not what they do, but what their staff does and how well, that determines the success of the event. Therefore, it is essential that you find suitable employees and place them in the appropriate jobs. To do this, you must determine what work has to be done, what skills are required, and how the tasks should be accomplished.

Job Description

The first step in hiring catering personnel is to identify the jobs that need to be done in order to perform the services offered. Your basic crew is composed of the minimal staff needed to sell your services, prepare the food, and serve your clients. Each of these tasks should have a job

description that identifies the basic function and the specific duties and responsibilities of the job. Keep the language simple and to the point, and take care to clearly describe the job and not the person doing the job.

Job Requirements

The second step in hiring is to identify the specific characteristics needed to perform each job described. This analysis should include the skills, knowledge, personality traits, and physical abilities needed to do the job well. This time you are describing the person as opposed to the responsibilities or duties of the position.

Recruitment

Now that you have a clear picture of who you are looking for to fill the positions you require, you need to attract a pool of applicants from which to select the most qualified.

Internal Sources

Present and past members of your staff who have proven to be reliable are a good resource to tap when looking for help. Since they know both the operation and the people they recommend, they are in a position to suggest good choices. Not only should you ask for leads and information as to where to recruit, but you should offer financial incentives for reliable referrals.

External Sources

Job listings in publications and employment offices, as well as recruiting visits to schools, are among the "tried and true" sources used when looking for help. However, as the saying goes, "What's been tried is oftentimes no longer true." You need to do more than just list your job openings; you need to sell those opportunities. Treat job candidates like customers, for they are in fact shopping for a job. Use messages that sell; think about what the candidates want and meet those needs. Strong marketing messages incorporate lots of "you" language and explain what's in it for the applicant. Start off with a catchy opening such as "be the best you can be," "be part of a dynamic team," or "grow with us."

Investigate alternatives to the help wanted section of the newspaper such as the food section or the sports section. Advertise in school newspapers or trade and association journals and be competitive—know what the competition is offering and be prepared to define your unique competence. You may want to consider direct mail to members of student service organizations or the local chefs' associations. Don't put all your eggs in one basket; use a variety of recruiting activities to attract the best candidates.

Sources of Extra Help

The menu and type of service to be used for a function determines the personnel required. Sufficient personnel must be provided to set up, serve, and clear tables within a reasonable period of time. While your basic crew will be able to handle most affairs, there will be times when additional workers will be needed.

Undoubtedly, many sources of part-time skilled kitchen help are available in your area. Ask chefs and cooks in local hospitals, nursing and retirement homes, and public and private schools about their availability for part-time work. Many chefs in these facilities work a five-day week and would welcome an opportunity to make extra money. Other sources might be colleges, hotels, actors' guilds, state employment and unemployment services, and various community organizations.

Remember that you, the caterer, are responsible for the actions of your employees, whether they are full-time, part-time, or temporary. Select the right people for the job and be sure the employee knows what the job is and how you want it performed.

Application Form and Employment Interviews

Application forms and interviews have traditionally provided the interviewer with the necessary information to make the best choices. However, it is important for today's caterer to be aware of what the law allows you to ask and what questions are considered to be unlawfully discriminating. Information such as date of birth, religion, race, marital status, and number of dependents has been eliminated. To be fair and to avoid legal ramifications, make sure you ask only what you need to know to make the hiring decision. Consult your lawyer or the U.S. Labor Department to make sure you are following fair and legal hiring practices.

Orientation and Training

New hires are usually enthusiastic and anticipate liking their new job. The first day with you will either reinforce or negate their expectations. The National Restaurant Association's pamphlet called "The First Day: A Checklist for Employee

Orientation" is an excellent source of information in developing your orientation program (available from 150 N. Michigan Ave., Suite 2000, Chicago, IL 60601).

All new employees, regardless of their experience or ability, need some degree of training. They need a clear-cut explanation of their responsibilities and how you like things done. Although training takes time and costs money, it should not be viewed as an expense but as an investment. A National Restaurant Association survey found that half of the waiters and cooks who quit their jobs did so within 30 days of hire. If a strong orientation and training program can reduce that turnover, then it is money well invested.

The training program you develop for your new, and not so new, employees should be oriented toward what's in it for them. Stressing why they need the information and how they will profit from learning it will ensure that the experience is valuable and relevant to the needs of both the organization and the learner.

SERVING STAFF

Waiters and Waitresses

The main responsibility of waiters and waitresses is to serve food to guests. In many businesses, they are also assigned such side work as checking the linen inventory, refilling the condiments, and polishing tableware.

There are three types of food and beverage service, ranging from the simplest to the most elaborate: American, French, and Russian. Before you describe these services to your client and discuss what level would be appropriate for the menu and event, make sure that your staff is competently trained to handle the skill and responsibilities required.

American Service

In this service, the server brings food that has been preplated in the kitchen or served preplated from a banquet carrier to the seated guests. The rule of thumb calls for one server for 16–20 guests. However, some caterers put more staff on line for greater efficiency. Even though every client expects good service, the first cost-cutting measure they often suggest is cutting the service staff. It is important for you to be firm when discussing staffing. Good service depends on having enough staff.

French Service

This type of service from a *guéridon* (rolling table) is a slower and more elegant production; one capable server can give ten guests satisfactory service. Frequently, two servers will team up to care for two tables of ten each. Such cooperation should be encouraged since the service will be faster, more competent, and certainly more impressive. Guests will also be more aware of the presence of two people simultaneously engaged in the process of preparing or combining foods. French service can be a very elegant experience for the guest and a sign of the client's largesse.

Russian Service

This service, too frequently and mistakenly called French service, is a system of serving food from a hand-held, attractively arranged tray of silver or polished stainless steel. This type of service demands inordinate skill, requiring servers to hold a tureen of hot soup in one hand as they ladle the liquid directly into the guest's cup or bowl with the other; the server must also be able to balance a tray of food with one hand and skillfully serve the guest with the other hand. Servers must be dexterous and careful in their maneuvers to avoid physical contact with guests or spillage. In a crowded dining area, the completion of this type of service without incident is a tribute to the personnel involved.

Headwaiter and Captains

The *headwaiter*, or maitre d', is the chief administrator of all dining areas. (The term *maitre d'* is actually more correctly reserved for a hotel operator.) He or she is responsible for staffing and training all dining room personnel and for making out their work schedules. Since the kitchen is an extension of the dining room and vice versa, the headwaiter must work closely with the chef, with whom he or she must meet daily. The manager, who is the headwaiter's supervisor, often joins them.

The headwaiter must make certain that all accoutrements for party service, such as linens, silverware, glassware, and china, are available in the necessary quantities, at the time required. The headwaiter can delegate many of these responsibilities to the captains.

Captains are responsible for certain sections or for a fixed number of tables serviced by the waiters.

There are no set rules as to the number of captains and waiters needed—it depends on the type and quality of the service. Union establishments may have contractual stipulations. Some set the maximum of one server per twenty guests.

Busboys and Sommeliers

A *busboy* assists in setting up, serving water, clearing, and cleaning up. One busboy can service twenty guests, although the actual number needed is determined by house policy or the level of service requested by the client.

Sommeliers, or wine stewards, may or may not be needed, depending on the character of the affair, or whether selections (and sales) will be made at tableside.

KITCHEN STAFF

Kitchen duties vary in practically every establishment depending on the size, volume, and character of the business. Each staff member has a title and should understand the obligatory work identified with the title. However, conditions may require additional duties; for example, the broiler cook may also be responsible for the fry and roast stations. Delegation of responsibilities is, of course, governed by capabilities.

The kitchen staff is headed by the chef, who is responsible for all food preparation. Because of professional lobbying and government encouragement, the term *chef* is no longer a whimsical appellation. Members of the American Culinary Federation can now be officially certified as skilled professionals by meeting the qualifications and then passing a rigorous test. A foodservice chef can now earn highly respected certification as a C.W.C. (Certified Working Chef), C.E.C. (Certified Executive Chef), or C.M.C. (Certified Master Chef). However, while this certification is considered very prestigious, it is not an absolute requirement for the fledgling caterer or the chef. A noncertified chef may simply and accurately be known as the executive chef, head chef, chef steward, or working chef.

Executive Chef. This term is used in large establishments employing a full staff. In addition to writing the menus, the chef coordinates all kitchen activities and has regular meetings with the manager and the department heads responsible for foodservice—the purchasing agent and headwaiter. It is his or her responsibility to see that all foods, including baked goods, are prepared in accordance with the standards of the establishment.

Sous Chef. The sous chef reports directly to the executive chef and is responsible for the physical condition of the kitchen and the supervision of personnel. The sous chef must pass judgment on the food before the chef approves it.

Chef Steward. The chef steward is a chef who also does the food purchasing, which may require occasional absences from the kitchen. The chef steward can also act as meal hour and banquet service supervisor.

Working Chef. In smaller establishments, a working chef not only cooks but supervises all kitchen activities.

Chef de Partie. The title denotes a person in charge of a particular department, such as soups and sauces or a fry station.

Swing Cook, Roundsman, or Relief Cook. This person is familiar with and able to man each station as the occasion requires (due to days off, sickness, and so forth). The swing cook must follow the routine of the one being replaced and do the advance work, such as ordering the necessary supplies, for continuity.

Garde Manger (Cold Meat Department). The garde manger makes all salad dressings and cold sauces, prepares all meat, fish, vegetable, and seafood salads, as well as fruit displays. He or she prepares and decorates cold food platters for buffet services and makes appetizers and sandwiches. Ice carvings and tallow or butter modeling are the garde manger's responsibility, assuming he or she is endowed with artistic talent. At a buffet presentation, the cold food offerings are often the center of attraction and allow many opportunities for creative and impressive displays.

Pastry Chef or Baker. This chef makes all cakes, cookies, pies, puddings, French and Danish pastries, breads, rolls, and muffins. Ice cream and sherbet are also products of this department, as are other dessert items, such as baked apples, stewed pears, trifles, and ornamental pieces of sugar and dough. Talented bakers also carve ice and tallow pieces.

Butcher. In large establishments, the butcher breaks down primal cuts into service orders. Smaller establishments have little use for this skill as preportioned and oven-ready products are readily available and are frequently cheaper to purchase.

Fish Butcher. This profession is little used or entirely eliminated in kitchens since seafood packers have developed product portioning to rigid specifications, a service that is not only convenient but permits highly accurate costing.

UNIFORMS

Clean, crisp, attractive uniforms make a good impression on clients and staff members as well.

Uniforms must be spotless, so provide your kitchen staff with extra sets of whites when they are to serve off-premises.

Chefs, cooks, and kitchen personnel should also be in whites—white shirts, coats, and aprons. (Gray denim work pants are acceptable in some areas.) Hats, caps, or hairnets are a *must* for all kitchen workers.

Busboys should wear white or colored jackets. Waiters' uniforms are available in traditional and contemporary styles. The uniform for waiters and waitresses has traditionally been either all black, or black pants or skirt with a white shirt or blouse and a black bow tie.

Linen rental houses stock a wide variety of uniforms. Such service is not unduly expensive and ensures a clean and standard staff appearance—an asset in creating a good impression.

Many caterers require that the staff, especially part-timers, maintain their own uniforms. You should check your state's regulations regarding the responsibilities of the employee and company with respect to the purchase and cleaning of uniforms.

DETERMINING STAFF REQUIREMENTS

The number and variety of workers you assign to a job will depend on many variables, including the preparation and the amount of finishing-off necessary. More staff will be needed, for example, if the kitchen is involved with more than one party at the same time. Additional kitchen help will be required if the cooks are assigned to carve in the dining room.

Scheduling and assigning help must be done with concern for providing the client prompt and efficient service, with the number and type of employees needed sometimes determined from past records of similar situations. Union regulations, where applicable, must be complied with. Guest satisfaction must not be sacrificed by understaffing. But it is also prudent not to over-staff, as salaries and benefits can cut deeply into profits.

SAMPLE JOB RULES AND REGULATIONS

It is a good idea to compile a list of rules and regulations that you expect your employees to follow. These rules should be read carefully by all new employees and any questions discussed with their supervisor. Also, a company policy manual should be reviewed and approved by your attorney before implementation.

Attendance

1. All employees must report to work on time. In case of illness or other valid reason, you must notify your supervisor.
2. Employees must never sign another employee in or out, or punch another employee's time card. Employees must sign or punch in or out as their schedule dictates.

Personal Behavior

1. Meals are to be eaten only at the time and place assigned. No food is to be eaten at any other time, except for required tasting.
2. Smoking is permitted only in designated areas and avoided for at least a half hour before serving guests.
3. Chewing of gum, matchsticks, or toothpicks is not permitted while on duty.
4. Personal telephone calls are not to be made during work hours. Emergency calls will be accepted by your supervisor.
5. Accidents must be reported at once to your supervisor, no matter how insignificant you may think them to be. Because many accidents can be prevented, extreme care should be exercised at all times.

6. Newspapers or other literature should not be read or passed around by employees during the time of service or within view of guests.
7. No food, raw or cooked, is to be removed from any area. Bones for pets may be saved and packed personally by your supervisor, and only at his or her discretion and convenience.
8. Each employee is responsible for the cleanliness of his or her own working area as well as any other assigned area. Notify your supervisor immediately if your area has been left in an unsatisfactory manner by the employee preceding you.
9. Discuss any problems or complaints with your supervisor, and not with fellow employees. If the situation cannot be resolved, you then have the right to appeal to the manager or owner.
10. Be courteous, cheerful, and helpful to customers, guests, and fellow employees at all times. The guests or customers are your reason for being here. Compliments by any guests, written or oral, about a specific employee or the group, will be noted and brought to your attention individually or publicly posted on the bulletin board. Complaints about an individual will be handled in private, and kept strictly confidential unless they are serious enough to affect the whole crew.

General Appearance and Hygiene

1. Employees must be in uniform at the start of their shift.
2. Wash hands thoroughly before handling or serving food.
3. Bathe or shower daily and use an unscented deodorant.
4. Keep hands away from face or hair at all times while on duty.
5. Brush teeth frequently and use an antiseptic mouthwash.
6. Impeccable personal hygiene is absolutely essential at all times.

7. Report and cover any open sores or breaks in your skin such as cuts or scratches.

8. Injuries, cuts, or bruises of any kind, no matter how minor, sustained while on duty, must be reported to your supervisor immediately.

9. Report any coughs, colds, or other communicable infections to your supervisor; you will be permitted to work only at his or her discretion. Employees with a fever will not be permitted to work.

10. Spitting is not only forbidden by law, but can lead to immediate dismissal.

Personal Belongings

1. No jewelry may be worn except for the following:
   - Small, plain earrings not exceeding one-half inch in diameter.
   - Wedding bands and school graduation rings, providing they are not too massive (with discretion of supervisor). Rings with society emblems, or rings set with semiprecious or precious stones, are not permitted.
   - Fine neck chains. However, they may not have a pendant of any kind, except a religious medal. The pendant must be pinned to an undergarment and not allowed to hang free.
   - Ankle bracelets are not permitted.

2. Pens, pencils, or thermometers must not be carried in the breast pocket unless securely clipped. Keeping a writing instrument in the hair or behind the ear is forbidden.

3. Cigarettes, matches, combs, keys, and so forth must not be carried in the breast pocket.

SALES CONTRACT
JOHN DOE CATERING COMPANY
Poughkeepsie, New York 12538

Customer name: _____

Address: _____

Phone: (W) _____ (H) _____

Date of Event: _____ Type of function: _____

Approx. no. of guests: _____ Guaranteed minimum: _____

Guest arrival time: _____ Cocktail hour: _____ Serve time: _____

Theme: _____ Colors: _____

Menu @ _____ Per person

OPTIONAL SERVICES

Tables (round) _____

Linens _____ Color _____

China _____

Glassware _____

Silverware _____

Skirting _____

Ice sculptures _____

Champagne fountain _____

Entertainment _____

Decorations _____

Limousines _____

Flowers _____

Cake _____

Bar _____ Setups _____

Photo or video _____

Other _____

SPECIAL INSTRUCTIONS REQUESTED

_____

_____

Note:

Food and service _____ *

Beverages and services _____

Optional services _____

Gratuities _____

Subtotal _____

NY sales tax _____

Total _____

Deposit 25% _____

Balance due _____

Total costs will be adjusted accordingly ± upon confirmation of final guest count which will be due 10 days prior to the event. A 25% deposit will be due at the time of acceptance of this proposal. The balance will be due 10 working days before the event. If the event is cancelled before 30 days you will receive a full refund minus a 10% service charge.

*Based on _____ people

_____   _____   _____

Date   Director of catering sales   Customer

Figure 5-1. Sales Contract.

DETERMINING CHARGES

An important part of your contract is the client's acceptance of the cost of the event. There are probably as many ways to price a catered event as there are caterers, since there are so many tangible and intangible factors to consider. In addition to the direct costs of doing business such as food and labor, there are also many indirect costs such as licenses, office supplies, advertising, and insurance, to name a few.

In addition, you need to consider the going rate for your area, the type of party being given, the likelihood that the job might bring in new business, and how much in demand you are.

Although experience is necessary to measure what the market will bear and what the value of your services is, there are basic considerations

---

CONTRACT

JOHN DOE CATERING COMPANY

Poughkeepsie, New York 12538

Date: _____ , 19 ____

AGREEMENT between JOHN DOE CATERING CO., hereinafter called Caterer, and _____
_____, hereinafter called Patron.

Full name of patron _____ Phone number _____

    Address _____ City _____ State _____ Zip code _____

If club or organization, give name: _____

Principal address: _____

    Club president's name _____ Club treasurer's name _____

Address _____ Address _____

    Committee representatives: Names/addresses

        Name _____ Address _____

        Name _____ Address _____

        Name _____ Address _____

Guarantor: _____ Address: _____

Date of function: _____ Hours: from _____ to _____

Area of function: _____

Minimum number of guests guaranteed _____ Price per guest _____

Extra charges as attached $_____

Anticipated total bill $_____

    1. IT IS FURTHER AGREED as a condition precedent of the agreement that the patron will pay 25 percent (25%) of anticipated total bill as computed above upon acceptance of this contract.

    2. All details of the Menu are set forth in letter dated _____ and attached extra charges which are made part hereof.

    3. Patron agrees to inform Caterer at least 48 hours in advance, in writing, as to definite number guaranteed. Caterer will be prepared to serve 5 percent (5%) increase above guarantee.

_____   _____

Patron's signature   Caterer's Signature

Figure 5-2. Banquet or Party Function Contract.

that will serve as a guideline to get you started in establishing charges that are fair to you and your client.

Analyzing the Competition

A good place to start is in the yellow pages under Caterers. Call your competitors and ask for price quotes. Take care that you are researching caterers who sell food and services comparable to your own. It would be a waste of time to compare yourself to classic French caterers if your market is more home-style foods simply presented. Unfortunately, it is not a simple matter of merely adopting your competitors' prices. This research, however, will give you a cost range within which to work. Your next step is to analyze your own cost of doing business.

Using Your Income Statement for Pricing

Your income statement or profit and loss is your best gauge as to whether or not you are pricing effectively. Figure 5-3 shows a feasible breakdown of costs and profits and should be used only as a guide in determining your prices. Catering operations usually yield a gross profit (after direct expenses) of between 30 and 35 percent with a final net profit (after operating expenses) of between 10 and 20 percent. Although your accountant usually provides this information on a monthly basis, it is a good idea to calculate a "P & L" for each party. As you compare your charges with your expenses, you need to determine whether any difference between proposed and actual profit is the fault of incorrect pricing strategies or poor operating procedures.

Food Cost

Food cost represents the cost of all raw materials used to bring in your sales. When calculating this cost, it is important to keep in mind that you will be ordering more food than your recipes may call for to feed the guaranteed number. You need to figure in a 5–10 percent increase over the guaranteed number to cover the possibility of food being damaged in transport or a waiter dropping a tray or even extra guests showing up. Also, it is not always possible to predict exactly the quantity you will need. Salad greens are sold by the head as opposed to volume and may not always give you the same yield; strawberries that are sold by the quart make it difficult to order 100 perfect berries for dipping in chocolate. Build in a buffer of 10 percent to be safe. The food cost usually represents 25–35 percent of your sales. The higher percentage may represent times when expensive items such as veal or lobster are being purchased; however, because the preparation may not be labor-intensive you can expect a lower labor cost to compensate. In this case you will focus your attention on your gross profit percentage. As long as the high food cost is compensated by a lower labor cost, you can still make a profit.

Restaurants and hotels often spend up to 45 percent on food cost. The profit spread for caterers must be greater since the business is more sporadic and the work more physically demanding. In addition, restaurants, unlike caterers, can increase their gross profit margin by saving unused food products for the next day's lunch or dinner service.

Once you have learned to maintain a consistent food cost, you can develop a factor to use in determining your function charge. In other words, if your client chooses menu X, which has a food cost of $12 per person and your operating efficiency has yielded a food cost of 25 percent, then you will charge the client $48 per person (4 × $12 = $48).

If you have been successfully running your business with 30 percent of your income going to food cost, then you would charge your client $39.60 per person ($12.00 × 3.3 = $39.60).

CATERING INCOME			100	percent
Direct Costs				
Food and supplies	25	percent		
Payroll	35	percent		
Payroll taxes	—			
Purchased services	6.2	percent		
TOTAL DIRECT COSTS			− 66.2	percent
GROSS PROFIT			33.8	percent

Operating Expenses
Advertising and promotion
Auto and delivery expenses
Bank charges
Contributions
Depreciation: auto and trucks
Depreciation: furniture and fixtures
Freight and express
Gas
Water
Insurance
Laundry and cleaning
Light and heat
Maintenance and repairs
Permits, licenses, and fees
Professional services: accountant, lawyer
Refuse removal
Rent
Equipment rental
Replacement of china, silver, et cetera
Stationery and office supplies
Taxes: property, state, and business
Telephone
Miscellaneous

TOTAL OPERATING EXPENSES			− 19	percent
NET INCOME			14.8	percent
Summation				
Catering income	100	percent		
Minus direct costs	− 66.2	percent		
Gross profit			33.8	percent
Operating expenses			− 19	percent
NET PROFIT			14.8	percent

Figure 5-3. Income and Expense Breakdown.

If your operation's income statement is similar to that in Figure 5-3, then the $48 per person charge will be allocated as follows:

$12.00   food cost
 16.80   for payroll
  2.98   for purchased service
$16.22   gross profit
$ 9.12   total operating expenses
$ 7.10   net profit

Labor Cost

Since you are emphasizing service as well as food, you must analyze the personnel requirements of each function. How many employees and how much time will be needed for food preparation? How much time is required for travel, service, setup, and breakdown?* With all these points to consider, a 35 percent payroll cost is realistic.

Extra Charges

Include Travel Expenses
How far is the party location from your commissary? How long will the round trip take?

If you use your own vehicles for transporting food and equipment to an off-premises location, incorporate the per-mile cost, round trip, into your total charges. To determine a fair charge, check with local car and truck rental agencies for their rates.

Compute Charges for Your Managerial Services
Too many caterers forget to charge for their own managerial and professional services, which can be a costly omission. Skill and ability must be rewarded, and the value of your personal services should be double that of your highest paid employee.

*Some union contracts stipulate a lower rate for setup and breakdown time and a higher rate for actual service time. This plan works on a rotating basis, allowing all employees an opportunity to put in time for both procedures.

Since you are the leader and are responsible for overseeing the entire event, your true worth would become obvious immediately if illness or an emergency necessitated employment of a costly substitute. However, if your estimate did not include a charge for your services, you would have to absorb this cost and your profit would be reduced substantially.

Set a Use Charge for Dishes, Glasses, and Other Equipment
Check your packing list for the number of dishes, glasses, and other equipment required for the job and charge for their use. You cannot afford to ignore the costs involved in packing, transporting, washing, storing, and replacing damaged equipment. To figure how much to charge, contact local rental agencies to see their rates. Compare quality and cost, and if your dishes and other equipment are of higher quality, your charges should be greater. Many caterers who rent dishes and glassware charge their clients a service fee of 10 percent over the rental charge itself.

Review Factors in Delivery
Delivery is often overlooked when computing charges. Consider such labor- and time-consuming factors as a location inconvenient for loading or unloading; inaccessible driveways; inability to "dolly" equipment and, instead, having to carry it up and down steps. Since, under these circumstances, it will cost more to set up and break down, these costs must be passed along to your client.

Is There an Elevator?
If the party is to be held in an area accessible only by elevator, allow extra time for equipment delivery and return. Elevator space is limited, and if the elevator must be shared with tenants or other freight, the wait between loads can be time-consuming and expensive. When an elevator must be used, notify the building superintendent

beforehand to be sure it will be available when you need it. (To express appreciation and thanks for assistance, you may wish to give a gratuity to the superintendent.) To prevent scratching the elevator or damaging your equipment, insist that the elevator walls be padded with buffer blankets.

What Is the Duration of the Party?

When guests insist on lingering after a party is over, it generally indicates that the affair was successful. However, these guests can prevent you from cleaning up and removing equipment, as per contract or understanding, which can cut sharply into your profits. Therefore, prior to the affair, make it clear to the host, either orally or in writing, that you will serve only a specified number of hours. If the host subsequently asks you to remain longer, you must be paid for that time.

A home cocktail party usually lasts from three to four hours. A formal dinner should not last more than four hours, including speeches and entertainment. Considering setup and breakdown time, as well as commissary return time, you and your employees will still spend more than one-third of a day at a party.

Charge by Volume

The number of people being served has a significant effect on the price you charge. Oftentimes the more food you purchase, the better price you are able to negotiate with your purveyor. Large parties usually yield better productivity on the part of your staff, since rarely will you have to double your staff to serve double the number of guests. Under those circumstaces you may be able to lower your markup and cut the price per cover significantly and still yield a handsome profit. Conversely, if the number drops, it may very well cost more per person than anticipated and negatively affect your profit. For this reason, it is important to get a guarantee for the minimum number of guests expected. This is a major factor. If there are only a few guests, your charges must be greater in order to make your

desired profit. If the event is too small, it may not pay to book the party at all. Make sure your clients understand the relationship between volume and price. It is not uncommon for a client to cut the number of guests after you have quoted a price based on a higher number.

PLANNING THE MENU

A caterer's menu should not be a chance offering. It should contain not only the traditional beef and chicken dishes, but also items that reflect your awareness of changing food preferences. These preferences may be fads, legitimate consumer movements to promote healthful foods, or special diets; they may enjoy short lives or they may become standards.

People who are looking for quality and taste often rely on establishments that have a reputation for those characteristics. Your offerings, including such standards as chicken and roast beef, should be presented in such a way that the client cannot help but favorably distinguish them from your competition. You should try to establish an identity and an image in your locale by offering the best value for the price, the most artistic presentation, and the best-tasting food. Make every effort to be consistent in quality as well as dependable and honest in carrying out a client's wishes. If the affair has to be turned over to a subordinate, assure the client that the affair will receive the same meticulous attention that you would have given it.

MEETING WITH THE CLIENT

Whether you meet at the client's home, place of business, or your own office, be fully prepared with appropriate types of menus that will be of interest. Have pictures or slides, even letters of appreciation, and have samples of your dishware, linens, glassware, and other service equipment.

Many clients whom you interview may have no prior experience in negotiating for a catered affair, and thus may be naive regarding procedures. Do not overwhelm them with a recital of unfamiliar menu terms or trade technology. Try to put the client at ease immediately by patiently explaining the procedures necessary in this type of transaction. If you have preprinted menus, present them. Also, provide a fresh legal-size pad and sharp pencil so the client can make notes. Then proceed with your pertinent questions (refer to the Master Checklist later in this chapter, Figure 5-8).

If you are an on-premises caterer, it might be opportune to show the facilities you plan to use for the function (bar area, dining area, for example). Potential clients might even be invited to view this area when it is set up before a function—never during a function, as you will not be able to give them your undivided attention. Furthermore, you may be obviously anxious and the activity of staff and guests could distract and overwhelm the client, who should be shielded from the mechanics.

If any of the menu items have a foreign name or are not self-explanatory, describe the dish and state whether you think it is appropriate to serve. After you have explained the menu, discuss the ancillary services that may be required, such as table decorations, special lighting, printed menus, or souvenirs. Explain the special services and charges for the orchestra, florist, photographer, and cloakroom attendant and note any gratuities.

When all the points have been covered, give the client a copy of your contract. Go over the contract and explain the fairness and equitability of each item. In dealing with committees, try to keep the group to a maximum of three; the larger the committee, the longer it may take to make decisions. With three persons, a majority decision is arrived at more quickly.

Salesmanship may be necessary in certain instances but within limitations. The high pressure approach of selling more than is reasonable, even when the client is willing to pay, can result in ostentatiousness and garishness, which can reflect unfavorably on your establishment or services. You are obligated to advise a client if you believe he or she is exceeding the boundaries of good taste and dignity essential to the proper conduct of any affair.

KEEPING ACCURATE RECORDS

Large catering firms have standardized forms for banquet estimates and contracts (see Figures 5-4 through 5-7 for examples). When the contract is signed, copies are sent to all departments involved. Department heads then proceed to fulfill their responsibilities, under the supervision of the catering manager.

A lesser-volume or small operator has to assume many or all the responsibilities. You may have to schedule or sell the affair, order all necessary supplies, and schedule the food production by the chef, whom you may also have to help. You may frequently have to assume the headwaiter's duties in the dining room.

Printed forms adapted to a caterer's specific needs will aid greatly in recording the details and in expediting the function (see Figure 5-8). A packing list must be filled out whether the party is on- or off-premises (see Chapter 3), and a house check made to see that all equipment is available and in good condition.

You should make a journal entry for each item required for an affair, and each item should be checked off when ordered. This system provides a record of the items ordered so that they can be costed out, and visual evidence that the items have or have not been ordered. This also prevents slip-ups or double ordering. Do not depend on your memory to retain all this information.

As food represents a large dollar volume outlay, the purchase and control of raw or finished food must be on an exact per-need basis. This can be accomplished effectively by referring to the recipe file, which should be a priority source in determining quantities needed. Following recipes closely guarantees uniformity and is a most important component of quality control.

CANCELLATIONS

Preprinted contract forms with blank spaces for firm name, date, and terms are available from hotel stationery supply firms. However, some caterers prefer to print their own forms and insert specific stipulations, which may provide that cancellations for whatever reasons (such as illness, broken engagement, or death) will permit the caterer to retain the deposit plus penalty payments for "damages." The contract must conspicuously disclose the cancellation fee and it must be reasonable (see Figure 5-9). If the ca-

terer goes to court, the item of "damages" must be thoroughly detailed on the contract and fully substantiated in order to be collectible.

Cancellation of a party within weeks of the scheduled date can justify a caterer's demand for total compensation as costly arrangements and commitments to employees will have already been made. The caterer will be obligated to pay employees' salaries and benefits even though they will not be working. It would be highly improbable to re-let the premises at such short notice.

When cancellations have occurred because of a tragedy involving the principals, if time and other considerations favor the caterer, then he or she still has every legal right to be compensated for the loss. Allow a reasonable length of time to elapse and if the family, survivors, attorney, or executor have not taken the initiative to contact you, then the caterer should try to arrange a meeting so that an equitable settlement can be negotiated.

|_____|
Month   Year

BOOKING REQUEST FORM

☐ DEFINITE

☐ TENTATIVE/HOLD TILL _____

Copies ☐ File — White

☐ F.O. MGR. — Pink

☐ Sales Dir. — Blue

BOOKED BY _____ DATE _____

NAME OF GROUP _____

CONTACTS NAME _____ TEL. NO. _____

ADDRESS _____

CITY _____ STATE _____ ZIP _____

Figure 5-4. Booking Request Form. (continues on next page)

Day of Week	Date	Type Function	Start	Close	Room	Attendance	Rent
							$

REMARKS _____

_____

SLEEPING ROOMS   BLOCK OF _____ (TOTAL)

Arrival: Day _____ Date _____   _____ Singles @ $ _____

Depart: Day _____ Date _____   _____ Twins @ $ _____

                                                 _____ Suites @ $ _____

REMARKS _____

                                    RECAP: Room Nites _____

                           Food Covers: Breakfast _____

                                          Lunch _____

Entered by _____   Dinner _____

Date _____   RENTALS $ _____

Figure 5-4. Booking Request Form. (continued)

ESTIMATE

Contact's Name: _____
Name of Organization
_____

Address _____
City _____ State _____ Zip _____

Tel. No. _____

	FUNCTION:	TIME:	ROOM:
DATE OF FUNCTION:	_____	_____	_____
NO. OF PERSONS _____	_____	_____	_____
	_____	_____	_____
	_____	_____	
_____	COCKTAIL HOUR PKG. PLANS	@ (T) $ _____	$ _____
_____	DINNER PKG. PLANS	@ (T) $ _____	$ _____
_____	EXTRAS:	*@ (T) $ _____	$ _____
_____		*@ (T) $ _____	$ _____
_____	17% GRATUITIES ON EXTRA ITEMS ONLY	* $ _____	$ _____
_____	COATROOM CHECKING	@ (T) $ _____	$ _____
_____	LOUNGE ATTENDANTS	@ $ _____	$ _____
_____	PIECE BAND FOR FOUR HRS.	@ _____	$ _____
_____	PIECE BAND CEREMONY/RECEPTION	@ _____	$ _____
_____	FLORAL AISLE BASKETS FOR CEREMONY	@ (T) $ _____	$ _____
_____	FLORAL CANOPY FOR CEREMONY	(T) _____	$ _____
_____	_____	@ (T) $ _____	$ _____
	_____	@ $ _____	$ _____
	_____	@ $ _____	$ _____
_____	8% State Tax (on Taxable items only)	(T) _____	$ _____

MUSIC BY: EDDIE LANE   DON JOSEPH   TOTAL $ _____
                 PL3-5800   352-0174

FLOWERS BY: AVENUE J FLORIST
                 ES7-2002   ESTIMATE BY

Figure 5-5. Function Estimate.

BANQUET CONTRACT

Nature of Function: _____

Name of Room: _____

Day & Date: _____ Time: From _____ To _____

Name of Organization _____

Address _____

Name of Representative _____

Address _____

Telephone: Home _____ Business _____

No. Expected _____ No. Prepared for _____ No. Guaranteed _____

Cocktail Hour: From _____ To _____ Room _____

— FOOD —	— LIQUOR —
Type of Service: _____	Type of Service: _____
	Bartender Charge: _____
Price (per person) $ _____	Price (per person) $ _____
Menu: Service Time: _____	— WINES/LIQUORS/BEVERAGES —
Type of Service: _____	Type of Service: _____
Price (per person) $ _____	Price (per person) $ _____

Figure 5-6. Banquet Contract.

Linen _____ Napkins _____ Lace _____ Candles _____

Flowers _____

Cake _____ Filling _____

Vienesse Table _____

Room Rental _____

Music _____ Pieces For _____ Hrs.: From _____ To _____ Name _____ Price $_____

Show _____ Price $_____

Photographer _____ Price $_____

Checkroom _____ Lounges _____

Parking _____ Security _____

Cigars/Cigarettes _____ Mints/Nuts _____

Ice Carving _____

Special Uniforms _____

Special Decorations _____

Carpeting _____

Corkage _____

Overtime Charges _____

Gratuities (Incl./Not Incl.) _____

State and City Tax _____

Remarks _____

_____

(Reverse Side) _____

Copies to:

_____ HOSPITALITY OFFICE   _____ PUBLIC RELATIONS

_____ BLDG/MAINTENANCE   _____ BANQUET KITCHEN   _____ RECEPTIONIST

_____ SANITATION   _____ CATERING DEPARTMENT   _____ INSTRUCTIONAL MEDIA
                                                                      DEPARTMENT

_____ STOREROOM   _____ BAKING DEPARTMENT

_____ COOKING DEPARTMENT   _____ CONTROLLER   _____ BUFFET CATERING
                                                                      DEPARTMENT

_____ SECURITY   _____ F&BS DEPARTMENT   _____ PURCHASING

Figure 5-6. (continued)

— DETAILS AND REMINDERS —

___ Floor Plan	___ Blackboard/Chalk/Eraser	___ Dance Floor	___ Printed Menus
___ Table Numbers	___ Pointer	___ Piano	___ Printed Matches
___ Registration/Card Table	___ Amplifiers	___ Organ	___ Printed Tickets
___ Collection of Tickets	___ Motion Picture Projector	___ Flags	___ Printed Direction Cards
___ Microphone	___ Screen	___ Food for Band	___ Signs
___ Podium	___ Spot Lights	___ Printed Invitations	___ Favors
___ Lectern	___ Lighting Effects	___ Printed Place Cards	___ Bulletin
___ Easel	___ Platforms	___ Printed Seating List	___ Other

— CONDITIONS OF CONTRACT —

ALL RESERVATIONS AND AGREEMENTS ARE MADE UPON, AND SUBJECT TO, THE RULES AND REGULATIONS OF THE MANAGEMENT, AND THE FOLLOWING CONDITIONS:

1. The quotation herein is subject to a proportionate increase to meet increased costs of foods, beverages and other costs of operation existing at the time of performance of our undertaking by reason of increases in present commodity prices, labor costs, taxes or currency values. Patron expressly grants the right to the management to raise the prices herein quoted or to make reasonable substitutions on the menu and agrees to pay such increased prices and to accept such substitutions.

2. In arranging for private functions, the attendance must be definitely specified 5 days in advance. This number will be considered a guarantee, not subject to reduction, and charges will be made accordingly.

3. All federal, state, and municipal taxes which may be imposed or be applicable to this agreement and to the services rendered by the management are in addition to the prices herein agreed upon, and the patron agrees to pay them separately.

4. No beverages of any kind will be permitted to be brought into the premise by the patron or any of the patrons, guests or invitees from the outside without the special permission of the management, and the management reserves the right to make a charge for the service of such beverages.

5. Performance of this agreement is contingent upon the ability of the management to complete the same, and is subject to labor troubles, disputes or strikes; accidents; government (federal, state or municipal) requisitions, restrictions upon travel, transportation, foods, beverages or supplies; and other causes whether enumerated herein or not, beyond control of management preventing or interfering with performance.

6. Payment shall be made in advance of the function unless credit has been established to the satisfaction of the management, in which event, a deposit should be paid at the time of signing the contract and a substantial additional payment will be required forty-eight hours before the function. The balance of the account is due and payable at the conclusion of the function. A service charge of one and one-half percent per month is added to any unpaid balance over thirty days old.

. . . .

25% of total payment due on the signing of this contract. Total balance is due at the conclusion of the affair.

Name of Salesman	Date	Signature of Engager

(This Contract is subject to the terms and conditions stated.)

Figure 5-6. Banquet Contract. (continued)

FINAL BILL

ORGANIZATION _____   TYPE OF FUNCTION _____

CONTACT _____   DATE _____

ADDRESS _____   TIME _____

PHONE _____   NO. GUARANTEED _____

ITEM	COST	TOTAL COST	SUMMARY	
FOOD			FOOD	_____
BEVERAGE			BEVERAGE	_____
LIQUOR			EQUIPMENT	_____
BEER			ADDITIONALS	_____
WINE			SUB TOTAL	_____
SODA			TAX _____ %	_____
LABOR			LABOR	_____
EQUIPMENT			TOTAL	_____
ADDITIONALS			LESS DEPOSIT	_____
FLOWERS			BALANCE DUE	_____
PHOTOS				
PRINTING				
MUSIC				
LIMO				
ETC.				

PREPARED BY _____

DATE _____

Figure 5-7. Final Bill.

1. Contact person in charge of party
2. Address and phone
3. Type of function
4. Date of function
5. Time of function
6. Name of room assigned
7. Number of persons
8. Minimum guarantee
9. Serving time
10. Cocktail reception
11. Dinner
12. Buffet
13. Dancing/band/entertainment
14. Head table/mike/lectern (podium if no head table)
15. Seating plan (floor plan)
16. Guest list/place cards
17. Ticket collection
18. Gratuities (included/not included)
19. Menu
20. Decorations—banners, flags, signs
21. Draped tables for:
    a. Prizes/gifts (head table, bridal/cake table)
    b. Tickets/sign-in
    c. Place cards
22. Parking and checking arrangements
23. Tents
24. Dance floors
25. Kitchen or preparation area
26. Stoves
27. Pantry area
28. Lavatory facilities or porto sans (outside bathrooms)
29. Dressing room for help
30. Storage area for equipment and supplies
31. Electrical outlets and hookup
32. Service area for trucks
33. Chairs and tables
34. Entertainment (band with bandstand), platform
35. Air conditioning
36. Heating
37. Ancillary services:
    a. Flowers and accessories (fern, smilax leaves)

    b. Photographer
    c. Special lighting
    d. Police (protection, security, traffic direction)
    e. Audiovisual and sound equipment
    f. Novelties
    g. Souvenirs
    h. Cake boxes
    i. Limo
38. Printing:
    a. Menus
    b. Matches
    c. Stirrers
    d. Place cards
    e. Directionals
    f. Seating cards
    g. Tickets

ADDITIONAL ITEMS FOR STAFF CHECKLIST

39. Contract signed
40. Bill made up
41. Completed work "orders"
42. Distributed work schedules to:
    a. Chef and kitchen crew
    b. Headwaiter, captain and waiters, wine waiters, busboys
    c. Head bartender, bartenders, bar boys
    d. Food and beverage manager
    e. Steward
    f. Baker
    g. Butcher
    h. Housemen and porters
    i. Housekeeper
    j. Engineer
    k. Projectionist
    l. Electrician
    m. Parking lot attendants, drivers
    n. Mens and ladies room attendants
    o. Cloakroom attendants
43. Purchases—menu analyzed—broken down and ordered from purveyors and checked on arrival
44. Rentals for extra equipment needed
45. Check if food and beverage ready to serve
46. Check if equipment ready

Figure 5-8. Master Checklist for Catering.

47. Check if rooms ready:
    a. Function room
    b. Reception room
    c. Meeting room
    d. Chapel
    e. VIP room
    f. Checkroom
    g. Dressing room
    h. Bridal room
    i. Suites
    j. Mens and ladies lounge
48. Directional signs
49. Printed tickets (liquor, checking, parking, dinner, raffle)
50. Direction cards
51. Stationary bars
52. Portable bars
53. Raffle drums
54. Tables/work tables/cake tables
55. Catering equipment—visualize entire affair and make a packing checklist (chinaware, silverware, pots, pans, linens, plus all equipment needed)
56. Sanitation (dumpster/waste containers, compactor, mops, brooms, soap, dust pan, pails, wringer, shovel, large plastic bags, work gloves)
57. Washing area
58. Plate warmers
59. Plate chillers (ice)
60. First aid kit
61. Can and bottle openers
62. Coat racks, umbrellas, change and bills (tolls), petty cash
63. Make up schedule of events

Figure 5-8. (continued)

DEPARTMENT OF CONSUMER AFFAIRS CODE OF CONSUMER PROTECTION LAW REGULATIONS
REGULATION 518. CATERING CONTRACTS

(a) *Definition.* "Caterer" means any person or business engaged in serving food or beverages for private functions in New York City.

(b) *Cancellation.*
  (1.) If a consumer cancels a catering contract and the caterer can re-book the date, the caterer's cancellation fee may not exceed 5 percent of the total contract price or $100, whichever is less, plus actual expenses reasonably incurred.
  (2.) If a consumer cancels a catering contract and the caterer cannot re-book the date, the caterer's cancellation fee may not exceed the difference between the total contract price and the cost of performance, plus actual expenses reasonably incurred. The caterer must be able to show diligent efforts to re-book and must fairly calculate the cost of performance.
  (3.) It will be presumed that a caterer who receives notice of cancellation six months or more before the scheduled date of the function will be able to re-book.
  (4.) Cancellation occurs:
    (A) when the customer mails the caterer a notice of intent to cancel; or
    (B) when the caterer has actual notice of the consumer's intent to cancel.

(c) *Refunds.* As soon as reasonably practicable after cancellation, (and never later than 30 days after re-booking) the caterer must return to the consumer any sum received which exceeds the permissible cancellation fee.

(d) *Contract Forms.* Contract forms must conspicuously disclose the caterer's cancellation fee.

(e) *Delegation of Performance.* A caterer may not delegate performance of any contract to another caterer without the consumer's consent. This consent may be obtained only after the caterer advises the consumer of its inability to perform under the contract.

Figure 5-9. Cancellation Clause.

One of the axioms of the catering business is that the success and longevity of each establishment is determined by the amount of goodwill associated with that company. Reputation has concrete dollar value and can be traded as a commodity; it is often of greater intrinsic value than the physical assets.

An act of God such as flood, blizzard, hurricane, tornado, or catastrophic fire caused by lightning or volcanic eruption can often absolve either the client or the caterer (or both) from any legal responsibility; see Figure 5-10 for an example of an inclement weather clause. (If the caterer is covered by Business Interruption Insurance, the loss will be minimal or none at all.)

If you are just starting out, it is best to consult your attorney about these and other matters involving contracts between clients and your company.

A. In the event of such unusual weather conditions that local or state police agencies prohibit travel or public transportation of any kind, then the patron will be relieved of payment for guaranteed number of guests. Patron, however, is obligated to pay for any dated printed matter or such perishable items that have been specifically ordered for the affair (for example, flowers, highly perishable fruit or berries).

B. If travel is possible and only travel warnings issued, and affair is delayed for no more than one and one-half (1½) hours, then THERE WILL BE NO OVERTIME PENALTY.

C. If guaranteed number of guests do not arrive, then the caterer will only hold patron responsible for half of the difference between arrived guests and guaranteed number. Full payment must be made for printed dated items and/or flowers or items specifically ordered for this affair.

D. Caterer will freezer-pack for patron (upon caterer's return to commissary and at his or her discretion) such food items that will not have deteriorated and that would have been served to guests paid for but who did not arrive.

Figure 5-10. Snow Clause.

·6·

Sanitation

Preventing foodborne illnesses is not only the moral obligation of the professional caterer, it is essential to the success of the business. This responsibility cannot be taken lightly, for the health and welfare of your clients, employees, and ultimately the fate of your business, lie in the balance. One outbreak of food poisoning can ruin your reputation, financially burden you to the point of bankruptcy if a lawsuit is brought against you, and cause discomfort or even death to your customers and employees.

Although state and local boards of health set rigid standards for foodservice operation and inspect facilities routinely in the interest of public health, they cannot guarantee that every catered affair is safe; that is the responsibility and obligation of the professional caterer.

PERSONNEL

Every employee who comes in contact with food must be made keenly aware of his or her respon-

sibility for food safety. Of all the potential hazards found in a food production area, your staff presents the most danger to your clients. Human beings are perfect breeding grounds for potentially dangerous microorganisms. Poor personal hygiene and improper food handling techniques magnify the problem. Certainly it is the employer's responsibility to carefully screen applicants properly, train new staff, and enforce state and local health codes, but it is the ultimate responsibility of the individual food handler to practice good hygiene at all times, both privately and in public.

Personal Hygiene

It is critical that your employees understand and practice proper hygiene. Training, creating the proper work environment, and clearly defining standards and policies are the best ways to communicate what is expected. Use the following checklist as your guide.

1. When hiring, do you make note of applicants' personal hygiene habits and pride in appearance?
2. Do you require a physical examination of every new employee?
3. Do you provide a dressing room for employees, as well as a separate dining area away from production?
4. Do you supply proper uniforms and make provisions to ensure that an adequate supply of clean aprons, side towels, and hats are available?
5. Do you include personal hygiene and proper food handling techniques as an important part of employee evaluation?
6. Do you provide easily accessible handwashing stations that are always fully stocked?
7. Do you prominently post sanitation standards and policies in food production and warewashing areas?
8. Do you provide and require the use of tongs, spoons, and plastic gloves to limit personal contact with food?
9. Do you offer basic sanitation training, which is available through your local health department, as well as videos and manuals from reputable sources such as the Educational Foundation of the National Restaurant Association?
10. Do you serve as a proper role model of what you expect from your employees?

PREVENTING FOODBORNE ILLNESS

The key word to remember when developing a sound sanitation program is prevention. The following ten factors have been identified by the Centers for Disease Control as the leading contributors to foodborne illness outbreaks. Constant vigilance against their occurrence is the best way to reduce the risk of food poisoning.

1. Inadequate refrigeration.
2. Preparing foods far in advance of planned service.
3. Holding food in warming devices at bacterial incubating temperatures (45°–140°F).
4. Infected persons touching cooked food.
5. Inadequate reheating and use of leftovers.
6. Inadequate cleaning of kitchen equipment.
7. Cross-contamination.
8. Storing acid food in toxic containers.
9. Intentional or incidental additives.
10. Obtaining food from unsafe sources.

There are three sources of food contamination:

1. Chemical (insecticides, cleaning compounds).
2. Physical (paint chips, broken glass).
3. Biological (humans, insects, foods). These will cause one of two types of foodborne illnesses:
   • An intoxication, which is an illness produced by bacteria that discharges poisonous wastes into food that is subsequently eaten, or by any foreign substance, such as a chemical, that gets into food.
   • An infection, which involves either the consumption of a food that contains disease-causing microbes in great enough number to attack the gastrointestinal lining, or any parasitic attack to the human body.
   In other words, you either eat the poisonous bacteria in the food (intoxication) or you eat the disease-causing microbes themselves (infection).

Sound sanitation procedures must be followed from the time food is ordered from the purveyor to the time it is served to your guests. Use the following checklists* to review possible sources of contamination in your business.

*Derived from *Basic Food Sanitation*, The Learning Resource Center, The Culinary Institute of America, 1988.

Purchasing

Employees who have the responsibility of purchasing food and supplies should:

1. Deal only with reputable purveyors.
2. Purchase only inspected food. These foods must be inspected and certified by the appropriate U.S. food agency.
   - Meat is inspected by the U.S. Department of Agriculture (USDA) and carries a stamp on the meat carcass or a tag on poultry.
   - Milk, eggs, fruits, and vegetables are inspected by the USDA.
   - Fish and frozen food are certified by the U.S. Public Health Service. This agency also distributes a list of safe shellfish sources.
   - Fishing sources and fish processing are certified by the U.S. Department of the Interior.
3. Visit your purveyors' facilities to ensure that food is protected from contamination and spoilage during handling, packaging, storage, and transit.

Receiving

Ensure that employees responsible for receiving food and supplies:

1. Inspect and weigh all perishable incoming goods before checking the nonperishables.
2. Look for broken or punctured containers, mold growth, color and odor alteration, evidence of pests, and improper thawing.
3. Inspect delivery trucks for signs of insects and proper temperature control (0°–10°F for frozen foods, 35°–40°F for refrigerated foods).
4. Unload, weigh, and count quickly to avoid thawing and thus possible contamination.
5. Date all containers to help in rotating stock.

Storing Dry Goods

To prevent spoilage, cross-contamination, and pest infestation, it is critical that you take the following precautions:

1. Keep storage areas clean, well lit, and at the proper temperature and humidity levels (60°–75°F and 50%–60% humidity).
2. Keep food at least 6 inches off the floor and away from the wall.
3. Make sure all cans and dry food are labeled to avoid mistakes, especially if transferred to another container.
4. To avoid possible leakage, do not locate storage areas over sewer pipes.
5. Use shelves that are made of slatted rust-proof metal, since wooden shelves absorb moisture and are hard to clean.

Storing Refrigerated and Frozen Foods

Refrigeration slows the growth of bacteria and extends the lag phase (the 4–6-hour incubation period that precedes rapid bacterial growth); but will not kill existing bacteria. Consequently, it is important that all food handlers realize that:

1. Raw food should be stored away from and not above cooked food, so it won't drip on and cross-contaminate the cooked food.
2. Inadequate air circulation will distort temperatures and hasten chemical changes in food, so your refrigerator should be large enough to contain most of your food with an allowance of 6 inches from the bottom and 2 inches from the walls. Food stored in walk-ins should be off the floor and away from the walls to increase air circulation.
3. Ideally, each food category (meat, vegetables, dairy, fish) should have its own refrigerator, but if using one refrigerator, put meat, fish, and dairy products in the coldest section.

4. Temperatures need to be checked regularly and preventive maintenance procedures should be followed to ensure that refrigeration equipment functions properly.
5. Food should be wrapped or covered with plastic to avoid dehydration and odor absorption; avoid using aluminum foil because it is dissolved by highly acidic foods, such as tomato sauce.
6. Food will cool fastest if it is put into small, shallow pans and stirred occasionally.

Food Preparation

Everyone involved in the preparation of food needs to understand and follow these important guidelines:

1. Sanitize all equipment before using and immediately after use. Wipe off areas that have been exposed to raw meat.
2. Wash foods, especially vegetables and fruits, under cold running water to reduce the amount of chemical residue.
3. Do not wash raw chicken before cooking. Recent studies have shown that this additional handling of raw poultry increases the risk of cross-contamination from workers' hands, work surfaces, sinks, and utensils.
4. Keep food under refrigeration until it is ready to cook or prepare.
5. Check internal temperatures with a thermometer (see Figure 6-1):
   • Beef should be cooked to 130°F.
   • Pork should be cooked to 150°F.
   • Chicken should be cooked to 165°F.
   • All reheated food should reach 165°F.
6. Eggs, milk, and butter should not be left out, especially after food has been dipped in them.
7. Limit leftovers and cool all foods to 45°F within six hours and then cover tightly. Never mix leftovers with fresh food, nor freeze leftovers, nor reheat in a steam table. Use proper storage containers with lids (do

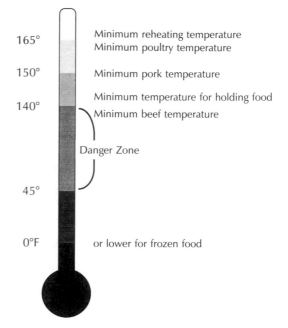

Figure 6-1. Safe Internal Temperatures for Cooking and Reheating Foods.

not reuse mayonnaise jars and other similar containers).
8. No eating, drinking, or smoking at work stations.
9. Never thaw food at room temperature. The four safest thawing methods are to:
   • Remove the food from the freezer and place it immediately in a refrigerator under 45°F.
   • Place under running water at 70°F or lower. Water should be running fast enough to remove loose particles of food.
   • Cook from the frozen state and increase cooking time by one-third.
   • Thaw in a microwave oven, followed immediately by cooking.
10. Avoid cross-contamination by using different cutting boards for raw and cooked foods. Sanitize the boards after each use.

Serving

Temperature control is critical and probably the most potentially dangerous of all the food handling factors. All preparation and service personnel need to understand safe procedures for holding and serving food.

1. Any food held in the danger zone (45°–140°F) for more than two hours must be discarded.
2. All cooked foods should be held at 140°F or higher. The key to preventing overcooking or the need for reheating or disposal is timing; therefore, stagger your preparation so fresh additions to the service area are progressively replacing depleted sources.
3. Long-handled ladles and tongs should be used so that employees' hands do not touch the food.
4. Baked goods that contain cream should be chilled and served as soon as possible.
5. Acceptable types of holding devices include:
   - Steam table or bain marie where food is surrounded by moist 140°F heat.
   - Cabinets that surround food with moist air at 200°–210°F and prevent the cooling of food. Hold service temperature at 140°F.
6. Hands should be washed often.
7. Parts of dishes, glasses, and utensils that come in contact with the customer's mouth should not be touched by employees. Plates should be held by the bottom or edge; cups and glasses by the handle, stem, or bottom; and silverware by handles.
8. Food that has been dropped or left on the plate should never be saved, nor should any product (including butter) that has been served to customers, since it could have been handled or sneezed upon.
9. Milk and milk products for drinking should be supplied in commercially filled, unopened packages or taken from bulk dispensers.
10. Sneeze guards should be placed over self-service stations. Keep quantities small and refill frequently. Arrange glasses, utensils, and food so customers have to touch only the one they are taking.

Warewashing

Warewashing is another important step necessary to ensure proper sanitation. Plates, pots, and utensils, if not cleaned properly, can contaminate the next customer's food. The individual in charge of warewashing and sanitizing therefore is one of the most important people in your entire organization, and it is necessary to hire a person who understands and is conscientious about this. This person should also be responsible for maintaining the warewashing equipment and know how to correctly store all equipment once it has been properly sanitized. This person's value to your organization should not be minimized. The training and salary paid to such an individual is a wise investment.

Dishroom and Utility Areas

Dishroom workers should:

1. Presoak all silverware and run it through the machine twice (the first time flat, and the second time in specially designed containers).
2. Check temperature gauges regularly. Post temperature charts for both machine washing and handwashing.
3. Ensure that toxic chemicals are clearly marked and stored away from food.
4. See that all pots and utensils are properly sanitized and allowed to drain and air-dry, and are then stored upside down.
5. Store dishes properly in clean carts.
6. Properly clean and maintain dishwasher. Dismantle and clean after each meal period or at least the end of each day.
7. Use a mop sink to wash mops. Mops and brooms should be neatly stored.

CLEANING AGENTS AND SANITIZERS

Cleaning Agents	Advantages	Disadvantages
Soap	Removes soil	Doesn't rinse well Leaves a residue
Alkaline Detergent	Highly rinsable Chemically compatible with other compounds Removes grease and wax	
Acidic Cleaner	Removes rust stains, tarnish, and dishwasher buildup	Can damage surfaces
Abrasive Cleaner	Cleans corroded metals and some porous surfaces	May scratch some surfaces

Sanitizers		
Chlorine-based	Inexpensive Not affected by water hardness	Corrosive on some metals
Iodine-based	Not affected by water hardness	Expensive Stains porous objects and plastics Affected by alkaline cleaners
Quaternary ammonium	Odorless Colorless Noncorrosive Long shelf life Effective on both alkalic and acidic kinds of bacteria	Effectiveness is decreased in hard water Certain quats are effective against only certain kinds of bacteria

8. Keep all dishroom surfaces (walls, floors, windows, and counters) clean, free of dust, dirt, and grease.
9. Make sure that grease traps are cleaned and maintained.
10. Do not eat, drink, or smoke in the dishroom area.

Cleaning

Definite cleaning schedules must be established to ensure a safe and sanitary work environment. A good cleaning schedule will include:

- A list of areas to be cleaned.
- When cleaning is to take place, how often, and by whom.
- Specific directions on how the cleaning should be performed.
- A checklist to ensure that everything gets cleaned.

It is also important that all employees understand the difference between cleaning and sanitizing. Removing soil from a surface meets the requirement for cleaning; however, only when bacteria is reduced to a safe level can all surfaces be considered sanitized. There are four kinds of cleaning agents and three kinds of sanitizers. (Immersing objects in 170°F water for 30 seconds is an alternative to using sanitizing agents.)

SANITATION INSPECTIONS

Local and state boards of health make frequent and unannounced inspections at all food establishments. The following areas of concern will be scrutinized:

1. *Foods:* Food must come from approved sources and be wholesome and unadulterated (game must be legal and USDA-inspected). Original containers must be properly labeled and identified.

2. *Food protection:* All potentially hazardous food must be kept in temperature-controlled areas during storage, preparation, display, service, and transport. There must be adequate facilities to maintain product temperature. Frozen food must be thawed properly. Potentially hazardous food must not be served. Food containers must be stored off the floor. Food handling must be minimal. Food-dispensing utensils must be properly stored. Toxic items must be properly stored, labeled, and used.

3. *Personnel:* Employees with infections must be restricted.

4. *Cleanliness of personnel:* Employees must have handwashing facilities, clean outer-clothes, and effective hair restraints. Good hygiene should be practiced and smoking restricted.

5. *Equipment and utensils (design, construction and installation):* Food contact surfaces must be properly maintained (avoid illegal use of wood butcher blocks or other porous substances). Counter surfaces must be clean. Nonfood-contact surfaces should be prop-

erly installed and maintained. Single service articles should be properly stored and dispensed, and *not reused*. Dishwashing facilities, both hand and mechanical, must be of approved design, adequately constructed, and properly installed and maintained (Figures 6-2a and 6-2b).

6. *Cleanliness of equipment and utensils:* Pots must be properly cleaned and free of grease and carbon accumulation. Only clean sponges and toweling can be used. All wash and rinse water must be clean and at the proper temperature. Thermometers must be integral to all mechanical washing facilities. Only approved chemicals can be used.

7. *Water supply:* Source must be adequate and safe. Hot and cold water must be under pressure.

8. *Sewage disposal:* Proper disposal of waste water and sewage must be available, particularly for septic tanks.

9. *Plumbing:* Must be properly installed, approved, and maintained, with no cross-connections, back-siphonage, or backflow.

10. *Toilet facilities:* Must be adequate, convenient, and accessible. Must have self-closing door; all necessary fixtures must be provided and be clean and in good repair.

11. *Manual washing facilities:* Suitable hand cleaners and sanitary towels or approved hand-drying devices must be provided, along with tissue and waste receptacles (Figure 6-3).

12. *Garbage and rubbish storage and disposal:* An adequate number of approved containers must be available that are covered, rodent-proof, and clean, and stored in an approved area. Rubbish rooms must be properly constructed and enclosed, and the contents must be disposed of regularly.

13. *Vermin control:* There must be no evidence of insects or rodents. Extermination control may be scheduled or as needed. Proof of last exterminator's visit should be available.

Sort and Scrape → Rack Prerinse → Wash 160°F → Rinse 180°F → Air Dry → Store

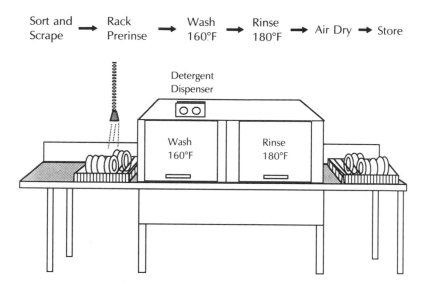

Figure 6-2a. Conveyor Machine Dishwashing.

Sort and Scrape → Prerinse → Wash Detergent 120°F → Rinse Hot water 140°F → Sanitize 170°F Water or Chemical solution for 2 minutes → Drain → Store

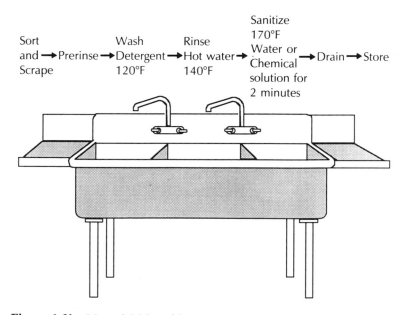

Figure 6-2b. Manual Dishwashing.

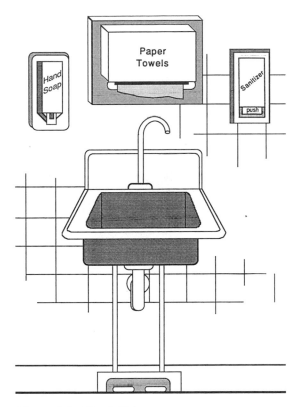

Figure 6-3. Hand Sink.

Outer openings must be protected against entrance of insects and rodents.

14. *Floors, walls, ceilings:* All floors must be constructed as required, in good repair, and clean. Floors must be properly graded and drained. Floors and walls should be properly junctured and covered. Mats must be removable, clean, and in good repair. All attachments to walls and ceilings must be properly constructed, in good repair, and clean. Dustless cleaning methods must be used and cleaning equipment properly stored.

15. *Lighting:* All lighting must be adequate and fixtures must be clean.

16. *Ventilation:* Preparation, storage and related areas must be free of steam and smoke odors. All room and equipment hoods must have ducts vented, as required.

17. *Dressing rooms and lockers:* All rooms must be adequate, all facilities clean, and lockers provided.

18. *Housekeeping:* Establishment and premises must be free of litter, insect or rodent harborage, and unnecessary articles.

19. *Laundry:* Clean and soiled laundry must be properly stored.

20. *Animals:* No live birds, turtles, other animals or pets are allowed, except police guard dogs.

Sanitation inspectors will score each area and give demerits where warranted. A final rating and grading will then be given, to be displayed in a conspicuous area of the establishment. The correction of violations, unless hazardous and flagrant, is allowed within a reasonable length of time.

THE ECONOMICS OF PROPER SANITATION

Since careless operations and lack of cleanliness can lead to damage claims against your business, you should place as much emphasis on sanitation standards as you do on food quality and cost control (see Figure 6-4). Moreover, proper sanitation saves money, saves time, aids safety, improves food quality and service, and projects a favorable public image for both management and personnel.

A Moneysaver

Properly maintained and used utensils and equipment last longer. Foods stored, refrigerated, prepared, and served according to sanitary rules enhance quality, improve appearance, increase customer acceptability, and prevent waste. The danger of food poisoning, with its consequent cost to management, is minimized.

Figure 6-4. Sanitation Steps to Clean and Sanitary Food Service.

A Timesaver

The sanitary way is the *right* way, and experience has shown that the right way is both the best and the quickest way. Consistent practice of proper sanitary methods has proven this.

An Aid to Safety

Regular mopping times and proper cleaning methods reduce the possibility of falls caused by wet, slippery floors or food spillage. Correct methods of handling sharp knives, dishes, glass-

ware, and silverware reduce the danger of cuts and subsequent infection. Strict adherence to sanitary procedures also prevents transmission of illnesses commonly associated with foodservice.

A Way to Improve Food Quality and Service

In addition to preventing the service of contaminated food, clean equipment and utensils ensure safe food with truly appetizing food flavors. Correct service is sanitary service. Make sure your employees realize this, as it will help them develop the confidence, poise, and pride inherent in quality service. And remember, high-quality food and service are the bases for building a successful catering business.

A Way of Projecting a Favorable Public Image

A clean, sanitary establishment always creates a favorable atmosphere. Your customers are certain to notice that correct serving methods are being used by your trained foodservice workers.

SANITATION CERTIFICATION

Although sanitation certification for all food handlers is not mandatory, it is an important standard to set for your staff. Knowledge of the practices and procedures central to the prevention of foodborne illness is an essential part of being a foodservice professional. It is important to realize that the trend is moving toward required certification for all food handlers. Many states, counties, and municipalities already require some type of certification and others are in the process of enacting appropriate legislation (Figure 6-5).

How to Become Certified

The Food Protection Certificate Program test, under the auspices of the Educational Testing

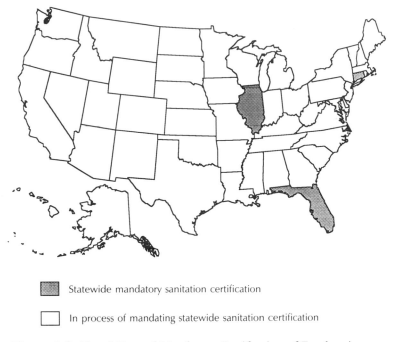

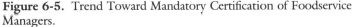
Statewide mandatory sanitation certification

In process of mandating statewide sanitation certification

Figure 6-5. Trend Toward Mandatory Certification of Foodservice Managers.

Service, is designed to test persons who have ongoing on-site responsibility for protecting the consumer. Candidates must demonstrate that they know how to protect against foodborne illness, detect breaches in a protection plan, and take appropriate corrective action when a breach occurs. The focus of the test is on the generally recognized standards, procedures, and practices necessary for the protection of public health, safety, and welfare as set forth in the FDA Model Food Service Sanitation Ordinance.

National Restaurant Association (NRA)

The Education Foundation of the NRA is still the foremost training and testing leader of food-

service sanitation throughout the country. The demand for this program (formally NIFI) is an indication of the trend towards certification.

The NRA's Applied Foodservice Sanitation course provides foodservice managers with basic sanitation principles and their application to practical situations, as well as methods for training and motivating employees to follow good sanitation practices. This program is used by many foodservice chains, community colleges, and professional organizations. Sponsors of this program can determine the appropriate time frame, location, class size, and instructor. Course books are then purchased from the Educational Foundation, which furnishes and corrects the final exam, issues certificates of completion, and maintains a permanent record of participants.

·7·

Setting Up a Kitchen

LEGAL REQUIREMENTS AND AREA RESOURCES

If after carefully analyzing the market you decide to go ahead and start a catering business, your next step will be to establish a commissary or kitchen. Before you make any investment, however, you must determine whether your business can be located in the area you have selected. Check through the following list:

1. Do the zoning laws permit the establishment of a commercial kitchen?
2. Is commercial traffic allowed to and from the facility?
3. Are there any restrictions regarding hours of operation?
4. Is parking space adequate for employees, for your vehicles, and for deliveries from vendors?
5. What are the relevant local board of health and building codes, and what permits are required?

6. Are the waste and septic systems adequate?
7. What utility services are available?
8. Are labor and public transportation available?

You may also want to discuss your plans with your lawyer and insurance agents for their advice and recommendations.

FACILITY REQUIREMENTS

After you know that your business can be legally operated and that the necessary resources are available, you can start to search for a facility to rent or buy. Use the following checklist to help you determine whether a site is suitable and what you must plan for in designing a kitchen.

1. Avoid establishing a kitchen in a building where you must use an elevator either to enter the kitchen or to go from one department to another.
2. Check all floors, walls, and ceilings for

cracks, holes, and peeling paint. (Do not use lead-based paint in any area.)

3. Check for possible fly and other insect infestation. All doors and windows should be properly screened.

4. Install adequate lighting. Cool white bulbs should be used in fluorescent fixtures because other colors tend to give food an unattractive appearance. Lighting fixtures should be easy to reach and to clean.

5. Carefully plan the placement of all equipment. Allow sufficient aisle space so that refrigerators, freezers, and ovens can open to their full swing and food trucks and dollies can move unimpeded.

   A good way to plan the placement of appliances and equipment is to make a scaled floor plan. Cut out templates—paper patterns scaled to the size of your equipment—and arrange the most effective layout on graph paper (see Figure 7-1). Architectural supply stores may have preprinted templates of kitchen equipment, or equipment measurements can be found in catalogs.* Templates are also available in computer software packages.

6. Check the natural ventilation. The ovens, ranges, and steam kettles should be placed so that the mechanical exhaust units above them can operate at peak efficiency and with a short "drag area."

7. Exhaust hoods above cooking areas should include automatic firefighting equipment.

8. Unlike a banquet-hall kitchen where the food is served on the premises, a commissary kitchen requires space for counting, organizing, packing, storing, and shipping food off-premises, besides the usual space needed for food production.

9. Be certain that the lavatory space conforms to local ordinances.

10. If possible, arrange to have one sink for the exclusive use by the chef, another for utility work, and a third for potwashing. Your local board of health may also require installation of a special hand sink in the kitchen.

11. Dishwashing, receiving and storage, and packing areas should, if possible, be separated from, but within easy access to, the kitchen.

In the beginning, be prepared for a shake-down period during which operations, cost patterns, and systems for performing functions will evolve gradually. This period can be chaotic and frustrating. Emerging business patterns may differ markedly from what you had anticipated and planned so carefully. And since this particular period can also be very costly, a new caterer must be prepared, both financially and otherwise, to cope with many unforeseen difficulties.

While careful planning is essential, no scientific formula exists to ensure smooth sailing. Do not be discouraged. In time, with constant attention to detail and objective evaluation, your business can become a very efficient and rewarding operation.

KITCHEN DESIGN AND LAYOUT

Good kitchen design is characterized by adherence to six criteria:

1. Grouping tasks of similar nature
2. Grouping equipment requiring similar utilities, especially ventilation
3. Maximizing labor utilization
4. Maximizing equipment utilization
5. Minimizing interdepartmental traffic
6. Maximizing sanitary conditions

---

*An excellent book about kitchen equipment is *Food Equipment Facts* by C. Scriven and J. Stevens, Van Nostrand Reinhold, 1989.

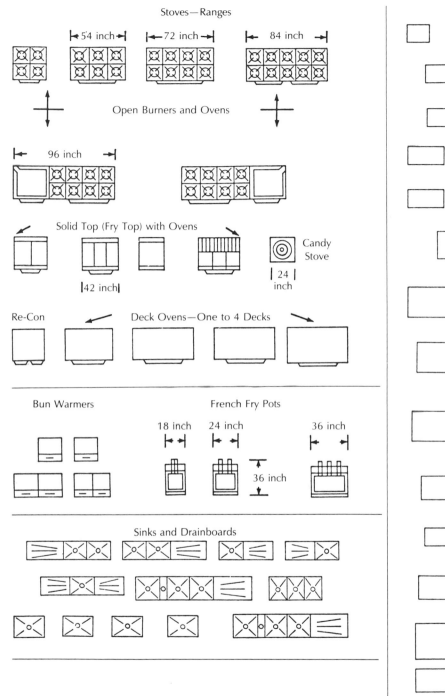
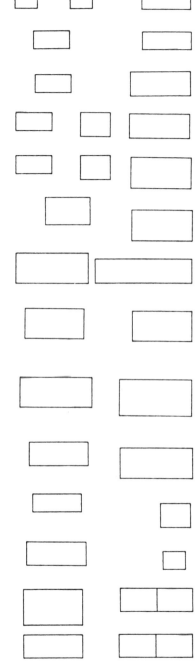

Figure 7-1. Kitchen Equipment Templates.

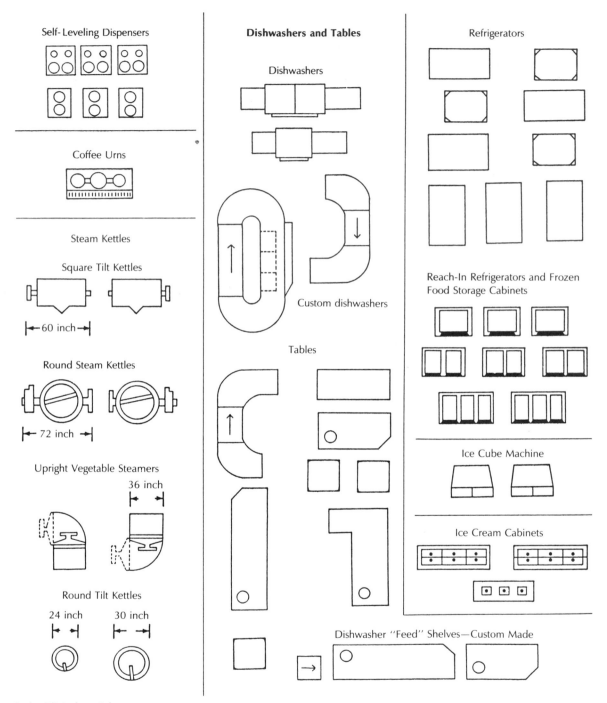

Scale: 1/8 inch = 1 foot

Figure 7-1. Kitchen Equipment Templates. (continued)

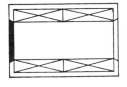

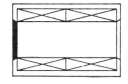

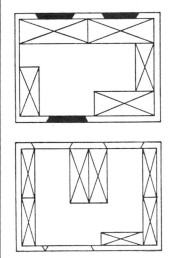

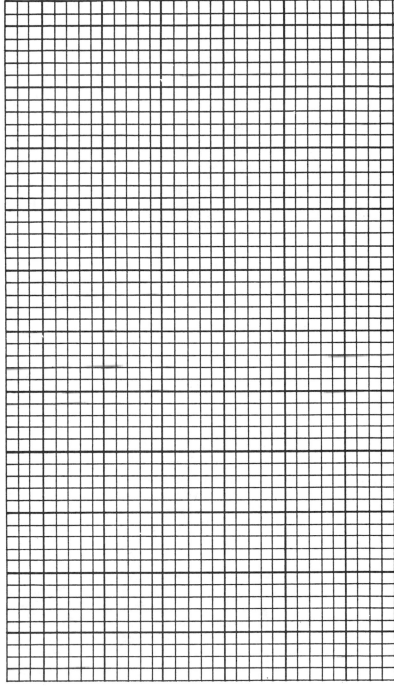

Scale: 1/8 inch = 1 foot

Sections within heavy lines on graph paper
equal to 5 square feet.

Figure 7-1. (continued)

Using these guidelines, the various kitchen functions are organized into the following foodservice departments:

Receiving
Dry storage
Refrigerated storage, including frozen foods
Meat preparation
Vegetable preparation
Salad preparation
Main cooking
Short-order cooking
Bake shop
Ice cream
Potwashing
Serving area
Dishwashing and dish storage
Dining area
Miscellaneous areas (office, employee facilities, storage, and ice manufacturing)

Not all catering businesses, of course, will contain all these departments. It depends on the size of your outfit, or on the extent to which you purchase and process raw materials or buy "convenience" foods that fit into your standards.

When planning the kitchen layout, you should consider the flow of food from one department to another—from receiving through preparation, production, and service, whether on or off premises—as well as supporting departments such as offices, dishwashing, potwashing, and sanitation. If food to go is to be sold, you will need to include the space and equipment for packaging, particularly if you are considering the new cook-and-chill system, or *sous vide* (see page 83). Figure 7-2 is a sample floor plan for an off-premises kitchen based on the grouping of related functions and activities. Note the generous space for packing and dolly storage.

If all food is to be served on-premises and you anticipate a large business, you should use banquet carriers and your planning should provide for storage. If your business will be off-premises, then you will need to check into the various types of dish and food-carrying equipment that are available and purchase the sizes and kinds appropriate to your needs, as well as plan for their storage.

Receiving

Receiving is one of the most important areas in your entire installation. The function of this department is to check the quantities and purchasing standards of all items that are delivered. Weights and counts must be verified, and any short count or short weight must be noted on the delivery slip and countersigned by the delivery person immediately. Specifications must be met by your vendors; if not, the shipment must be rejected. Receiving hours need to be established and posted. By allowing enough lead time on ordering, the receiving department is able to reject inferior products at the time of delivery. The receiving department can also function as the shipping department for off-premises caterers.

Receiving Department Equipment

1. A counter scale of 500-pound capacity with a large manual or digital read-out, and platform scale for items up to 1,000 pounds. The scales must be periodically checked by an outside service for accuracy. A set of test weights is also suggested (Figure 7-3).

2. A portion scale, to ensure that portion-control items meet the specification. Total weights may be exact but portion size could be inconsistent (Figure 7-4).

3. A table (not to exceed 5 by 8 feet) large enough to inspect incoming products and to count those items not to be weighed. The table may be used to assemble items for off-premises catering.

4. A stand-up desk or shelf for checking packing slips and other paperwork.

5. A heavy-duty hand truck, identified with your company name, for moving goods. (To

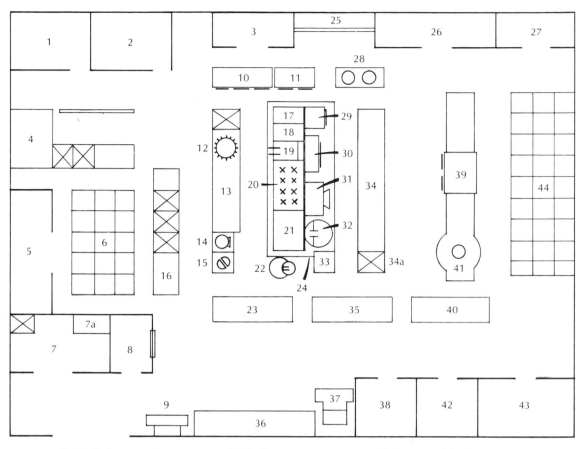

1. Men's dressing room	17. Broiler	32. Steam stock kettle
2. Ladies' dressing room	18. Re-con oven	33. Meat grinder
3. Chef's office	19. Fryer	34. Work tables
4. Pot washing area	20. Surface burners	Shelves under
5. Cart washing area	2 ovens underneath	34a. Hand sink
6. Cart storage	21. Deck oven	35. Assembly table
7. Trash room with sink	22. Mixer	36. Receiving and sorting table
7a. Compactor	23. Assembly tables	37. Ice machine
8. Receiving office	Also #35 and #40 (for	38. Merchandise storage
9. Receiving scale	cart packing	39. Dishwasher
10. Reach-in refrigerator	24. Exhaust canopy over	Hot-water booster underneath
11. Reach-in freezer	25. Vegetable-fruit storage	40. Food assembly tables (for
12. Suspended pot-pan hooks	26. Walk-in refrigerator	cart packing)
13. Chef's work table	27. Walk-in freezer	41. Disposal
Shelves and bins underneath	28. Coffee makers	42. Storage, dishes, silver, props
14. Chopper	29. Microwave oven	43. Storage, linens, etc.
15. Slicer	30. Oblong tilt steam kettle	44. Glasses, cups, dishes, storage
16. Work sink with	31. Vegetable steamer	in mobile racks
drainboards		

Figure 7-2. Floor Plan of Kitchen for Off-premises Caterer.

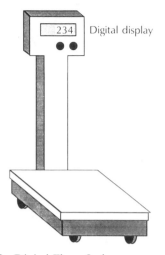

Figure 7-3. Digital Floor Scale.

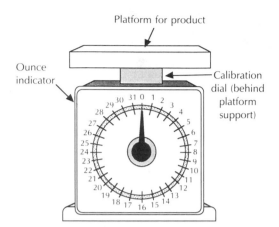

Figure 7-4. Portion Scale.

avoid injury to the receiving clerk, insist that nothing be carried that can be put on wheels.)

6. Platform skids with detachable jacks may also be necessary.
7. A pallet jack bearing your identification may be useful for high-volume caterers.
8. A thermometer for checking whether refrigerated and frozen products were delivered at the correct temperature.

Dry Storage

When planning your installation, safeguard your dry storage from deterioration, adverse temperature or temperature changes, adverse moisture or moisture changes, pilferage, and dust, dirt, insects, fire, or other damage.

The dry-storage stockroom should be dry, well ventilated, out of direct sunlight, and maintained at a temperature of 55° to 65°F. Since freezing or excessively warm temperatures can damage canned goods, an accurate wall thermometer should be placed in a prominent place and checked regularly to prevent wide temperature fluctuations.

Dry-storage shelves ought to be at least 8 inches off the floor and made of heavy-duty metal. They should be arranged to provide "first-in, first-out" distribution, to allow maximum circulation of air, and to avoid high stacking of such items as cereal, flour, and sugar. No food should be stored directly on the floor. Platforms should be constructed or merchandise kept on skids. Portable bins, either plastic or metal, make good storage containers. The ones with attached wheels are the easiest to clean and move.

The dry storage area should also contain a valuable-items storage cabinet, separate and locked, for the safekeeping of expensive foods or equipment. Records and files of the storeroom clerk can also be kept here.

You should also reserve an area for communications equipment, such as a telephone, which is a must. An intercom is equally important and possibly a TV screen to monitor the activity area.

Refrigerated Storage

In many installations there are refrigerated storage areas at several points from receiving to service. In small installations, one unit may suffice. Larger installations may have separate refrigerators for meats, dairy products, vegetables, and fish, plus a separate freezer (usually a walk-in). The size of these units is determined by the volume stored, menu requirements, and the frequency of delivery.

Unnecessarily large refrigerators and freezers waste valuable energy and increase operation costs. However, when a facility is in an outlying district, when extra delivery charges are incurred for small quantities, or when deliveries are infrequent, greater refrigerated storage requirements may be justified.

COOKING EQUIPMENT

While careful consideration must be given to budgetary considerations, equal attention should also be given to equipment quality. Economically, the purchase of high-quality equipment is a smart move. In addition to giving superior performance, there should be fewer breakdowns and lower repair costs.

The equipment in your kitchen is the heart of your facility, and it must be planned and designed for the best service. Your decisions must be guided by the tasks each unit is expected to perform. The placement of each unit is also crucial as you must consider stepsaving and traffic flow. Before purchasing any equipment, consult industry professionals at restaurant equipment and supply houses and from your local gas and electric companies.

Menu Demands

Your menus must be analyzed to determine what and how much equipment you should purchase. The kitchens that are built around the menus are kitchens that have the best chance for success. A quick look at the fast food industry is a good indication of this premise; space is maximized to execute the menu items. This planning process cannot be left to conjecture or to the discretion of high-pressure equipment salespeople, who usually mean well but do not have to work in the facility after they have made the sale. Otherwise, without careful planning, you may find yourself working in a kitchen with surplus equipment that collects dust and takes up space. You also may wish you had selected something different, or perhaps could recover the money that you spent.

From the largest refrigerator to the smallest measuring spoon, you must carefully visualize and plan so as to avoid painful, costly pitfalls later. Keeping this in mind, we need to look at the area of the kitchen that would have the largest impact based on your menus, the cooking battery.

Cooking Battery

There are eight basic commercial cooking methods, and a specific unit of equipment for each method. Some units incorporate two methods in a single design. For instance, a stove with open top grates, or with a French-type or solid plate surface, will have a fully functional and thermostatically controlled oven underneath.

The eight cooking methods are:

1. Surface cooking
2. Top and bottom cooking ovens
3. Griddling—full solid surface cooking with heat controls for each quarter of the assembly
4. Immersion cooking—deep-fat frying
5. Radiant cooking—broiling (broiling units can be free-standing or mounted over ovens)
6. Steam cooking (This is becoming increasingly popular because of its versatility. Practically all models can be purchased with built-in steam-generating units requiring no remote source of steam supply.)
7. Steam convection or combi ovens (convection oven with steam injected)
8. Microwave cooking

Figure 7-5. Battery of Cooking Equipment (hot top, open top, griddle, deep fat fryers, char broilers, and convection oven).

Figure 7-5 is an example of a cooking battery using six of these methods in one installation.

The main cooking battery will require the highest financial investment and reflects the largest operating expense because of the highly skilled labor required and the high cost of utilities. Accurately anticipating your potential needs will help you avoid buying excessive equipment with high operating costs or acquiring inade-quate equipment with insufficient capacity. For example, if you are outfitting a commissary devoted exclusively to off-premises food preparation, you may only need one broiler or salamander. (Mounted over an oven, this is a small broiler that saves valuable floor space.) This unit could be used for top browning or marking. For a banquet hall kitchen, you may need to install a battery of these broilers.

Surface Cooking

Ranges

Heavy-duty commercial ranges are built to withstand constant use as well as the weight of heavy
cooking utensils and their contents. Their
greater gas input enables them to cook large
amounts of food in a shorter time than home
ranges.

Heavy-duty ranges may have a solid hot top,
a set of open top burners (called a grate top), or
a solid griddle for frying. Solid griddles are also
available as separate units (Figure 7-6). Beneath
these tops there is usually an oven for roasting
or baking, or you can special order a skeleton
range with shelves and storage cabinets in place
of the oven.

Heavy-duty ranges usually have double-deck
high shelves that also function as flueways to
carry off the combustion products from the
oven and top shelf burners. These ranges can
be grouped together with spreader plates to
provide additional working surface between
units. Heavy-duty range sections, from 28 to
33 inches wide and 24 to 42 inches deep, are
available in stainless steel, black and gray Japan
finish, and porcelain enamel finish in black or
a color.

Power Burner

Gas ranges are now available with power burners
which feature a 50 percent more usable heat
efficiency in range top cooking. Optimum combustion, obtained by mixing air and gas, results
in faster cooking time and lower operating costs.

Candy or Stock Pot Stove

These ranges are usually 24 inches or less in
height and are designed for heavy stock pots.
They are also used in the bake shops to supply a
high-intensity gas flame for sugar and candy
work (Figure 7-7).

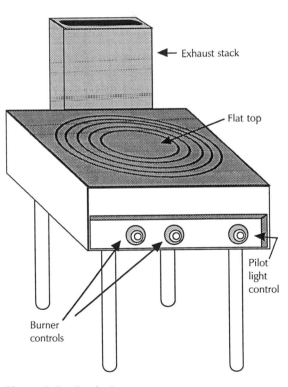

Figure 7-6. Griddle.

Grease trap

Temperature controls

Exhaust stack

Flat top

Pilot
light
control

Burner
controls

Figure 7-7. Candy Stove.

Ovens

Range Ovens

These ovens are below the cooking tops, and are used mainly for roasting. They are also available in separate units and can be constructed in pairs, one above the other, known as double-deck range-type ovens. The oven space ranges from 13 to 15 inches in height to permit roasting large cuts of meat. Oven volume varies from 5.4 to 6.3 cubic feet and can handle as much as 130 pounds at one time.

Deck-Type Ovens

Deck or peel ovens, constructed in sections, have special baking (7-inch) or roasting (12-inch) decks that can be combined in any desired arrangement. Decks may be supplied with hearth tile for special baking purposes. Each oven has an individual temperature control (Figure 7-8).

Convection Ovens or High-Velocity Forced Air Circulation

This oven offers the most up-to-date design for baking and roasting for commercial purposes. The rapid circulation of air, due to a motor-driven fan unit, permits food to be cooked on multiple racks rather than on a hearth. The full oven space can be utilized and production

greatly increased. This oven is equally efficient for both baking and roasting. Most caterers find it to be the most frequently used unit in their kitchen (Figure 7-9).

Recent models have improved oven heat retention because of more effective insulating materials, including stainless steel doors. Additional features are the cook-and-hold controls that offer the convenience of advance starting of roasts. Meats are automatically held at serving temperature after the cooking time is completed. These ovens can be mounted on stands or in cabinet bases, and double stacks. Gas models are available with pilotless ignition.

Combi Ovens

Extremely versatile, this relatively new oven roasts or steams in the same cavity or combines

Figure 7-8. Deck Oven.

both cooking methods simultaneously. It is often recommended for use with the new cook-and-chill system or *sous vide*, a method which has proven to be a big labor-saver. Preparation is done ahead of time, and food is refrigerated in sealed, airtight bags which can be reheated in baths of hot water. The FDA has strict regulations that are product-specific and must be met by anyone preparing foods by the *sous vide* method.

Revolving Tray or Reel Ovens

Large-volume caterers will find this type of oven beneficial to their operations. The unit is really a large chamber with revolving shelves (similar to a ferris wheel), mounted on a longitudinal axis, with flat trays suspended between them. Food is loaded on these trays as they appear opposite the door opening. Heat loss is kept to a minimum by built-in diffusers that prevent the heat from escaping (Figure 7-10).

Cook-and-Hold Ovens

Slow cooking has the advantage of reducing the amount of shrinkage during the roasting process. Cook-and-hold ovens not only result in better yield, but also save energy over the more traditional shorter cooking time at higher temperature. These ovens should be considered if you roast a lot of meat. (Figure 7-11).

Salamanders and Heavy-Duty Broilers

Salamanders are really miniature broilers mounted above the cooking surface of a heavy-duty range, often in pairs to provide additional broiling capacity. Salamanders have practically every feature of a heavy-duty broiler including ceramic radiants. They are particularly valuable in limited areas because they require no floor space (Figure 7-12a and 7-12b).

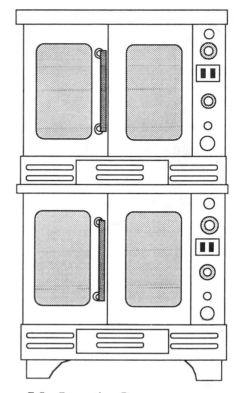

Figure 7-9. Convection Oven.

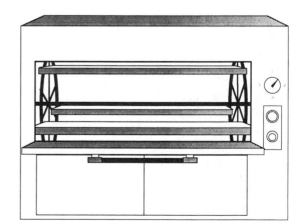

Figure 7-10. Revolving Oven.

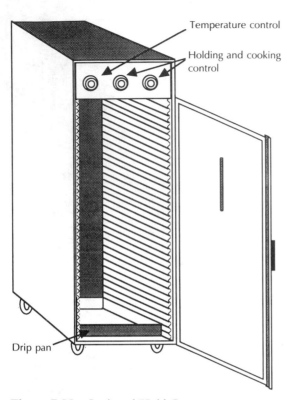

Figure 7-11. Cook-and-Hold Oven.

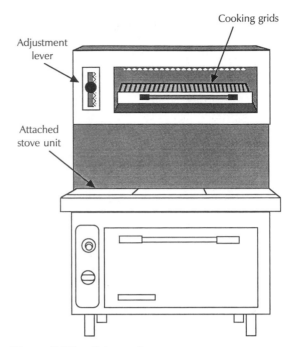

Figure 7-12a. Salamander.

In large-volume banquet or on-premises catering establishments, a heavy-duty broiler can be a valuable production tool. In area, it occupies the same space as a heavy-duty oven. The burners are equipped with ceramic radiants to provide the intense uniform heat that is so essential for mass production. Infrared burners are available for very high production requirements. Some models have overhead ovens, heated by the burners in the broiling compartment, that are integral to the unit. They serve as warming compartments, precook chambers, and finishing ovens, and greatly increase the broiler's capabilities.

Grills, an option to broiling, are heated from the bottom and have the advantage of full-view cooking which is easier to tend (Figure 7-13).

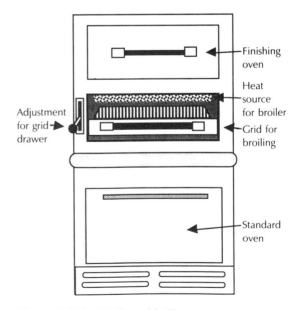

Figure 7-12b. Broiler with Oven.

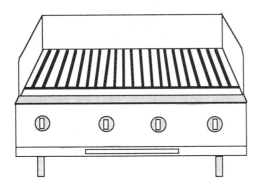

Figure 7-13. Gas Grill.

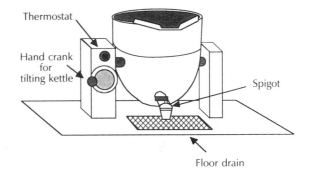

Figure 7-14. Steam Kettle.

Immersion Cooking

Deep-fry kettles have limited use in most commissaries; a two-basket unit is usually more than sufficient. A banquet-hall kitchen might require a battery of fryers. Built-in time-temperature controls allow precise, consistent cooking and reduced fuel consumption. Internal ignition models are recommended over the standard pilot light. Some models have built-in filters for convenience. Modified pressure fryers increase the efficiency by covering the heating well and should be considered especially if your menu calls for large quantities of fried chicken or other deep-fried products.

Steam Cooking

The tremendous design advancements in steam-cooking equipment warrant considering it for your kitchen. Quantity cooking can be achieved in less time and with better results. Color as well as valuable vitamins and minerals, which are so often lost in other methods of cooking, are retained. It is almost impossible to burn or scorch foods in a steam kettle. This method saves time and eliminates the messy job of cleanup (Figure 7-14).

Every piece of steam-cooking equipment is now available with a self-contained, steam-generating unit that requires minimal connecting expense. One of the most popular units is a tilting skillet that comes in 23- and 40-gallon sizes. Ten-gallon and lesser capacity, hand-tilted skillets for minimal requirements are also available. These versatile skillets increase kitchen productivity by boiling, steaming, braising, sautéing, simmering, grilling, stewing, and pan-frying—all in a single unit (Figure 7-15).

There are compartment steam cookers that cook foods in standard cafeteria pans, eliminating the need for transfer and cleanup. Different foods, such as poultry, seafoods, eggs, rice, pasta, and vegetables, can be cooked in separate pans simultaneously. These units outperform full sections of range tops in cooking capacity and energy savings (Figure 7-16).

Chinese Cook Stoves

Chinese cook stoves are the most satisfactory method of preparing stir-fried foods of every nature. The food is cooked in woks, which are bowl-shaped utensils, usually of black steel. The stoves can develop abnormally high temperatures. They are heated from underneath by a high-intensity gas flame and have heat-retentive ceramic walls, resulting in rapid food preparation.

Microwave Ovens

Although their uses are limited, some caterers will find a microwave oven crucial. They are

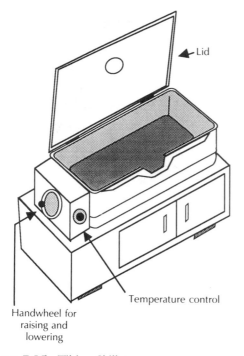

Lid

Temperature control

Handwheel for
raising and
lowering

Figure 7-15. Tilting Skillet.

convenient and effective for heating small amounts of hors d'oeuvres, thawing small portions of frozen foods, baking a dozen potatoes, or heating the contents of two 9-inch dinner plates at one time.

Microwaves can be of value at house parties where the contents of ceramic casseroles have to be heated. However, many do not top brown so the desired surface appearance may not be achieved.

Since the unit weighs only about 150 pounds and uses household current, some off-premises caterers take one along on their jobs. On-premises caterers might find a microwave beneficial in emergencies—for example, quickly heating a few additional portions that may be needed at a banquet.

When purchasing a microwave, make certain that it is fully approved and carries a minimum two-year guarantee against "burnout."

PREPARATION EQUIPMENT

Food Cutter or Buffalo Chopper

This is one of the most versatile machines in any kitchen and reputedly long-term trouble free. It

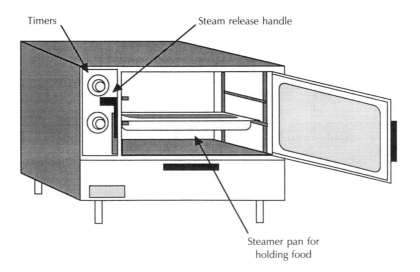

Timers

Steam release handle

Steamer pan for
holding food

Figure 7-16. Steamer.

chops onions, potatoes, celery, and other vegetables from coarse to extra fine, depending on the length of operation (in seconds). It is also excellent for chopping chicken, shrimp, tuna, eggs, liver, and other salad bases. It will make bread crumbs using fresh or dried bread and produce properly sized potatoes and corned beef for hash. A meat grinder head or vegetable slicer can be attached (Figure 7-17).

Mixers

This is an essential machine for every food preparation establishment. There are bench models available in 5- to 20-quart capacities; floor models are available from 20 quarts to 140 quarts. Paddle attachments of every type and for any purpose are available, including mixing, whipping, and a dough hook for kneading. Mixers are either belt driven or gear driven; however, gear-driven models are the most popular. Mixers also come equipped with grinders and vegetable slicer attachments (Figure 7-18).

Slicers

A slicer is essential for every catering kitchen. Select one that suits your production needs. Manufacturers now provide a wide variety of slicers ranging from hand-controlled gravity-angle feed, to those that are completely automatic and will portion out specified amounts of product onto a conveyor belt (Figure 7-19).

Blender Sticks and Food Processors

Blender sticks or mixing wands and food processors reduce the amount of labor and provide a uniformly minced product. A blender stick has the advantage of doing the job right in the cooking utensil. For example, you can purée soup in the pot it was cooked in rather than transferring it to a food processor (Figures 7-20a and 7-20b).

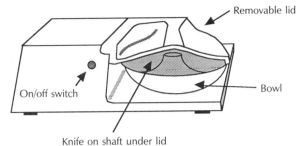

Figure 7-17. Buffalo Chopper.

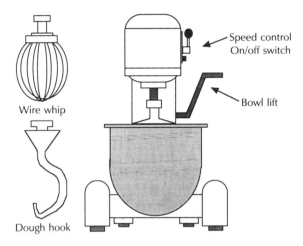

Figure 7-18. Table Mixer.

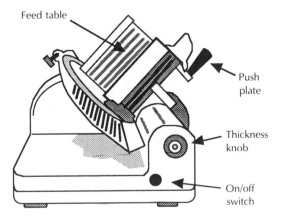

Figure 7-19. Slicer.

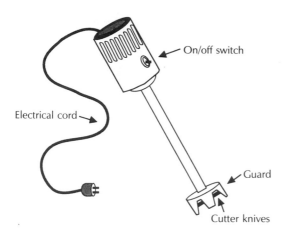

Figure 7-20a. Blender Stick.

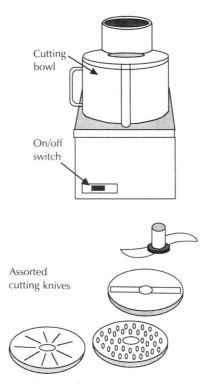

Figure 7-20b. Food Processor.

Tables

Kitchen Work Tables

Kitchen tables come in standard 30-inch widths and 34-inch heights. Overall lengths range from 4 to 10 feet. The tops should always be of polished stainless steel (14 to 16 gauge), with turned or rolled-down edges and welded and polished corners. The tops, as well as the undershelf, should be reinforced and sound-deadened. The undershelf can be eliminated to allow clearance between legs for mobile storage bins, thus utilizing the vertical height. The legs are made of steel tubing, with adjustable feet from 37 to 42 inches high. Tables mounted on casters allow flexibility and ease of cleaning the surrounding floor areas. Production tables with back splash and adjustable heights are available, the latter permitting increased flexibility and productivity. Drawers are an option; since they tend to become junk collectors and add to the cost, they might better be dispensed with.

Maple Tables

Many states outlaw maple-topped tables because of the difficulty they present in complying with maximum sanitation requirements. The newer plastic composition table tops are now in favor, although they often are not durable enough to withstand heavy work loads.

Mechanical or Assembly Line Tables

Some institutions, food manufacturing plants, and airline catering kitchens have tables that are equipped with a motorized driven belt for dealing with high volume. It is an excellent way to increase your productivity as long as you have your *mise en place* set.

Packaging and Wrapping Machines

There are many different kinds of machines and packaging materials. A vacuum-packing machine is most common. Vacuum-packed foods have a longer storage life and also save storage space since containers are not usually necessary.

Mobile Racks and Dollies

Mobile items such as platform trucks and rack dollies save time, ease work loads, and take the strain out of handling heavy stock, supplies, and equipment. They can be used in preparation, staging, transportation to and from the function, as well as for storage. These mobile pieces of equipment will save labor as well as reduce employee injuries. Racks, enclosed and open, are available in many shapes and sizes.

KITCHEN VENTILATION

A good kitchen ventilating system must be engineered for full efficiency. Many local fire and health authorities require hood and duct design before granting a permit.

No two ventilating conditions are alike. Many factors must be considered. Air intake or replacement source, its effect on the surrounding area, and the most effective method of exhausting heat and grease-laden vapors must be planned. Exhaust ducts from kitchen hoods must be independent of any other ventilating system. This sometimes requires expensive and complicated duct work, frequently extending outside a building and above the roof.

Exhaust hoods are intended to capture as much of the odors and heat as possible and to contain them until the integral fan exhausts them (Figure 7-21). The fan may be a propeller, mushroom, or centrifugal type. The National Fire Protection Association (NFPA) requires that all hoods be equipped with a grease filter. Grease filters must fit tightly, against each other and against the holding frame, to prevent the exhaust air from bypassing the filter and depositing grease in the hood. Grease filters should be readily accessible to permit regular cleaning and replacement.

Improper venting of water heaters in kitchen areas, or ineffective venting in the dishwashing area, can adversely affect the proper functioning of a kitchen ventilating system.

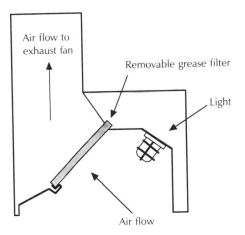

Figure 7-21. Exhaust Hood (side view).

Island-type cooking battery installations are particularly susceptible to cross-drafts and require special attention. Aprons may have to be attached to deflect the draft. If an adjoining dining room is air-conditioned, improper kitchen venting can cause an overload of the system and waste valuable energy.

The NFPA (Standard no. 96) and local authorities having jurisdiction also require that all hoods be equipped with a fire-extinguishing system of inert gas, dry chemical, or fine water spray. An auxiliary hand-held extinguisher must be accessible nearby. In addition to standard motor controls for the fans, sensors must be installed that will automatically shut down the fan in the event of overheating or burnup.

All electrical installations must meet the National Electrical Code (NFPA no. 70). It may be possible to conserve energy by rerouting the kitchen heat to heat water or limited areas.

For further information about ventilation, consult the following references:

Design of Kitchen Ventilation Systems, U.S. Public Health Service, Atlanta, Georgia
Guide for Kitchen Ventilation Systems, Virginia Department of Health, Richmond, Virginia

Standard no. 96, Ventilation of Restaurant Cooking Equipment, National Fire Protection Association, Boston, Massachusetts

SINKS

A sink must be provided for rinsing out utensils and for the various washing and water-source operations necessary in a kitchen. A separate sink is required for potwashing, and another sink of two or three compartments is needed for general kitchen use. A separate handwashing sink is now mandatory in many areas. Sinks are subject to abuse and, consequently, should be constructed of 14- to 16-gauge stainless steel. Corners and edges should be rounded to prevent harborage of residue. Unless there are unusual space configurations or protrusions, you may be able to purchase fully fabricated units with 10-inch splash and integrated drainboards.

Perforated swill guards with removable standard overflow should be considered an essential adjunct to a sink. Heavy-duty faucets are a wise investment to replace the commercial type normally furnished with an installation.

Small-volume caterers who cannot afford a mechanical dishwasher can purchase gas and electric heaters that can be installed under a sink unit to convert it into an operational dishwasher. Baskets for dish immersion are available, as are hang-on thermometers for measuring the water temperature.

REFRIGERATORS

One of the most important pieces of equipment in the commissary or banquet kitchen is the refrigerator, which should be carefully chosen as a part of the overall food handling system. Its function, of course, is to retard the growth of molds and bacteria as well as to inhibit internal changes that can make food less nutritious, unpalatable, and unsafe.

Refrigerators are available to suit any specialty phase of the industry and fit any space. There are reach-in, reach-through, under-counter, and walk-in refrigerators, all of which come in a variety of sizes. The reach-in or reach-through models come in one, two, or three sections. Most have self-contained compressors and range from ¼ to ½ horsepower. The approximate capacities are 22 cubic feet for a single door, 48 cubic feet for a two-door, and 73 cubic feet for a three-door.

No matter what the type—reach-in, roll-in, or walk-in—each unit should be evaluated on how well it meets basic requirements for air circulation, humidity, temperature, sanitation, and adaptability.

Air Circulation
The unit should have multiple cold air outlets to cool quickly and uniformly under maximum loading. The best refrigerator, however, loses its efficiency when food is packed too closely, preventing the proper circulation of inside cooling air. Outside air circulation is equally important to allow the compressor to function properly and effectively. The placement of the refrigerator should take into account convenience as well as the accessibility of outside air, which, if inadequate, can cause food spoilage.

Humidity
Relative humidity should be maintained at 80 to 85 percent to keep food from drying out.

Temperature
The refrigeration system components and how they are assembled affect efficiency and economy. The internal cabinet temperature must be maintained at 38° to 40°F.

The compressor or pump, which circulates the refrigerant at a determined pressure, is controlled by the temperature needs of the cabinet interior. There are two types of compressors—standard and high torque. For maximum capacity and to meet sudden high-power demands, a high-torque compressor is preferable.

The following popularly sized reach-in refrigerators, for example, should not have compressors with a horsepower rating less than stated:

Cabinet Size	Horsepower Rating
19.7 cu. ft.	1/4
36.5 cu. ft.	1/3
45.5 cu. ft.	1/3
71.8 cu. ft.	1/2
96.5 cu. ft.	3/4

The condenser, which cools the refrigerant, should be located in an easily accessible place where it will be exposed to air. The condenser must be cleaned regularly. Accumulated dust and dirt can impede proper air circulation; this can cause overloading of the compressor and lead to a breakdown.

Both fiberglass and polyurethane are good insulating materials, but today most manufacturers use polyurethane because it is stronger. The effect of proper insulation, however, can be diminished if air leaks through seams and door gaskets.

While most commercial units are equipped with thermometers, the reading refers to the air within the cabinet and not the product itself. To get a more accurate reading of the unit's efficiency, insert thermometers into glasses of water or into vegetables or fruits placed in different areas of the cabinet. For further protection, install a battery-operated alarm system with visual or audible signaling devices for either or both high and low temperature warnings.

Sanitation

A cabinet that is difficult to clean is a potential health hazard. Reach-in cabinets should have few, if any, interior seams. The better models are seamless. Interior construction must be covered all around and made from stainless steel, aluminum, or bonded vinyl on steel.

The shelves should be zinc-covered, anodized aluminum, stainless steel, or chrome, and be adjustable and removable. There should be a minimum of corners, extrusions, and few crossings in shelves, shelf standards, clips, trays, or pan slides; these collect spillage which, if not adequately cleaned, can lead to bacterial growth and mold. Walk-ins should have tight and durable junctures to reduce the possibility of food spillage or debris forming under and between panels.

Adaptability

Refrigeration equipment must be evaluated not only on its food preservation function, but also for its contribution to other kitchen operations. For instance, tray slides are designed for 18- by 26-inch baking pans or 14- by 18-inch cafeteria trays. Thus, salads, desserts, and other preportioned foods can be prepared in advance, put in a pan or tray, and stored in the refrigerator. The items are more accessible, and the capacity of the unit is more fully utilized.

Regardless of what type of refrigerator you buy, be sure that the door has safety grip handles, rather than a latch, to eliminate the chance of clothing catching on the latch.

Walk-in Coolers

Walk-in coolers can be made to any size, in single or multisection units, using modular panels. They can be made for outdoor stationing entirely, or for partial outdoor stationing with the entrance indoors. There are exterior and interior ramps that allow easy access for wheeled food carriers and sealed glass windows for interior observation.

Light switches and thermometers are usually built into the door frames. Reach-in service doors that provide access to smaller shelves are available and should be considered as they will prevent the extensive cold air loss that occurs each time the main entrance door is opened.

The standard inside height is 7 feet 6 inches with optional heights to 8 feet 6 inches and 10 feet 6 inches. Depths are standard at 5 feet 10 inches (normally 6 feet), and in 11½-inch increments. The most effective insulation is 4 inches of high-density polyurethane, foamed-in-place insulation. The entire door opening should be protected by anticondensate heaters (to prevent condensation and frost formation) for easy opening.

Freezers

What is popularly referred to as a freezer is really a frozen food storage cabinet. Although its basic use is to store (at 0°F) those foods that are already frozen, the common practice is to use this unit to freeze foods for future use. This can be a potentially dangerous practice as the time required to reduce the product to a safe temperature and frozen state is critical to both quality and food safety.

There are combination units available that store refrigerated foods on one side and frozen foods on the other. However, this type of unit is generally not practical for the catering kitchen. A freezer should be a separate unit with easy-to-open doors.

Self-defrosting units are slightly more expensive to operate but because they function without temperature fluctuations, they offer more product protection. Also, this unit does not need frequent shutdown for removal of ice build-up. Although exterior and interior features of frozen food cabinets are similar to refrigerators, their compressors are at least twice as large.

True freezers (air blast units designed for commercial freezing of food products) are not essential unless you freeze large quantities for long-term storage or operate a frozen food carry-out business. When used properly, following approved technical procedures, a blast freezer will produce professionally frozen products.

Walk-in Freezers

Walk-in freezers have practically the same specifications as refrigerators. However, they are equipped with heavier capacity compressors and condensers, and have air curtains to minimize cold air escape.

DISHWASHERS

Unlike other equipment that becomes operational when plugged in, a dishwasher requires a connection to an energy source (electric or gas). It also requires an attachment for a water inlet from a water heating unit, and quite frequently from a self-contained or auxiliary booster unit. A direct connection to a waste or sewer outlet is also necessary.

A good installation requires a prewash unit and waste disposal. Soiled and clean dish tables have to be fabricated individually for each installation to ensure adequate storage space for dishes waiting to be cleaned and dishes waiting to be put away. They must often be designed to fit around columns and other obstructions.

A dishwashing system is actually engineered for each facility, depending on the space available, the volume of business, the layout, the traffic flow, the amount and type of food soil and the length of time it will remain on the dishes (from completion of dining time to conveyance to washing area), and the hardness of the water. There are so many options available that you can virtually design your own system.

The amount of floor space required is determined by combining the lengths at the loading and unloading ends. Dishwashers may have straight-line feeding or angle-feeding or return. All are equipped with automatic controls for wash, dwell, and rinse. Some models require that the doors be opened before the racks are inserted. Closing the door automatically starts the cycle for rinsing, washing, and sanitizing. At the end of the cycle, the power is shut off and the door has to be opened for removal and reloading. There are larger, fully automatic models in which the racks are engaged at the entrance by arms that convey them through a flexible strip curtain, through the entire wash cycle, and then discharge them at the opposite end (Figure 7-22).

Plastic dishware is not processed satisfactorily in conventional machines. High-temperature, high-velocity, blower-dryer units must be installed to dry such dishware quickly.

The heat generated by dishwashers can be a problem, but expensive exhaust ducting can often be avoided by installing a condenser over the dishwasher. The condenser exhausts the dishwasher vapor, condenses it, and releases the air back into the dishroom.

Flight Type Machines

The unit is similar to the rack conveyor machine, but instead of placing the dishes on racks, they are loaded on an endless belt constructed of rubber, plastic, or composition "fingers" that hold the dishes in place as they pass through the prerinse, rinse, and wash cycles. Upon completion, the dishes are removed and placed directly on dish trucks or storage shelves, a method which is very efficient for large operations.

Water Heaters

An adequate hot water supply is absolutely essential for proper dishwashing. Although hot water may be available from the primary system, it must be boosted to at least 180°F for sanitizing. If feasible, the booster heater should be installed under the dishwasher or placed not more than 5 feet away. The unit, which can be either the instantaneous or automatic storage type, guarantees that the proper water temperature will always be available on demand.

Racks and Tables

Dish racks are not normally supplied with dishwashing machines. Needs vary since different sized dishes, cups, glasses, and supremes may be used in each operation. For example, if you want the racks to be stored with the dishes, cups, or glasses in them, you will probably need a different size rack for each.

Dish tables for the entrance or exit areas of the machine must also be purchased separately. They should be large enough to allow for proper rack loading and for clean stacking and packing. The tables should be made of heavy-gauge stainless steel or fiberglass. Make certain they are tightly fitted into the machine at the entrance and exit areas. Improper fit will result in dangerously wet, slippery floors.

Slanted overhead shelves for holding cups, glass racks, and other odds and ends should be installed on either side of the dish tables. There should also be a small drain at one end of the shelves.

If space permits, provide two soaking sinks—one for silver, the other for dishes. These are particularly useful to the off-premises caterer who may be bringing back dirty dishes encrusted with dry food if there are no dishwashing facilities available at the catering site. If there is not enough space for fixed sinks, two large, heavy-duty plastic tubs will be adequate.

WASTE DISPOSALS

A garbage disposal, a valuable time and labor saver, is usually part of the dishwashing layout. Depending on the complexity of the dishwashing system, the disposer can be installed under the prerinse sink or in a special trough with running water. A disposal can also be useful in the preparation area, particularly if a lot of fresh food is processed and prepped. Peelings and other food waste can be conveniently thrown into the disposal.

Before investing in a disposal, make sure that the local code allows for their use (some do not because of sewage problems). Be sure that the disposal's capacity is adequate for your needs. The electrical supply must be able to

Flight Type-Endless Belts
6600 to 9000 dishes per hour
Standard Widths—25 in.; extra wide—30 in.

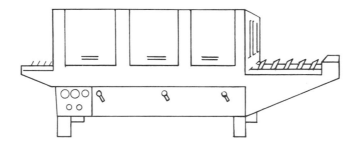

Rack Conveyor Types

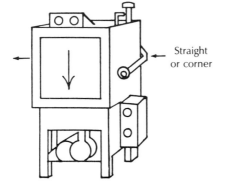

Straight
or corner

50 racks per hour
Can fit in areas 28 in. or wider

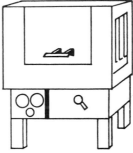

194 racks per hour
Can fit in areas 44 in. or wider

Conveyor speeds
can be adjusted

234 racks per hour
5850 dishes

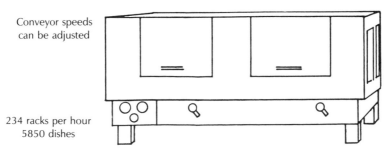

Figure 7-22. Flight Type and Rack Conveyor Dishwashers.

handle both the disposal and the dishwasher if the two are turned on simultaneously. Since the disposal will be used with and around water, the electrical controls should be properly safeguarded so that no danger exists for the operator. It should have a reversing switch, a very handy feature when the disposal gets jammed or clogged. In case of a problem, keep on file the name of the company responsible for the service and warranty on the unit.

DISH AND UTENSIL STORAGE

The most desirable system for storing dishes and utensils after they have been cleaned and sanitized in the dishwasher is one that requires the least amount of handling between the time the utensils are washed and their next use, and the most protection for cleanliness. For this reason, storage of uncovered utensils in a cupboard is not recommended.

If possible, portable carts should be used in the dishwashing area so that sanitized and dried items can be stored quickly. Protected by a sanitary cover until needed, the cart can then be wheeled to the proper place and uncovered. Portable carts are available in various sizes and types to meet any requirement. Choose a cart in which the sanitized utensils can be easily stored, that is durable, portable in relation to its size, and is equipped with casters and a locking device, if necessary. See page 98 for more information about this subject.

CLEANING EQUIPMENT

A heavy-duty tank-type vacuum cleaner with a 10- to 12-foot flexible hose is an invaluable tool. It can be used to clean hard-to-reach areas, such as behind ranges and other appliances and equipment. The vacuum cleaner should also be used frequently to keep refrigerator coils from plugging up with dust, which reduces the unit's efficiency. It is also effective for the superficial cleaning of filters.

Tank-type liquid absorption vacuum machines do an excellent job in cleaning quarry and asphalt tile, concrete, and similar surfaces.

SMALL TOOLS AND UTENSILS

The exact type of small tools, pots, and pans that you will require is impossible to forecast. But as business develops, your needs will become evident. However, all kitchen utensils should be regular institution ware of either standard or heavy-duty gauge construction. While the initial cost is high, this ware is more durable than lighter weight housewares. Porcelain or enameled ware should be avoided since it chips and stains easily.

Today, many utensils covered with a nonstick coating are on the market. These resist abrasion from metal spatulas and spoons and are virtually scratchproof and easy to clean. However, for certain types of cooking, especially those requiring the "crusts" of cooked particles to make a tasty sauce or gravy, this type of cookware is ineffective. In those cases, rely on stainless steel or anodized aluminum pans.

One of the most versatile and valuable utensils is the "squarehead," a heavy-duty aluminum roaster, approximately 18 by 20 by 7 inches, with a heavy-duty flat cover that can also be used as a heavy-duty grill. These roasters can be heated on the range or in the oven, and hold a substantial quantity of food (approximately 42 quarts). Squareheads stack beautifully in refrigerators and trucks.

Vacuum pots or airtight transfer containers with a 3- to 10-gallon capacity are useful containers for storing and transporting foods (see Figure 7-23). They can effectively retain heat or cold for 24 hours or more. These containers are very attractive, and can be used on the buffet

CHECKLIST FOR SMALL TOOLS AND UTENSILS

Braziers—5 to 24 quarts

Can openers—heavy-duty manual or heavy-duty electric (with additional gears and cutters for replacement)

Cast iron skillet—up to 14 inches in diameter

China caps—fine to coarse

Clean-up equipment—brooms, brushes, mops, squeegees, buckets, pails

Colanders—1 to 16 quarts

Commercial duty blenders—for pureeing

Dish or salad pans—14 to 40 quarts

Double boilers—(can be improvised by using available pots)

Dredges—for sprinkling sugar, cinnamon, flour

Food storage containers—round and square, from 1 quart up, made of metal or plastic

Foodmill—grinder or foodmill

Fry pans—6 to 14 inches inches stainless steel or anodized aluminum

Funnels—3/8- to 1½-inch opening or higher

Garbage containers

Heavy-duty foil

Hot food service pans—approximate size: 12 by 18 by 2½ inches

Ice cream scoops—assorted sizes and shapes

Mallet—of solid aluminum, used to break down fibers or flatten meat

Measures—1 cup to 4 quart, aluminum, stainless steel, plastic but not glass

Meat saw/cleaver—for flattening purposes; *do not chop bones with cleaver*

Mixing bowls—1½ to 12 quarts

Piano wire whips—assorted sizes

Plastic self-sealing wrap

Portion scales—1- to 16-ounce capacity, to achieve uniform individual portions

Receiving scale—this is a necessity; see pages 76 and 78.

Roast and bake pans (squareheads)—with a heavy-duty cover that can also be used as a grill; approximate size 18 by 21 by 7 inches

Roasting pans—standard weight and heavy-duty from approximately 12 by 20 inches to 17 by 26 inches. (Check your ovens for largest size they will hold.) Purchase some half-size roasters also.

Rubber composition cutting boards

Sauce pans—1½ to 10 quarts

Saucepots—4 to 24 quarts (Larger sizes are available but they are too awkward and difficult to handle.)

Scoops—for bulk flour, sugar, rice, and other dried goods

Sharpening stones

Sheet pans—approximate size: 18 by 26 inches (Mobile racks to store these will be helpful.)

Skimmer—6½ inches

Soup ladles—2 to 10 ounces

Spoons—wood; solid, slotted, and perforated

Stockpots—with or without faucets, from 24 to 40 quarts

Strainers—to 5 quarts

Thermometer—one for roast beef; another for candy, jelly, and frostings

Tongs—7 to 10 inches

Utility pans—2 to 10 quarts

Waxed paper

table as coffee, tea, or punch dispensers, or for transporting and dispensing ice cubes. Moreover, when kept clean and shined, these metal units are more pleasing to the eye than those made from plastic materials.

COMMISSARY KITCHEN EQUIPMENT

Since food and equipment must be organized and packed to go in an off-site business, the commissary kitchen needs to be equipped with more tables than a banquet facility. To avoid confusion, separate tables, holding racks, and cabinets may be needed for each affair under preparation. There must be room for in-kitchen storage for these racks and cabinets. Aisles and areas must be wide enough to allow for unobstructed and free movement of these conveyances either to the refrigerator, freezer, or truck.

Larger businesses, with high volume require walk-in refrigerator and freezers with ramps. The cabinets, tray racks, and dollies can be rolled in, saving double handling. This also reduces the possibility of mix-up and damage to preportioned items.

Unlike on-premises catering, where food is served directly to the diner as soon as it is finished in the kitchen, off-premises caterers sometimes have to finish the food on the job. To avoid transferring foods from the original roasting or baking pans to other pans for shipping, it is recommended that you use roasters and bakers with covers. These pans can be easily stacked for storage or transport. Also available are tote boxes with covers that can be packed in the commissary and stacked safely and securely.

Holding units, which keep food warm during transport, are excellent for maintaining uniformly controlled temperatures and for prolonging food quality during transport (see Figure 7-24). If the units are disconnected from their power source for several hours, these carriers are

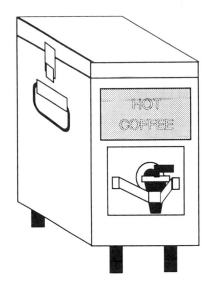

Figure 7-23. Hot Beverage Container.

capable of holding the food to the original kitchen-fresh goodness. These units are so efficient at keeping the food warm and ready to serve that employees do not have to guess or judge for themselves the food's quality.

Cold food cabinets, which incorporate all the features of the hot cabinets, are a wise investment. They could eliminate the need to purchase or rent a refrigerated truck.

There are so many sizes and models available you should consult your equipment dealer and/or factory representatives, who are trained to solve problems of food transport.

PLATFORM TRUCKS, DOLLIES, AND RACKS

Platform trucks and rack dollies will save time, ease work loads, and take the strain out of handling heavy stock, supplies, and equipment. As morale aids, they demonstrate your interest in making your employees' jobs easier. They are also an element in your favor should an injury

Figure 7-24. Insulated Food Cabinets.

claim arise because of heavy lifting or moving—you will be able to prove that you have provided a means to prevent such injury.

Dollies

An investment in rack dollies for stacking and conveying cups and glasses will result in greater productivity; a dolly can hold many more units than a person can carry and can be moved for long distances with minimum exertion and fatigue. (Note: Cups should always be packed in cups racks and should never be nested, which causes breakage and roughening of the cup rims. Rough rims can transmit germs more readily and can also cause mouth injury.)

Dollies are also useful for moving large stock-pots, heavy pails used in cleaning, and large, filled garbage cans.

Open Tray Trucks

These trucks are versatile and can save steps and time in any business. Trays of cooked or raw foods can be easily moved from the area of preparation into a walk-in, or to another area for finishing or serving. The trucks can also be used as portable shelving.

Enclosed Tray Trucks

Most tray trucks are no more than 24 by 34 inches wide and 72 inches tall, and can carry up to twenty trays (Figure 7-25). Available insulated and in various sizes, they are invaluable in pretraying all types of food. For buffet presentations, they allow the showpieces to be completed in the kitchen or commissary and taken to the area of service, either on- or off-premises. Portioned foods, hors d'oeuvres, pastries, and tall layer cakes can be transported great distances in tray trucks with minimal damage to finished surfaces. They reduce packing time by eliminating the search for special containers. Good housekeeping is maintained because the food is under cover and in one place.

Insulated trucks will keep foods at the required safe temperatures for hours if thermo containers are placed in the truck.

Tray trucks are constructed of stainless steel and are easy to keep clean. Colored vinyl can be bonded on the exterior to match any desired decorating scheme.

Dish Dollies

Considerable time and labor can be saved by removing dishes from the dishwasher and storing them directly on dish dollies (Figure 7-26). This eliminates double handling in shelving, and the dishes can be moved directly to the point of service.

Dollies can hold as many as 240 11-inch dinner plates. The dollies are only 32 inches high, and the outside dimensions rarely exceed 24 by 40 inches. Dividers can be adjusted to hold any size dish. Some models have self-contained elements that keep dishes hot until service time—a valuable feature for operators concerned with meticulous service.

Fully enclosed models prevent dust and dirt penetration and are excellent for off-premises catering. Open models are more practical for

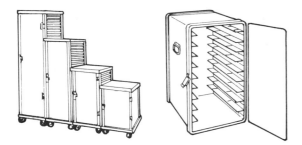

Figure 7-25. Enclosed Tray Trucks (available insulated and in various sizes).

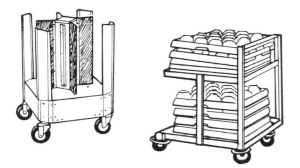

Figure 7-26. Dish Dollies.

on-premises catering. (Factory-furnished dust covers are available.)

High or Low Roll-in Racks

Open-sided, roll-in racks are a great convenience in any kitchen or bake shop. Full size roasting and baking pans can be placed therein directly from the ovens to cool off. Adjustable shelves allow for vertical packing and stacking. They can be rolled into walk-in refrigerators or freezers and will fit into many sectional roll-in or roll-through refrigerators and freezers.

Bake Shop

Since high-quality baked goods are so readily available fresh or frozen from commercial spe-

cialty bakeries, many caterers dispense with setting up a full-scale bake shop in their facilities. If you do decide to do your own baking, you will need some special bakery equipment, some of which you probably already own and use in your main kitchen.

The following equipment may be necessary if you decide to incorporate a baking department in your kitchen:

> Bake oven
> Proof box
> Fryer
> Mixer
> Scale
> Pastry stove
> Tilting kettle (could be table mounted)
> Portable bins for storage
> Work tables, polyurethane or marble
> Work tables, stainless steel
> Spice bins
> Sinks and drainboards
> Racks for proofing and cooling
> Landing table or dump table
>   (wire rack–topped table designed for cooling baked products)
> Storage facilities for flour, sugar, and sifting equipment
> Refrigerator and freezer storage; dough-retarding refrigerators

NEW VERSUS USED EQUIPMENT

As a beginning caterer with limited funds, you may consider purchasing used equipment. Do not do so, however, just because it seems to be a bargain; if it does not fit your needs exactly, do not buy it no matter what the cost.

If you do consider used equipment, make sure it is a brand name you recognize and that it is approved by the National Sanitation and American Gas Association Foundation and by

Underwriters Laboratory. It should be energy efficient, insulated properly, and if gas, have an electronic ignition rather than a pilot light. It should be easy to clean and accessible for minor adjustments, and there should be an authorized dealer or supply house located nearby for parts and service. Make sure you have recourse if the item does not work to your satisfaction, and get a warranty if available.

Aside from the cost of the equipment itself, you will probably have to pay for delivery and setup (new equipment normally includes these charges). Add all this up and ask yourself again if you are really getting a bargain.

·8·

Service Equipment

Caterers need to either buy or rely on local rental companies for most of their "front-of-the-house" event equipment. Because of the tremendous cost of buying your own equipment, it probably is best to rent when you first begin. However, once you are in a position to purchase your own distinctive china, flatware, and linens, there are a number of factors you'll need to consider when making a selection.

CHINA

China is the generally accepted medium in dinnerwear, and no substitute has as yet been found for its elegance. China should be considered using the following criteria: replaceability, durability, and appearance. The first rule when buying china is not to buy close-outs or discontinued patterns, although their low price may make them seem tempting. Doing so is very poor economy because when it is necessary to replace

broken dishes or to increase your stock due to business expansion, the original pattern may not be available. You will then have to purchase an entirely new set of dishes, for a collection of assorted shapes, sizes, and patterns would make for a very unprofessional presentation. Also standardized dish weight, design, and shape lead to more efficient washing, handling, stacking, and storing.

The heaviness or thickness of china is often assumed to be an indicator of its durability. But this is not always so, since employees are prone to be less careful when handling heavy dishes. Medium-weight dishes are much more practical, and are generally more attractive. When packed in racks, they are lighter and more easily handled. Heavy dishes, when stacked, tend to rub against each other and the glazed surface becomes marred. Also, if a stack of heavy dishes is moved, the weight can cause shock waves, resulting in a greater number of cracked and broken dishes. (When packing for transport or storage, never stack more than 20 to 24 dishes high.)

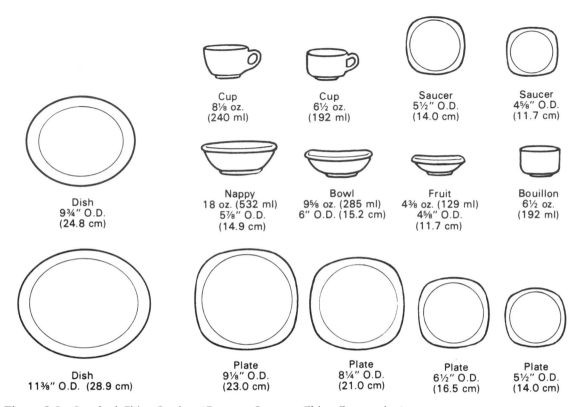

Figure 8-1. Standard China Service. (Courtesy Syracuse China Corporation)

Avoid purchasing dishes with raised patterns. Raised surfaces chip more easily, and can also be dust and dirt traps that require more attention in cleaning. Rolled-edge dishes are a plus, however, because the rounded edges act as bumpers, protecting the dishes from chippage and breakage.

The dinnerware you select for guest service is "table-top" merchandising. Properly presented, it can help your service appear distinctive and original, creating an effect pleasing to your clients. There are countless shapes and theme patterns available in open stock, so your choice can appear custom-ordered (see Figure 8-1). If you purchase your china and plan to have your personal logo or monogram inscribed in the pattern, it should be discreet and not appear as an obvious bit of advertising.

Size

One of the most objectionable features of any food presentation is a crowded plate. Foods must not run into each other, and there must be sufficient room to allow for cutting food without it rolling off the edges. In selecting dinner plates, consider choosing the 10¾-inch (brim to brim) size. This size makes an adequate show plate to use as a base for starter courses at banquets, as well as a satisfactory meal-presentation plate. It is large enough to present the food course without

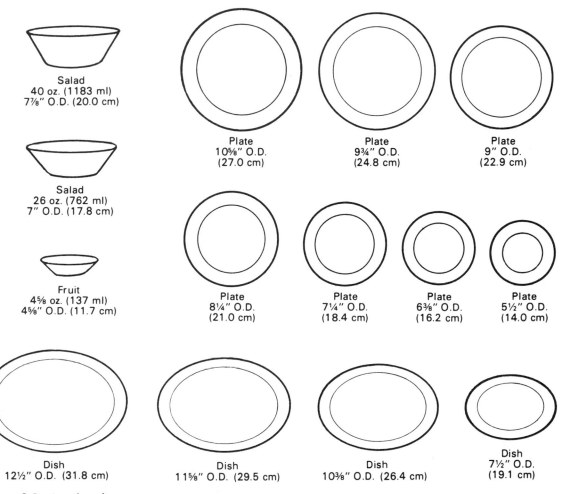

Salad
40 oz. (1183 ml)
7⅞" O.D. (20.0 cm)

Salad
26 oz. (762 ml)
7" O.D. (17.8 cm)

Fruit
4⅝ oz. (137 ml)
4⅝" O.D. (11.7 cm)

Plate
10⅝" O.D.
(27.0 cm)

Plate
9¾" O.D.
(24.8 cm)

Plate
9" O.D.
(22.9 cm)

Plate
8¼" O.D.
(21.0 cm)

Plate
7¼" O.D.
(18.4 cm)

Plate
6⅜" O.D.
(16.2 cm)

Plate
5½" O.D.
(14.0 cm)

Dish
12½" O.D. (31.8 cm)

Dish
11⅝" O.D. (29.5 cm)

Dish
10⅜" O.D. (26.4 cm)

Dish
7½" O.D.
(19.1 cm)

Figure 8-1. (continued)

crowding, giving a desirable impression of spaciousness. For oversized beef cuts or pasta presentations, you may use a 12½-inch steak platter.

Coffee cups come in various shapes and sizes: low cups, high cups, tea cups, and mugs. Many mugs are footed, giving them a graceful appearance and allowing them to be used without saucers (Figure 8-2). Cup sizes range from 4½ ounces (the after-dinner or demitasse size) to 7, 7¼, 7½, 7¾, and 8¾ ounce capacity.

Coffee and bouillon cup handles are not molded with the cup, but are applied separately during the manufacturing process. Check these handles very thoroughly. They should be able to withstand the abuse of packing and delivery. (When packing cups, do not nest them. Cups should be packed as a single layer in individual racks.)

Check to see whether the cup bases have separately attached rings, or if the bases are an

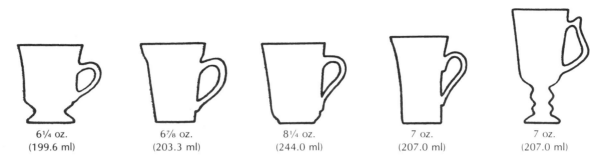

| 6¼ oz. | 6⅞ oz. | 8¼ oz. | 7 oz. | 7 oz. |
| (199.6 ml) | (203.3 ml) | (244.0 ml) | (207.0 ml) | (207.0 ml) |

Figure 8-2. Five Popular Styles of Mugs.

integral molded part of the cup. Also look to see whether the base of the ring is fully glazed or if it is rough. A rough ring can become a magnet for dirt, and can make cleaning very difficult.

Basic Dish Requirements

The type and quantity of dishes needed depends on the type of service, the dishwashing facilities, the availability of dishes for reordering, the number of dishes you can store in reserve, and the amount of money you have to spend. These are the basic requirements:

Dinner plates
Underliners or salad plates
Bread and butter plates
Platters (optional)
Cups and saucers
Soup bowls or cups
Sugar bowls and creamers

STAINLESS STEEL FLATWARE AND SERVING PIECES

Stainless steel equipment is acceptable in most establishments today. However, it should be quality stainless, a metal that has good feel, substance, and body. Pattern details should be articulated and finished-off, not just "punched out" as is sometimes the case.

Reputable silver manufacturers have lines of stainlessware comparably priced to their silver-plated line. The advantage of stainless over silver is, of course, the upkeep. Polishing and burnishing are practically eliminated. Harder than silver, stainlessware shows fewer signs of abuse.

These are the basic flatware requirements:

Dinner knives
Butter knives
Dinner forks
Salad/dessert forks
Fish forks
Soup spoons
Teaspoons
Iced-tea spoons

You may, on occasion, resort to cheap stainlessware and be justified in using it; for example, to serve a large outdoor party where costlier flatware may be carried off or inadvertently discarded. In such instances, heavy-duty disposable plasticware could also be used.

Serving Pieces

The type of service offered will determine what you need. However, for general service, you must have a good supply of the following:

Large serving spoons
Cold meat forks
Salad tongs or large salad forks and spoons
Cake knives or servers

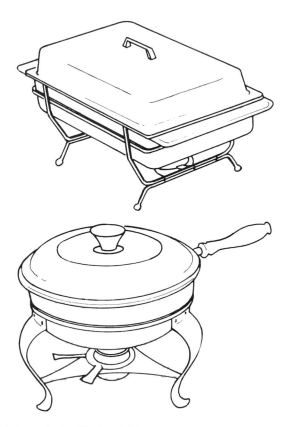

Figure 8-3. Chafing Dishes.

ADDITIONAL SERVICE EQUIPMENT

Chafing Dishes

You will want to stock an assortment of chafing dishes in different shapes and sizes for buffet service (Figure 8-3). Available in round, oval, and oblong shapes; in sizes ranging from 2 to 8 quarts, and larger, and in a variety of metals (silver, stainless steel, and combinations of copper, brass, and aluminum), they add a decorative note to your buffet.

Trays

Select heavy-duty metal, plastic, or fiberglass utility trays for use by service staff, cooks, and bartenders. For serving hors d'oeuvres and for the buffet table, choose stainless steel or silver round, oval, and oblong trays that will complement the food (Figure 8-4).

Tea and Coffee Service

To serve tea, you will need a silver or stainless steel tea service, which includes a tea server, hot water pot with a warming unit, creamer, sugar bowl, and matching tray. To serve coffee, you will need a silver or stainless steel coffee urn with a self-contained heating unit, and a matching creamer, sugar bowl, and tray.

Polished silver pitchers have long been used in foodservice operations for serving coffee and

Figure 8-4. Serving Trays and Tureen.

tea to seated guests. Although decorative, they are heavy to handle and are not insulated. You may prefer to use lighter weight insulated pitchers with heat-resistant handles.

Glassware

A caterer requires a large and varied supply of glassware to meet the demands of service and to replace the breakage. The type and number of glasses required depends on the service offered. Figure 8-5 illustrates standard stemware styles. (See page 158 for further discussion of glassware needs.) The following list may be helpful as a basic guide:

> 3- to 5-ounce juice glasses
> 8- to 10-ounce water tumblers or goblets
> 12-ounce iced tea glasses
> Sherbet glasses
> Parfait glasses
> Champagne glasses
> Wine glasses
> Supreme glasses and liners (Figure 8-6)
> Relish trays
> Compotes for candy, nuts, petits fours
> Sugar bowls and creamers
> Ash trays

Glassware has emerged as an important component in merchandising food and beverages. There is such a vast array of styles, shapes, colors, weights, and sizes that the potential use of any one unit is overwhelming.

The basic function of glasses, that is, to hold liquids only, is obsolete. Glasses are an aid in portion control, in merchandising a house beverage, and are a distinctive way of serving fruit or seafood dishes. They add style and showmanship to bar offerings and to the presentation of spectacular desserts, and they can add substantially to income revenues.

Some caterers, both on- and off-premises, promote their business by offering individualized house drinks and special desserts in large

footed hurricane glasses, 12½-ounce brandy glasses, or oversized parfait glasses that have been etched or imprinted with the business name. Guests are allowed to take them home, and the unusual container becomes an advertising medium as well as a souvenir. The basic cost should be absorbed in the price of the meal, or a portion charged to advertising expenses.

Linens and Napery

A fledgling caterer will probably find it best to rent linens rather than make an immediate cash outlay for cloths. The disadvantage is that you are always at the mercy of the laundry service, most of whom are unable to furnish the array of colors paramount to distinctive presentations. As a result, you may be forced to compromise on quality, and, on occasion, have to accept patched, mold-stained, torn, or improperly folded and ironed cloths and napkins. Also, your offerings will be the same as other caterers who use the same service; thus, you will not have that "linen edge." In response to this situation, a relatively new service specializing only in table-top decor has developed. Your clients may prefer to make their own arrangements with specialty linen rental companies that offer a wide range of high-quality party linens ordinarily not available from commercial laundries. Owning your own linens, of course, has certain advantages. You can choose your own colors, quality, and sizes.

Most rental laundries supply 72-inch-square cloths as standard for 54- and 60-inch round tables. The drop (that is, the amount of cloth that hangs down from the table) on a 54-inch table is adequate, but the drop on a 60-inch table is skimpy. If you wish to order larger cloths it will cost more, but the aesthetic value of a more generous size may be well worth the extra charge.

The synthetic polyester fabrics used to make most tablecloths and napkins are of such fine quality that they are appropriate for even the most elegant affairs. Many are spot and stain

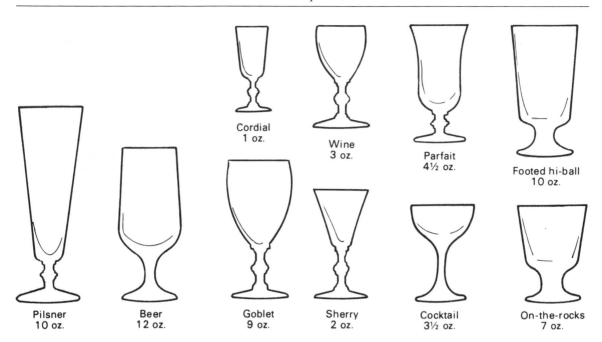

Figure 8-5. Standard Stemware. (Courtesy Libbey Products)

Figure 8-6. Supreme Rings and Insets.

resistant and flame-retardant and, if handled as directed, require no ironing, which is a tremendous boon to caterers who own their own linens.

Furthermore, laundering these synthetics may not require commercial laundry service.

Linens can be laundered and finished in isolated areas of any catering business, requiring only enough room for a washer and dryer and for a place to store soiled and cleaned linen. The size of the washer and dryer depends on volume; the use of a small mangle (a rolling press for ironing linen) would enhance the appearance of the finished product. With this equipment you can save the cost of carrying a large inventory, plus avoid crises caused by delayed linen deliveries. The cost of the equipment and installation would be self-liquidating through the elimination of commercial laundry costs.

These standard cloth sizes fit the following tables.

Cloth Size	Table Size
54″ square	Bridge table or 30″ round
90″ round	30″ round cocktail table
72″ square	48″ square or round

Cloth Size	Table Size
108″ round	48″ round
72″ square	54″ square or round
114″ round	54″ round
90″ square	60″ round
120″ round	60″ round
90″ square	72″ round
120″ round	72″ round
60″ × 120″	30″ × 96″ rectangular banquet

Disposable Serviceware and Paper Products

Disposable serviceware and paper goods have become indispensable in many areas of catering; they are not only pleasing, but extremely functional. Large quantities of disposable goods can be stored in comparatively little space. Since they often weigh less than similar quantities of their conventional counterparts, they are easier to move and handle. Safety is another factor, as disposable products do not shatter and leave sharp edges. Theft is also greatly reduced because disposable goods have no value to souvenir hunters. Furthermore, the repetitive chore of dishwashing can be eliminated or reduced. Moreover, disposable serviceware can generate additional income because they make it feasible for even the most elegant catering businesses to sell their foods for takeout. It is important, however, that today's caterer be sensitive to the environmental problems caused by the amount and type of disposable products being used. Biodegradable and recyclable products make sense in today's world, and a growing number of your clients will appreciate and sometimes demand their use.

Paper napkins, plates, tablecloths and placemats come in all colors, sizes, and textures. The proliferation of choices guarantees many acceptable settings and combinations. Composition, plastic, paper, and styrofoam containers and trays are available in all shapes and sizes. They can be manufactured to meet the needs of any product presentation (imprinting a company message on the containers is a valuable method of low-cost advertising). Many disposable containers have excellent thermal qualities for heat and cold retention so that complete meals can be packaged in your kitchen and delivered for group consumption. If necessary, these meals can be reheated in microwaves or in conventional ovens, in the original containers. Sturdy, reinforced disposable platters can be used at clambakes. The weight of heavy clams, oysters, and lobsters does not cause the platter to buckle and the sauces do not soak through.

PORTABLE EQUIPMENT

Portable electric ovens, electric woks, electric coffee makers, thermalized plastic or cloth carriers, and washing tubs, are examples of back-of-the-house equipment. While most of these can be easily rented on a per-day basis, many caterers purchase these items outright.

Off-premises caterers will need to find portable replacement for just about everything they use in their commissary. Some caterers even purchase mobile kitchens to work from, enabling them to bring back-of-the-house equipment wherever they need it.

Food-Carrying Equipment

Your operation will often be judged by the type of equipment you use. In view of this, as well as sanitation hazards and your desire to have food arrive at its destination in the best possible condition, you should use the best food-carrying equipment available.

Many excellent, insulated metal food-carrying cabinets are available today. Some can be hand-carried and have drop handles. Larger ones may require two persons to carry them, or they may be mounted on rubber wheels; companion dollies can be used for moving and stacking. These square and solidly constructed containers pack beautifully in the delivery truck or van. Because they are enclosed on all sides, food is well protected from contamination. They can hold standard sheet and hotel pans securely, ensuring that food will arrive at the point of service in good condition.

By far, the best food transport carriers are made from plastic or polyurethane. These materials are light, easy to clean, and keep food hot or cold for hours at a time. Some caterers use cloth-insulated bags, like those used for pizza delivery, to keep foods in a safe temperature zone.

Corrugated cardboard boxes should be used only in emergencies and should never be placed on the floor of the truck. If the truck floor is wet, the bottom of the boxes could fall out when they are lifted, which could ruin the contents and necessitate cleanup and repacking. Furthermore, the glued areas of the cardboard boxes can be a haven for roaches.

Wooden tote or carrying boxes are available, but they have many disadvantages. They retain moisture, have a tendency to mold, are difficult to clean, and may have slivers that can injure the handler.

Since it may be very easy to confuse your equipment with similar equipment at the facility where you are catering, you should mark your equipment with your name or other identification as soon as you buy it. A good engraving tool is an inexpensive investment. Its use will save you embarrassment and will help your employees identify your equipment when on a job. Some caterers use special stick-on labels for the same purpose.

When purchasing holding equipment for transporting food, consider the following:

- How easy is it to store?
- Can it be disassembled and stacked without marring?
- Is it lightweight but rugged? Will it show abuse?
- Do vulnerable parts protude in a hazardous manner?

- Are locking devices easy to use?
- Are companion dollies available to facilitate handling?
- Will it be easy to clean?

Portable Coffee Urns

Although some facilities where you will be catering will have coffee urns in their kitchens, do not assume they will be adequate for your needs. Therefore, plan to have enough portable urns in inventory to provide two cups of coffee for each guest you anticipate serving.

There are many excellent portable coffee urns available today. They not only make good coffee, but are decorative and easy to clean and handle. For catering in private homes, a 30- to 50-cup coffee maker is generally adequate.

Some caterers use metal or plastic thermalized coffee carriers that permit them to make the coffee at their kitchen and then transport it to the event site ready to use.

VANS AND TRUCKS

Unquestionably, the most practical vehicle for small catering purposes is the cargo van. In addition to rear doors, many vans have side doors that slide or fold open to more than half the vehicle length; they permit easier loading of large and bulky pieces of equipment. The new mini-vans are also popular, especially in large metropolitan areas where heavy traffic and crowded alleys make the larger vans more difficult to manuever.

Caterers who do large-scale off-site catering may need to use a truck to handle high volume. However, the size of whatever you buy should depend on the volume of business anticipated. What is the largest party you are equipped for and capable of handling? How many times during the course of a year would you be handling such large parties? It might be advisable to rent a larger truck for these few occasions rather than "drag around" unused and wasted space. The larger the body, the more expensive the initial cost, license fees, and insurance; the more weight, the more motor drag and the more gas it will use. Longer truck bodies are more difficult to maneuver and access to home driveways could sometimes be impossible. Dual rear wheels, even on the shortest body, are necessary.

If you do select a truck, step-in or platform trucks are best. A step-in has the advantage of accessibility, but more expertise must be used in loading to prevent top-heaviness. In windy conditions, step-ins are more difficult to control.

Vans and trucks must always be impeccably clean, both inside and out. Have a graphic artist design the message you want on the truck and suggest the colors. This important one-time investment can be a very effective advertisement for your business.

Specifications

Instead of the number of passengers or cubic-feet capacity, you should find out how much weight, or payload, can be carried. Remember, dishes, silverware, and equipment are heavy; in addition, you must also consider the weight of any passengers. For very heavy loads, check to see whether the van or truck can be equipped with an optional heavy-duty engine, suspension, and tires. Unless you plan to routinely haul loads exceeding the rated capacity of the vehicle, this probably will not be necessary.

The body should have a side door and the interior should be insulated against adverse and extreme weather conditions. In extreme cold, foods can freeze during transit. Dishes, glasses, and silver will "sweat" when taken from a cold truck or van into a warm room, and handling will leave fingermarks. In hot weather, the interior temperature is intensified, rapidly increasing the possibility of food spoilage. Unless man-

dated by law, it may be possible to avoid buying an expensive refrigerated truck, providing you have adequate cold retention equipment (see pages 14–15).

Purchasing

Purchasing a vehicle requires a substantial cash down payment, as well as monthly payments over a period of several years. Before making this investment, consult your accountant to determine whether your cash assets are sufficient to meet this obligation, and to learn the dollar depreciation and other tax advantages of such an acquisition. A less costly alternative is to buy a good-quality, reliable used vehicle.

Owning your own vehicle has many obvious advantages, but you must be prepared to accept the responsibility for proper maintenance. Your vehicle must be mechanically sound, and kept in top-notch condition—immaculately clean and always at the ready. You should have a dependable garage nearby for maintenance and repair and know of a 24-hour towing service. If you are catering an event more than 25 miles from your commissary, provide your drivers with a list of garages in those areas that can be called for emergency towing and service.

Leasing

Leasing is beneficial because you are only required to pay a small down payment, and maintenance problems are reduced. There are also tax advantages to leasing, but these vary according to the profitability of each business.

There are two basic types of leases—open-end and closed-end. An open-end lease calls for small payments each month, (usually for three years), with a balloon payment for the balance due at the end. Some leases also contain a maximum mileage stipulation, and if this is exceeded, there is a mileage penalty. Most leasing companies will not contract for less than a two-year period. Termination of this contract before the lease expires can be expensive because repainting, removing dents, and other work must be paid for by you as stipulated by the lease agency.

A closed-end lease requires larger monthly payments but no balloon payment at the end of the contract. The vehicle is returned to the leasing agency, which disposes of it—probably selling it back to you at a price.

Renting

Renting is often the best solution. If there is a reputable truck rental agency in your area, one that has trucks available on demand, consider renting a truck as you need it. If you do rent, check costs every few months to determine whether it is more economical to continue to rent or whether you should lease or buy your own vehicle.

If using a rented truck, spray its interior with a nontoxic insect spray after the completion of each job, but prior to your return. This spray will work while you are driving back to your commissary, and greatly reduce the possibility of transferring roaches and other insects that may have already been in the truck back to your facility. All the equipment you used and carried in the truck should be thoroughly washed and sterilized before being placed in storage.

·9·

Special Events

No event is routine, and in many ways every event is special to the client. However, some events—particularly banquets, buffets, clambakes, picnics, and weddings—will need special arrangements and will require special attention from the caterer.

BANQUETS

A banquet is an elaborate and often ceremonial meal for a large number of guests, often in honor of someone. While all banquets are lavish to some degree, the extent of extravagance may be limited by the type of occasion or the budget. Formalities such as grand entrances (dignitaries, bride and groom), patriotic renderings, ritual invocations, acknowledgments, or a formal speaker are often integral parts of each point of service.

All diners at a banquet are to be served the same food at predetermined courses. This helps with purchases, preparation, and control of food and related items. (Exceptions are guests whose food intake is restricted because of health or religious reasons. Arrangements for such guests are made in advance, either by the client or by a committee.)

It is necessary to know the number of guests since this will determine the space, personnel, and equipment required. Knowing the place and time is also important in order to ensure the availability of a dining area (for establishments having multiple dining rooms) and to schedule adequate personnel. Proper staffing minimizes the possibilities of excess help "hanging around" or too few personnel being rushed and unable to give proper attention to details; it also avoids overtime charges due to understaffing.

The price of the banquet must be determined beforehand, and all charges fully negotiated.

Basic Banquet Menu Construction

There are innumerable banquet presentation possibilities and various sequences. Deviations from the normal presentation and increases in the number of courses can add considerably to your overall profit. The standard dinner consists of four courses, called the Basic Four.

1. Starter course: fruit, seafood, soup, small antipasto
2. Main course or entrée: meat, fish, poultry, filled crepes, or even a substantial salad (with accompanying vegetables)
3. Dessert: cake, pie, ice cream
4. Beverage: coffee, tea, milk

Adjunct Courses

Basic Cocktail Reception

This normally precedes the meal by at least a half hour. Seating is restricted to chairs in strategic areas. The reception can consist of prepoured cocktails, such as Manhattans, martinis, whiskey sours, or an appropriate white wine, and an assortment of "finger nibbles," such as potato chips, peanuts, pretzels, bacon crisps, cheese cubes, and so forth. This type of service eliminates the additional charge for a professional bartender. One server may be required in the beverage area to keep the area clean and to handle refills. Another server may be assigned to the food area with similar duties.

In addition to "nibbles," hot or cold hors d'oeuvres can be offered by a server from a silver tray, as a butler would do—hence the term "butler style." Charges are computed on the cost of food and service involved.

Partial or Mini-Reception Preceding Dinner

This reception, which generally lasts about an hour, involves a greater variety of finger and fork foods, dips, and at least one hot chafing dish item requiring the use of forks and dishes. Ad-

ditional hors d'oeuvres may be passed butler style. The tables for displaying and serving the foods should be covered with fine linens and display showpieces of ice, tallow, or salt dough. When computing the charges for this reception, take into consideration (besides the cost of food) the additional time required to set up the tables, extra personnel, linens, display pieces, dishwashing costs, fuel costs, and use charges.*

Full Reception

This type is generally served at lavish weddings, expensive fund-raising events, and VIP honorings. Buffet tables are set with expensive linens, a profusion of display showpieces, a wide diversity of expensive foods, plus four or more chafing dish items. In addition, one to three chefs are present to carve and slice hams, beef, turkey, pastrami, and smoked salmon or sturgeon, or to cook and serve filled crepes, omelets, and hot quiches (this is called exhibition cooking). Foods used for a reception must not be sweet—they should be salty, spicy, and drink-compatible. There should be a complete bar setup, with an extensive inventory of appropriate liquor, tended by a ratio of at least one bartender to 40 guests. Small cocktail tables seating four should be placed in all available areas for the convenience of the guests. A reception of this type should last approximately an hour and a quarter; it is the time in which guests do their greatest amount of socializing. Once the guests are seated for dinner, the opportunities to visit with friends or relatives are curtailed.

---

*Use charges are additional charges for items that are not normally supplied and that require special handling and preparation. For example, chafing dishes must be polished and cleaned after each use and must be kept in good repair. Another example is a candelabra with two, three, or five prongs. These are beautiful to look at but extreme care must be taken in handling; repairs and replacements are often necessary. (The use of candles is sometimes illegal during public events. Check with your local fire department for regulations.) Extra charges must always be made for higher quality flatware, crystal, and china.

Charges for this type of reception, which precedes the actual dinner, can be as much as, and even more than, the charge for the basic dinner itself. Each component of this grand reception, including your planning time, use charges for equipment, extra costs for expensive and unusual foods, and extra costs for personnel engaged in carving or cooking at the buffet tables, must be taken into consideration when estimating charges. You must realize that when you borrow skilled kitchen help for the buffet presentation, you could be depleting the kitchen crew and jeopardizing the production of dinner. Therefore, your kitchen crew must be augmented, at least for the time of the reception. (Check with your local labor boards to determine the rules regarding overtime when staff are sent to work at a different location after working in your kitchen.) Figure 9-1 is an example of a work allocation and schedule for a lavish reception and banquet. An event of this complexity and detail requires skilled staff and meticulous advance preparation.

Liquor Arrangements

The method and charges for serving liquor quite often depend on the type of license you hold. If your facility holds no license, then your client may bring in liquor (if the law so permits).

In those instances, you will supply the bartender, all glassware, ice, and soft drinks necessary, and charge what is known as corkage. The client either pays a flat rate for the entire affair, or the charge is set at so much per guest. You can charge extra for the service of the bartenders, or include this price in the corkage fee.

If your premises are licensed to sell and serve liquor, you have the following options:

1. A public cash or pay bar where guests purchase their own liquor and pay for their drinks individually.
2. A limited bar where each guest is allowed a certain number of free drinks upon presen-

tation of a tab or ticket for each drink (tickets furnished by the client to the guests).
3. An unlimited bar where guests may drink at no charge. Payment is made by the client at a flat rate per guest. A flat rate is the best arrangement for both client and licensee as it eliminates the possibility of "padding." In any case, there should be an understanding as to whether the liquor will be standard or premium quality.

Enhancing the Basic Four

Starter Course

This course is enhanced by the use of crystal glasses or silver coupes. Juices and fruit cocktail may be surrounded by crushed and colored ice and decorated with a fresh flower; for a wedding dinner you could use a large, fluffy, white ribbon bow or little gold-colored wedding bells. Affairs of state could have appropriate tiny silk flags. The possibilities are limited only by your imagination and resourcefulness.

Mini Course or First Entrée

This course would follow the starter course. It might be a small portion of seafood in a pastry shell, a small roulade of sole, ravioli with sauce, or any other food not in the same category as the main course.

Salad or Soup

It is now proper to serve a salad or soup following the mini course or first entrée, if the client so desires.

Intermezzo

At this point in a banquet, it has become fashionable to offer an "intermezzo," an intermission or pause before the main course. This is the time to cool and prepare the palate for the fine food to follow by serving a dish of ices slightly granular in texture and slightly tart in flavor (for example,

ESCOFFIER DINNER
April 26, 19____

Uniform For All Service Personnel

    White shirt or blouse
    Black slack or skirt
    Black shoes (shined)
    Black bow-tie
    Gold coats
    White apron
    White service gloves

Number Of Service Personnel

    20 Waiters
    10 Sommeliers
    5 Bus Boys
    5 Captains

Service Instruction

    Reception: Time (S) 5:00 p.m.   (F) _____

    Place: Student Lounge

    Set Up: Two (2) bars each to serve the following:

           Moet et Chandon Brut Imperiale
           Beaujolais Blanc
           Lillet Blanc
           Kir (Cocktail)
           1/3 Glass of white wine
           2 Drops of Creme de Cassis

    Equipment for Bars: 75 each Champagne Tulips
                   75 each White Wine Glasses (8½ oz.)
                   1 pkg. Cocktail Napkins
                              Ashtrays (not displayed)

Figure 9-1. Work Allocation and Schedule of Duties for a Banquet.

This is an excellent example of work detail, which can be adapted by operators to suit their particular establishment. The Escoffier Dinner is a classical and prestigious event; the participants are considered gourmands. Not only must the meal be perfect but the service must be impeccable and served with eclat.

The kitchen brigade and the dining room personnel have overwhelming responsibilites. A great deal of time must be spent in planning, planning, planning! The chefs must perfect their recipes and predetermine cooking and service time precisely. Dining room attendants must have exact knowledge of their duties also. There is no room for assumptions or error. Each guest is presumed to be an expert who anticipates that the service will be on the same plateau of perfection as the food to be served.

Even if top professionals are employed, the chronology of service and the accoutrements for each course must be thoroughly explained. A "dry run" is an effective way to attain the perfection sought.

Instructions:
1) All glassware is to be steam cleaned.
2) Bars are to be set up on Friday, April 25, 19_____ .
3) Champagne and wine should be placed in cooler on Friday, April 25.
4) All beverage served from bar only.

Student Bartenders:

(1) _____   (3) _____

(2) _____   (4) _____

Buffet Setup

Location of Table: Center of room

Type: Two-station buffet (see floor plan)

Draping done by: Mr. Steve Beno and crew

Buffet served by: Mr. Fritz Sonnenschmidt and crew

Maitre d': _____

Waiters assigned:

_____   _____   _____

_____   _____   _____

Instruction:
1) Set up small round tables with four (4) chairs at each around room (see diagram)—12 tables.
2) Alternate table cloths red and white.
3) Supply 150 7"-plates for buffet table; also supply 150 salad forks. (Be sure all items are spotless.)
4) Have a supply of ashtrays (but, do NOT display).
5) Supply 100 linen napkins displayed on tables.
6) All food will be served from buffet table. (No item on table to be passed.)
7) All waiters are to clear soiled dishes and glasses during reception—Cork Bar Trays.

Dinner

Time: (S) _6:00 p.m._   (F) _____

Number of Covers: 100

Floor Plan: See Diagram

Number of Tables: 10 ten-covers per table

Linen: Alternate tables with red and white cloths—90 × 90 size. Red tables will have white napkins; white tables will have red napkins.

Table top: (in order of placement)
1) Show Plate
2) To right of show plate, knife and consomme spoon
3) Next to the show plate, Escoffier Room
   (a) White wine glass   (b) Red wine glass   (c) Red wine glass   (d) White wine glass
4) To left of show plate, dinner fork

Figure 9-1. (continued)

    5) Napkin center of plate (top)

    6) Menu displayed on show plate for each cover

Centerpiece: Bouquet of vegetable flowers—one per table

Side Tables: A side table will be placed in each alcove and will contain the following items in the order of requirement:

    a) Dinner fork (Lamb)

    b) Dinner knife (Lamb)

    c) Teaspoon (Granite)

    d) Butter knife (Cheese)

    e) Teaspoon (Souffle)

    f) Teaspoon (Coffee)

    g) Ashtrays

    h) Sugar packs (Raw from Escoffier Room)

    i) Extra napkins

    j) Water pitcher (in case requested)

    k) Water goblet

Procedure of Service

Instruction:

1) There will be two (2) waiters per table, one (1) sommelier per table, one (1) bus boy per two tables and one (1) captain per two tables.

2) All waiters, bus boys, and sommeliers will receive instruction from their captain.

3) When not involved in the act of service, waiters/waitresses will stand by assigned station, feet slightly apart, arms behind back.

** THERE IS ABSOLUTELY NO TALKING AMONG CO-WORKERS DURING THE SERVICE.

Procedure:

	Step 1.	Waiters will assist guest when seating begins.
SOUP served from Gueridon.	Step 2.	Upon command from captain, waiters will proceed to hot cart and pick up hot soup cup and saucers.
	Step 3.	Upon command from captains, waiters and bus boys will clear soup cup and saucer and spoon.
	Step 4.	Sommelier upon command from captain will pour first wine, Corton Charlemagne, in white wine glass nearest the plate. 1/3 of the glass is to be poured.
FISH course plated by Chef.	Step 5.	Upon command from captains, waiters will proceed to entrance of Great Hall and pick up fish course, five plates each, which will be plated; bus boy to pick up sauce and pass. "Sommelier Check Wine Glasses"
	Step 6.	Upon command, waiters are to clear show plate and fish plate all in one step, along with fork and knife; bus boy to take tray to dishroom.
2nd WINE served.	Step 7.	Sommeliers to pour second wine, Chateau Lafite Rothschild, in glass (b), upon command.
	Step 8.	Waiters are to place dinner knife on right side of guest, and dinner fork on left side of guest.
LAMB plated by Chef.	Step 9.	Upon command, waiters are to proceed with captain to service area, pick up and serve main entree, making sure lamb faces guest; bus boy to pick up additional jus and serve from left of guest. "Sommelier Check Wine Glasses"

Figure 9-1. Work Allocation and Schedule of Duties for a Banquet (continued).

Step 10. Bus boy and one (1) waiter clear white wine glass *used;* bus boy takes glasses to dishroom.

Step 11. Upon command, waiters and bus boy are to clear dinner plates; bus boy takes plates to dishroom.

Step 12. Waiters to place show plate in front of guest and teaspoon on right side of show plate.

Step 13. Waiters to pick up Granite, five each, and place on show plate.

Step 14. Waiters to clear all plates, upon command from captain; bus boys remove to dishroom.

Step 15. Waiters place butter knife on right side of guest.

Step 16. Sommelier to serve next wine, Bonnesmares, in remaining red wine glass.

CHEESE served from Gueridon.

Step 17. Waiters to pick up plates for cheese, captain to pick up cheese, cut and plate from Gueridon.

DO NOT REMOVE WINE GLASS FROM LAST COURSE.

"Sommelier Check Wine Glasses"

Step 18. a. Upon command, waiter to clear cheese plate and knife; bus boy removes to dishroom.
b. Waiter to crumb the table.
c. Waiter to place two (2) teaspoons to the right of the guest.
d. Bus boy to remove centerpiece—put in Pantry area.

Step 19. Sommelier to pour last course wine, Chateau Climens, in white wine glass.

Step 20. Waiters to pick up Souffle Glace and serve, five each waiter; Captain to pick up sauce and serve one spoon over souffle.

Step 21. Sommelier and waiter to remove BOTH RED WINE GLASSES.

Step 22. a. Captains designated will prepare Gueridon for liqueurs and cordials; there will be four Gueridons serving; one (1) waiter to assist each captain.
b. Waiters to place coffee cups and saucers to right of guest, sugar and cream center of table, serve coffee.
c. Bus boy to pick up Corbeille de Mignardises (Pulled Sugar Baskets with sweet goodies) and place in center of table.

Step 23. Waiters clear dessert plates.

Step 24. STAND BY STATIONS.

Instruction for Sommelier

1. All wines will be issued from Pantry 2 in order of service.

2. All empty or partially used bottles must be returned to the Pantry and given to wine stewards.

3. When serving wine, fill glass 1/3 full only.

4. Keep an eye on the tables that you are assigned to in case the guest might require more of the wine being served.

5. a. When serving all wines, make sure that each guest has seen the label.
b. Remember!! (Four steps when serving)
   (1) Pour
   (2) Stop
   (3) Twist
   (4) Retrieve

Figure 9-1. (continued)

6. The white wine glass that the Corton Charlemagne was served in is removed once the main course (Lamb) has been served, NOT BEFORE.

7. Both RED WINE GLASSES, the one with the Chateau Lafite Rothschild and the one with the Bonnes Mares, will REMAIN ON THE TABLE until the dessert has been served.

8. All commands for wine service will come from the captain assigned to your station.

9. ABSOLUTELY NO DRINKING BY ANYONE BEFORE OR DURING DINNER.

10. a. All wines to be decanted will be done under my supervision.
    b. Wines and time of decanting will be discussed at a later date.

11. ORDER OF WINES SERVED

    1st.... Corton Charlemagne—Served after soup is cleared and before fish is served.
    2nd... Chateau Lafite Rothschild—Served after fish is cleared and before lamb is served.
    3rd... Bonnes Mares—Served after the Granite is cleared and before cheese is served.
    4th.... Chateau Climens—Served after the cheese is cleared and before the dessert is served.
    REMEMBER, COMMAND WILL COME FROM CAPTAIN.

Instruction for Wine Stewards

1. You will be responsible for all wines, liqueurs, and champagne.

2. All white wines must be refrigerated by Friday night, April 25, 19_____ .

3. Cork screws will be supplied by myself.

4. All wines will be issued by you and emptied or partially full bottles will be returned to you.

5. If you should issue ten (10) bottles of Corton Charlemagne, make sure you receive ten (10) bottles back.

6. YOU ARE NOT TO DRINK, nor are you to serve any wine to any staff, to include instructors.

7. All beverages used during the reception should be returned to you by the assigned bartenders.

8. A list of all beverages issued and returned must be kept. A form is attached for this purpose.

9. Wine for the Dinner to be issued in the following order:
    (1) Corton Charlemagne
    (2) Chateau Lafite Rothschild
    (3) Bonnes Mares
    (4) Chateau Climens

WINE STEWARD CHECK LIST

RECEPTION

ITEM	No. on Hand	Issued	No. Returned
Moet et Chandon Brut	_____	_____	_____
Beaujolais Blanc	_____	_____	_____
Lillet Blanc	_____	_____	_____
Creme de Cassis	_____	_____	_____

Figure 9-1. Work Allocation and Schedule of Duties for a Banquet (continued).

DINNER

Corton Charlemagne _____ _____ _____

Chateau Lafite Rothschild _____ _____ _____

Bonnes Mares _____ _____ _____

Chateau Climens _____ _____ _____

V.E.P. Chartreuse _____ _____ _____

Cognac Hennessy Bras d'Or _____ _____ _____

Liqueur de Poire _____ _____ _____

Creme de Menthe _____ _____ _____

Assigned Wine Stewards

_____ Group # _____

_____ Group # _____

TABLE ASSIGNMENTS

Maitre d':   Mr. _____ Tables 1, 2, 3

             Mr. _____ Tables 4, 5, 6

             Mr. _____ Tables 7, 8, 9, 10

Captains: Mr. _____ Tables 1 and 2

             Mr. _____ Tables 3 and 4

             Mr. _____ Tables 5 and 6

             Mr. _____ Tables 7 and 8

             Mr. _____ Tables 9 and 10

Bus Boys: _____ Tables 1 and 2

             _____ Tables 3 and 4

             _____ Tables 5 and 6

             _____ Tables 7 and 8

             _____ Tables 9 and 10

Figure 9-1. (continued)

Table 1	Table 2	Table 3
W _____	W _____	W _____
W _____	W _____	W _____
S _____	S _____	S _____

Table 4	Table 5	Table 6
W _____	W _____	W _____
W _____	W _____	W _____
S _____	S _____	S _____

Table 7	Table 8	Table 9
W _____	W _____	W _____
W _____	W _____	W _____
S _____	S _____	S _____

Table 10
W _____
W _____
S _____

Figure 9-1. Work Allocation and Schedule of Duties for a Banquet (continued).

lemon or raspberry). Many gourmets insist on this service when making their own arrangements while others abhor the idea. If handled properly, this course adds a weighty percentage to your profits. Intermezzo *should never be served following the starter course*. It must be preceded by at least two courses.

Main Course

If the food for the main dish is preplated in the kitchen, the service is called American service. It is a quick method but lacks a certain elegance, which some people desire and are willing to pay for. There are two more elegant alternatives:

1. *French service:* Servers serve each guest from a guéridon (a rolling wagon) which may be equipped with a Rechaud burner (a little stove used to keep foods hot). The servers display a great deal of personal flair in each aspect of the service, with guests made to feel that this show is just for them. The servers must know the anatomical construction of seafood, meat, and poultry in case tableside filleting or carving is required and use the proper tools in a skillful manner. Another aspect of French service is flambéed food offered as a main course or dessert.

Foods are flambéed with warmed brandy or trademarked liquids made especially for this purpose. This procedure must also be handled skillfully and carefully. When prepared properly, it is a thrilling sight and worth the extra charges entailed. *Flambéed* service should never be attempted in low-ceilinged areas—flames and smoke could activate the sprinkler system. Your insurance agent should be notified when you plan to use this type of presentation because you may need additional liability coverage.

2. *Russian service:* Food is served to guests from hand-held and artfully decorated trays. The trays may contain the main entrée plus the appropriate garniture, or another server may follow with the garniture of vegetables. It is not uncommon to find servers for this type of meal wearing white cotton gloves. Russian service requires a great deal of skill and dexterity on the part of the server; one hand holds the tray while the other hand is used for serving. (Never employ an inexperienced or clumsy server for this type of service, as guests may be injured by hot liquids or tipped trays.)

Bread Station or Bread Cart

Another extra service is to have a bread station (or several) in conspicuous areas of the dining room. This is a fixed and decorated table offering a variety of breads (guests slice their own), rolls, and crackers. A bread wagon may also be rolled tableside.

Relish Station or Relish Wagon

A variety of relishes may be offered in the same manner as the breads.

Cheese and Fruit Presentation

A popular and profitable course for a supplemental dessert (or as *the* dessert) is the presentation of individual trays containing a variety of cheeses, fruits, and nuts for each table. A guéridon cheese service is also effective but much slower to dispense and might require a number of guéridons and additional servers, which could increase labor costs considerably. It has also become popular to serve a combination of fruit, cheese, and salad as a follow-up to the entrée.

Viennese Dessert Table

Only superlative adjectives like dazzling, overpowering, overwhelming, and awe-inspiring properly describe a real Viennese dessert table. A Viennese table is a magnificently decorated table or tables often containing as many as fifty desserts, including petite French and Danish pastries, layer cakes, pies, chocolate mousse, gelatin molds, ice cream with a variety of sauces, strawberries Romanoff, crepes suzette, baked Alaska, cherries jubilee, watermelon balls, cantaloupe slices, simmered pears in chocolate sauce, petits fours, and cookies. The table is filled with carvings of ice, butter, sugar, and wax. The food is displayed on silver stands and in compotes of various heights. The cherries used for the jubilee are contained in chafers and are constantly flamed; concealed blocks of dry ice are set in water baths to produce clouds of vapor. These exquisitely draped tables must remain out of sight during the meal—they may be kept behind screens and wheeled in for presentation. Tables that are integral parts of the presentation can be so arranged to "break away" so they can then be rolled over to individual guest tables.

At the moment of presentation, these tables should be brilliantly spotlighted and the rest of the room temporarily darkened. The orchestra can be called on for a trumpet fanfare and a roll of drums. When the excitement diminishes, an announcement should be made by either the maitre d' or the orchestra leader inviting guests to go to the Viennese table, when notified, to select their own desserts. This will eliminate long lines and result in crowd control. There should be sufficient attendants behind the table to assist the guests.

All pastries presented should be smaller than usual, and all cakes and pies should be cut in smaller than normal portions to yield at least 50 percent more per unit. You should estimate that each guest will take at least three units. The cost of producing this extravaganza is expensive per guest. It takes a tremendous amount of planning and preparation. It is time-consuming to set up each tray in a beautiful manner. Some show-pieces can only be prepared and finished off at the last moment.

Storage up to the time of service can also be a problem. The staff required to set up the table in an artistic manner requires premium compensation. Your charge should include a most liberal markup for each item you have produced or purchased. Fragile pieces of ice, sugar, or butter should be charged for at a rate at least three times your cost to compensate for possible breakage or replacement. You personally should be liberally reimbursed as the architect of the project.

Beverages

The coffee served at the end of a banquet should be brewed a little stronger. There is little opportunity to sell additional foods or services at this point, but some additional revenue may be gained by selling coffee laced with brandy or orange peel, or Irish coffee. This can provide a gracious final touch.

An effective finale can be offered at this point with the service of brandy. A European touch is the service of brandy in chocolate cups instead of glass ponies, allowing the guests to sip their brandy and then eat the chocolate container. This type of cup is available from fine restaurant supply companies.

THE BUFFET

The buffet, where foods are presented so guests can serve themselves, is not only popular for receptions and cocktail parties, but also can be a spectacular way of presenting an entire meal. It is particularly appropriate in homes where space is limited and many people are to be served. The buffet can be elaborate and elegant enough to suit the most sophisticated tastes, or can add a special flair to the simplest of breakfast, lunch, or dinner menus.

Successful buffet catering must use the basic principles of merchandising, since well-displayed merchandise sells itself. The food display, garnitures, and serviceware all enhance the appearance of the table and act as attention-getters. Ice carvings, flowers, tallow or salt dough, or sugar or nougat work can be used as supplementary showpieces. There are "come-ons" that attract guests to the table. Also popular are cascading mounds of fresh fruit and vegetables, baskets of breads, and whole salamis and cheeses. These are not only colorful but also express freshness and quality.

The buffet table is a miniature marketplace because its charm, magnetism, excitement, flavor, and food stimulate the diner's appetite. As guests approach the table, their minds subconsciously photograph the entire display; if it is artistically and attractively presented, they are entranced with the picture. Tempted by a wide choice of food, beautifully offered, they become impulsive and enthusiastic.

Table-top Cooking

No matter how beautiful the table may be, its appearance will be enhanced by human animation. Having employees serve food from chafing or other service dishes is not only a gracious gesture, but one that speeds up service. A chef carving a roast or slicing a salmon has great customer appeal, but one actually cooking a variety of omelets, crepes, or deep-fried specialties kindles a curiosity that is hard to resist, and practically all onlookers are intrigued by the action. Remember that cooking for many people has become a spectator sport.

Table-top or exhibition cooking should be used when practical. That means giving serious consideration to such elements as price, time, equipment, and safety.

Price

The costs involved in table-top cooking are higher because the person selected to do specialized cooking has to spend the entire time at the buffet. Since this person's skill is great, his or her wage rate will be higher. Therefore, consider whether your monetary return is sufficient to warrant this service.

Time

Table-top foods should not take too long to cook because waiting guests could create a traffic jam, interfering with service to others. Small crepes should be prepared in the kitchen, then taken to the buffet for final touches. Each pan should contain at least a dozen crepes so that a number of guests can be served within a short time. Filled omelets should be made large enough to be cut into 12 fork portions. Eggs foo yung, made in a 12-inch pan, for example, will yield approximately 25 appetizer portions.

Small table-top grills, heated by propane gas tubes, can cook from 40 to 60 cocktail franks or 40 cocktail hamburgers, which can be served on finger rolls or cocktail breads. These grills also work very well for Japanese teriyaki served on bamboo skewers, or Thai sates. A cheese fondue in a 2-quart chafing dish or fondue pot is enough for at least 50 bread cubes. A Mongolian fire pot might be more attractive to today's diet-conscious guests. The fire pot is a do-it-yourself stove in which guests can cook vegetables, meat, and fish in a broth heated by gas or charcoal. The food is placed in little dippers that are then lowered into the simmering stock. These suggestions are but a few of the different items that can be prepared quickly, but in quantity.

Equipment

In addition to table-top grills, cooking equipment such as electric fry pans, electric woks, waffle

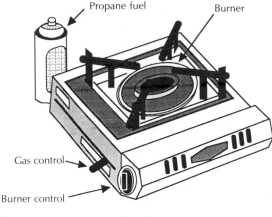

Figure 9-2. Table-top Gas Burner.

irons, chafing dishes, fondue pots, deep-fat fryers, and the new table-top gas burners can also be used for buffet catering (Figure 9-2).

Table-top deep-fat fryers are excellent for exhibition frying. The most effective and convenient are stainless steel–clad with a 4-quart capacity (do not use a larger one for buffet service), with a rating of no more than 110 volts and 1500 amps. Be sure that the electrical system can carry the load, which undoubtedly will already include many lights and other electrical equipment, without blowing fuses or tripping switches. Another option would be to use electric woks. Before using the fryer or wok at a party, give it a dry run. Remember to be extremely careful about guarding against accidental spills.

When using a deep-fat fryer, firmly set the fryer on a table and fill it to the factory-suggested line. Products to be deep-fried must be free of water and lowered carefully into the shortening. Avoid overcrowding; this allows the product to cook faster and prevents the hot grease from overflowing.

Some items that lend themselves well to table-top frying are shrimp in beer batter, tiny potato puffs, ravioli, wontons, corn fritters, tiny apple fritters, eggplant sticks, fillet of sole fingers, and boneless chicken wings.

Fondue cooking on a buffet is still popular, and fondue is a comparatively simple dish to prepare. A cheese fondue is the most popular type. Crusty French bread or croutons—each speared by a long bamboo skewer or a two-pronged fondue fork—are placed on a tray so guests can dip their own. Large paper napkins and 4-inch plates should be available. An attendant should be nearby to replenish fondue or bread. Dessert fondue is another option; fruit and pound cake can be dipped in chocolate, caramel, or marshmallow sauce. Bagna cauda, a traditional Italian mixture of warm anchovies, garlic, heavy cream, and truffles, creates a similar activity as guests dip raw vegetables and pieces of Italian bread into the rich sauce.

Space is another important consideration. Traffic must be able to move around the table freely. There must also be enough table space for the table-top cooking, and sufficient open space around the preparation area so that the heat generated by the unit will not adversely affect other foods.

Safety

Safety is a paramount consideration at all times. Since table-top cooking involves hot liquids, cooking apparatus must be firmly anchored and set on a tray that is at least one-third larger than the unit used. The table must be rigid and stand steadily on the floor. Never use a wobbly table.

If using a knockdown or collapsible table, make certain that the leg hardware is firmly locked in place. Then take the additional precaution of tying or wiring the leg hardware together to avoid the possibility of the table collapsing. Tie any electrical wiring and appliance cords to the table leg so that if anyone trips over the wire, the grill or fryer will not slide or move. When an extension cord must be on the floor—whether in

a traffic area or not—cover it with 4-inch adhesive firmly fastened to the floor; thus, the wire cannot be kicked and no one can trip over it. There are also rubber covers designed to cover wires that can be reused and look nicer than the tape.

All these precautions will be nullified if an employee becomes careless when operating any table-top equipment. Only permit the most competent and skilled personnel to do any table-top cooking.

Decorative Pieces

Whether a simple affair or a spectacular showcase, the buffet provides you and your staff with the opportunity to display artistic and culinary talents. Ice carvings, tallow work, decorated foods, colorfully garnished food trays, specialty cakes, spun sugar, and nougat designs can be used alone or in combination to dramatize and individualize buffet tables. Salt dough sculptures have become popular since they are easy to store.

Ice Carvings and Molds

Because of their size and the effort needed to execute and move them, ice carvings are generally used only for very special occasions and those held in hotels, clubs, and banquet halls. Furthermore, large ice carvings can be done only in an icehouse or in a large walk-in freezer. Ice carvings are always a big hit, especially if you come up with something different. Ice carving can also be functional when made into the shape of bowls or trays designed to hold trays of food or bowls of punch (Figure 9-3) or even a wine rack for champagne* (Figure 9-4). Small ice molds can be made in a commissary kitchen; however, molded ice will never have the clarity of professionally frozen ice blocks.

*Actual-size templates for this and many other ice carvings are available from the CIA Bookstore, Hyde Park, NY 12538 and from Mac Winker's book *Ice Sculpture: The Art of Ice Carving in 12 Systematic Steps* (Memphis, TN: Duende Publications, 1989).

Caviar on Ice. Caviar lends a touch of elegance to a reception or cocktail party buffet. It is most frequently set on an ice mold, presented in the original can so the brand can be shown (Figure 9-5).

To make an ice display for caviar, fill a large gelatin mold, round bowl, or saucepan with water to a depth of 4 inches. Place it in a freezer until solidly frozen (for two to three days). To unmold, set the pan in hot water for a moment or two, then quickly invert it on a tray covered with a plastic doily. (The diameter of the tray should be at least 8 inches greater than the mold.)

Using hot water, half fill a can or pan having approximately the same diameter as the caviar can. Place the container of hot water in the center of the ice mold for a few minutes so the ice will melt sufficiently to accommodate the

1. Fill a stainless steel bowl with crushed ice, place a smaller bowl filled with water in the center of the ice. Fill the crushed ice with water and freeze until solid.

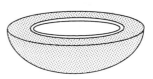

2. Remove the outer bowl and the ice from the center bowl. Serve punch from the center bowl.

Figure 9-3. Ice Punch Bowl.

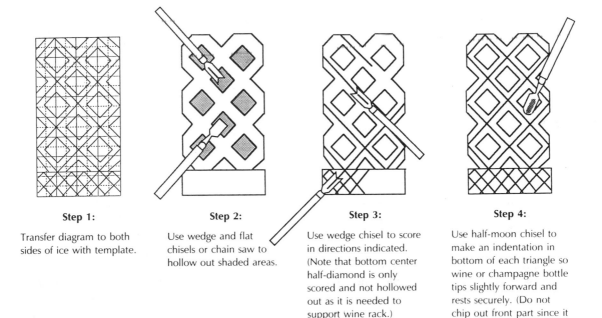

Step 1:

Transfer diagram to both sides of ice with template.

Step 2:

Use wedge and flat chisels or chain saw to hollow out shaded areas.

Step 3:

Use wedge chisel to score in directions indicated. (Note that bottom center half-diamond is only scored and not hollowed out as it is needed to support wine rack.)

Step 4:

Use half-moon chisel to make an indentation in bottom of each triangle so wine or champagne bottle tips slightly forward and rests securely. (Do not chip out front part since it holds bottle in place. Use an empty bottle to test each opening.)

Finishing touches: Clean ice with water. Return to freezer.

Figure 9-4. Ice Wine Rack.

1. Fill a stainless steel bowl with water and freeze.

2. Remove ice from bowl. Set a bain marie filled with hot water, the same size as the caviar can, to melt an indentation.

3. Place a small towel in the indentation and set the can of caviar on top. Set the ice mold on a napkin on a tray. Garnish with lemon shells filled with chopped onions, egg whites, and sour cream.

Figure 9-5. Caviar Ice Mold.

1. Cut a cone from styrofoam, cover it with green cloth, and secure it in the bottom of a bowl with florist's clay. Insert toothpicks to help hold the fruit.

2. Arrange fruit in an attractive display.

Figure 9-6. Fruit Display.

caviar tin. Decorate the presentation of caviar using a simple pan-made ice mold as the base.

Before placing the caviar on ice, fold a small white napkin or piece of cheesecloth and place it in the melted area. This will prevent the can from rolling or sliding. Decorate the mold with lemon leaves. Hollowed-out serrated lemons, filled with finely chopped hard-cooked egg whites or finely minced onions and sour cream, make a very effective garnish. Add lemon wedges or arrange them in a separate dish next to the mold. Caviar is traditionally served with cold toast or

blinis, small buckwheat pancakes. Having one of your service people making fresh blini on a table-top griddle is a nice touch.

Keep a large dry sponge and small pan nearby. About once every half hour, use the sponge to absorb the melted ice and squeeze the water into the pan. (Do this as unobtrusively as possible.)

Fruited Ice Molds for Punch Bowls. In the bottom of a heart-shaped pan, loaf pan, or ring mold, arrange sliced fruit or mint leaves with strawberries or cherries. Pour in plain or tinted

 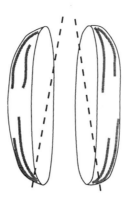 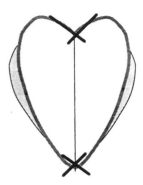

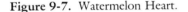

1. Cut watermelon in half from end to end.

2. Cut halves on the bias. The two larger pieces are hollowed out and used for the heart. The remaining two pieces are used for the base.

3. Secure two watermelon quarters with bamboo skewers to make the heart. Use the other pieces turned flatside down for the base. Fill center with cut fruit.

Figure 9-7. Watermelon Heart.

water, ginger ale, fruit juice, or lemonade to a depth of ¼ inch and freeze. When frozen, fill the mold with additional liquid and refreeze. To unmold, dip the pan in hot water to the rim and invert it over the punch bowl.

Edible Centerpieces

Edible, or partially edible, centerpieces can highlight different sections of the table or can be attractive focal points of the buffet. For a large, elaborate buffet table, they may be supported by an elegant floral arrangement or an ice carving, or perhaps a centerpiece of fruit or carved melon.

Fruit Centerpieces. Using florist's clay, anchor Styrofoam shapes inside a medium or large silver or glass bowl (Figure 9-6). Insert bamboo sticks or club toothpicks in the Styrofoam and "hang" leaves, grapes, pineapple stems, melon balls, strawberries, and other small fruits from them. Fill the bottom of the bowl with shredded coconut, walnut or pecan meats, lemon leaves, or other greenery.

Carved Melons. Melons, particularly watermelons, can be made into festive, eye-catching centerpieces. Because of their size and shape, watermelons can be arranged either vertically or horizontally, depending on the amount of display space allowed and the effect desired. Watermelon displays make a colorful, inexpensive focal point for the buffet table while producing a functional container for mixed fresh fruit. Simplicity should be the rule, keeping the cuts made into the melon few and clean. Avoid overdoing it by adding too many details; this may give the finished carving the appearance of having been handled too much. Also avoid using materials that are inappropriate to the fruit being served, like olives for eyes or a bed of parsley around the base. Melon carvings supported by whole fresh pineapples and clusters of grapes and other fruits give a sense of freshness and color that is hard to match. Figures 9-7 through 9-9 are examples of carved displays made with watermelons.

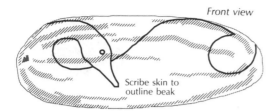

1. Cut through the rind of the watermelon as illustrated.

1. Cut through the rind of the watermelon as illustrated and remove top.

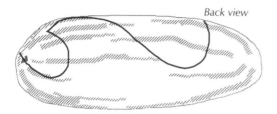

2. Cut through skin, remove top of melon, and carve out inside.

2. Peel skin on head and cut eye and bill. Make fan from toothpicks, melon balls, and pineapple triangles.

3. Peel skin on head, cut eye and bill, and fill with fruit and melon balls.

Figure 9-8a. Watermelon Swan (Horizontal).

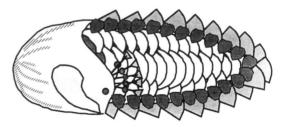

3. Fill back of peacock as illustrated, using pineapple triangles, strawberries, and canteloupe slices.

Figure 9-9. Watermelon Peacock.

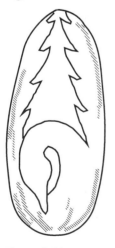

1. Carve a slice from the bottom of the watermelon, stand on end, and cut through rind as illustrated.

Figure 9-8b. Watermelon Swan (Vertical).

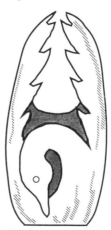

2. Remove excess rind, cut out eye, and fill center with cut fruit and melon balls.

CLAMBAKES

Clambakes or steams are a traditional New England happening. Originally a seashore function, they are now held in backyards, parks, and other picnic areas.

To prepare a clambake for 100 or more guests, dig a pit about 3 feet deep and 4 to 5 feet in diameter and line it with large rocks. Next, place wood on top of the rocks and allow it to burn until it is white-hot. Depending on the size of the stones, pit, and type of wood, this procedure could take up to three hours. But from here on the process requires speed.

Embers should be removed and the stones swept clean of ashes. About 6 inches of seaweed should then be put on the stones. Next, place a layer of heavy wire mesh over this.

For every 50 guests, add a bushel of well-washed soft-shell clams. With these, place one live lobster and two ears of corn for each guest. Pull down the corn husks to remove the silk, but then replace the husks around the ears. Washed but unpared white potatoes may be added if desired. As a "topper," add chicken quarters or halves that have been parboiled, buttered, and wrapped in foil. Gutted trout, mackerel, bluefish, or chunks of cod may also be foil-wrapped and used with, or in place of, the chicken.

Top the food with a thick layer of seaweed, then cover the entire area with wet canvas or burlap. Weigh down the canvas securely with large rocks or heavy planks and allow the food to steam for one to two hours. Figure 9-10 is an illustration of a traditional clambake; Figure 9-11 shows an updated version using screen-bottomed boxes.

Although this can be a gala and exciting presentation, it calls for detailed planning and meticulous follow-through. Since all seafood items spoil quickly, they must be properly refrigerated and given priority attention.

In determining charges for a clambake, a number of unusual conditions must be considered.

1. Do you have the proper tools and personnel available to dig the pit? (This takes considerable time and requires the services of individuals who are physically able. Remember that at the end of the clambake, the pit must be refilled, smoothed over, and all excess stones and dirt carted away.)
2. Where will you get the proper stones? How will you get them to the site of the clambake?
3. Will you be able to get sufficient quantities of seaweed?
4. Will you personally have to pick up the wood? Since your order will probably be small, the company from whom you purchase it may not make a delivery.
5. Do you have heavy wire mesh for the base, as well as heavy canvas or burlap bags for the top?
6. If the bake is to be held on public land, is a permit required? If it is to be held on private property, will you need written permission from the owner?
7. Ample space must be provided for dirty dishes, as well as for scraping and rinsing, if possible. Because of the informality of this event, be prepared for greater dish loss and breakage. Also, remember that because of the large area to be covered and the unevenness of the terrain, your employees will tire more easily and may become more careless with equipment.
8. If disposable dishes are used for the main course, then select heavily coated and rigidly constructed 10- to 12-inch oval plates. This is necessary because clams, lobsters, corn, and chicken are heavy, hot, and juicy.
9. The most inexpensive stainless steel forks, knives, and spoons should be used. Heavy-duty plasticware can be substituted if it will not snap or break.
10. Rugged paper or plastic tablecloths are particularly appropriate for a clambake. Provide mountains of paper napkins because these

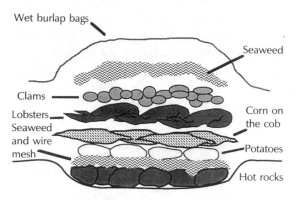

This type of clambake works best with a small number of portions because heat is difficult to control.

1. Dig a 1½-foot-deep hole in the ground.
2. Build a fire and add large rocks. Allow the fire to burn down to coals.
3. Place seaweed and wire mesh on top of the hot rocks and coals.
4. Place potatoes (already three-quarters cooked) on top of the seaweed.
5. Place corn on top of potatoes followed by lobster and clams.
6. Top clams with seaweed and cover with wet burlap bags.
7. Allow food to steam approximately 1½ hours. Uncover layers and serve.

Figure 9-10. Traditional Clambake.

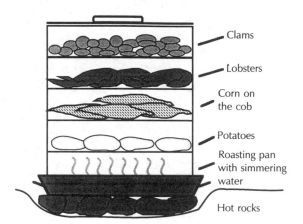

This is a more practical clambake method where the food is placed on screen-bottomed boxes and stacked on top of each other. This method makes it easier to control cooking and serving.

1. Dig a 1½-foot-deep hole in the ground.
2. Build a fire and add large rocks. Allow the fire to burn down to coals.
3. Place a roasting pan on top of the coals and fill three-quarters of the way with water.
4. Set the boxes on top of the roasting pan (the longest cooking items should be closest to the heat).
5. Steam until all food is cooked.
6. Serve with broth that has collected in the roasting pan.

Figure 9-11. Clambake Using Screen-bottomed Boxes.

foods are wet and sticky. Also, have a sufficient supply of heavy-duty rubbish bags that will not rip when lobster shells, clam shells, and corn cobs are packed in them.

BARBECUES

Barbecuing, a great American tradition, involves both preparation and presentation skills. Like other types of showmanship, the more flourishes and props there are, the more effective and impressive the service. Props can include showy grills, decorative and oversized tongs, giant salt and pepper shakers, colorful sauce bowls, gaudy aprons, extra-large padded gloves and hot pads, plus a beautiful but functional carving knife, fork, and sharpening steel. These props should be displayed prominently and used with flourishes to add to the guests' enjoyment.

When catering a private home barbecue, you can use any of the many gas or charcoal grills on the market. However, since most of them were meant for home use their production capability is limited, and the number of guests that can be served at one time is small.

In catering home barbecues, you have the advantages of on-site refrigerators, freezers, water, gas, and electricity. And in some homes, you may find permanently installed grills, a situation that works to your advantage.

Home barbecues add much pleasure and diversity to home entertaining. In parts of the country where weather conditions are favorable and predictable, barbecues are held throughout the year. As a result, there is a greater variety of equipment available to rent through your local rental agency.

The quantity and type of briquettes needed will differ, based on the amount and kind of food to be served. Thick steaks or roasts need a deep bed of coals, whereas franks or burgers call for shallow fires.

Prior to cooking, rub fat trimmings or bacon over grill rods or wire baskets to prevent sticking. If drippings flare up during the cooking process, sprinkle them lightly with water from a plastic squeeze bottle.

Whenever you are doing outside cooking, whether it is a barbecue, table-top grill, or fully set-up kitchen under a tent or canopy, make sure you have a fire extinguisher handy in case of an accident.

Portable Gas Griddles

An average size (18 by 42-inch) gas-fired restaurant griddle can be used to cook more than 100 orders of griddle cakes or more than 500 orders of franks or hamburgers per hour. It makes an excellent portable cooking surface for outdoor barbecues. Secondhand models are often available from restaurant supply houses.

To convert the griddle for outdoor use, have a plumber connect a 4- to 6-foot flexible brass gas hose to the gas line on the griddle. If necessary, have it permanently brazed to that spot. The coupling on the opposite end can be fastened to a 20-pound portable propane gas tank, available from most suburban gas companies.

EQUIPMENT LIST FOR BARBECUE PARTIES

Asbestos gloves
Assortment of wood or bamboo skewers
Brushes: one for butter, one for sauce
Canvas gloves for use in setup and cleanup
Cloth towels and aprons
Fancy carving knife, fork, and steel
Fire extinguisher
First aid kit
Heavy frying pans—cast iron is most
    functional
Hibachis for use as supplementary grills
    for appetizers, side dishes, or small items
Hot pads
Large metal-shielded skewers
Large pepper mill and salt shaker
Large wooden spoons
Long tongs: one for meat, one for coals
Long-handled fork, spoon, and turner
    (spatula)
Meat thermometer
Paper towels
Paring knives
Roast beef slicer
Sturdy work table with cutting boards for
    food preparation and service
Wire basket grills—adjustable to accommo-
    date meat, fish, and chicken; and with
    long handles for holding over heat

Chain an appropriate wrench to this hose so that it will be readily available. Buy a sheet of scrap steel larger than the griddle dimensions, and set the unit on it before placing it in the working area. When completed, test the griddle. You may need to adjust the valve openings if they were not originally intended for use with propane gas.

This same procedure can be used for setting up a cooking range and oven on a mobile base.

Mount the range on a steel-bottomed dolly with heavy-duty wheels. It can be platform-lifted on or off a truck and wheeled to the desired area. Using a range in this way will require a portable auxiliary chimney.

When using propane gas with portable equipment, it is always advisable to carry a spare tank with a gauge showing the amount of gas remaining. If there is no gauge, weigh the tank when full. Then weigh it again and mark that weight on a piece of masking adhesive taped to the side of the tank. To better gauge this figure, check with a propane dealer in your area to find out how much the tank weighs when empty.

Charcoal Grills

When using large barbecue grills for quantity production, it is essential that you give the fire area constant and undivided attention. In this type of setup, you do not have fingertip heat controls, so you cannot get the immediate heat elevation or reduction possible with conventional ranges.

Because of the many variables in outdoor parties, cooking time can only be estimated. Charcoal or compressed fuel packages can take as long as 45 minutes to reach the proper temperature. If you try to rush them, you either burn the food or undercook it.

To achieve that special "barbecue" flavor in food, you can scatter wood shavings like hickory or mesquite that have been soaked in water on the fire at the proper time to produce a smoky flavor.

Remember, all meat cookery calls for glowing coals—no flame. The fire should burn until a gray ash covers the charcoal or briquettes before you add the food. With grills that have crank handles, the proper heat can be achieved by adjusting the grill to a high or low position over the fire. However, most commercial grills only have hooks at fixed positions on each end, which limits the elevation of the cooking rack. Hand

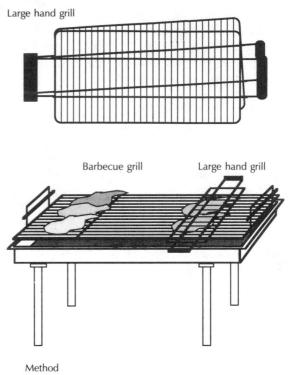

Method
1. Place food items between the two grills.
2. Place the hand grill on top of the grill rack.
3. Turn the hand grill by using the handles.

Figure 9-12. Hand Grill.

grills or racks make turning large numbers of chicken, sausage, ribs, and fish efficient and safe (Figure 9-12).

If you do not have a thermometer to determine the temperature, you will have to resort to the "field-mess detection method." To do this, hold your open hand a couple of inches above the grill and count one and two, two and three, three and four, and so on. If you must remove your hand by the end of the one and two count, you know that the fire is very, very hot. In other words, the higher the count, the lower the temperature. (Determining the temperature in ovens without a thermostat can be done in the same way. Insert your hand halfway between the deck and the top of the oven and count, in the same manner, up to eight. If you must remove your hand before reaching the count of eight, you can be certain that the oven is hot enough for roasting, 350°F.)

Starting a Fire

Starting a good barbecue fire requires practice and skill. The following methods are practical.

1. If using an electrical starter, follow the model directions explicitly. If liquid starter fuel is used, sprinkle it on the coals at least a full minute before applying the starter. *Never* use gasoline or kerosene. And remove all aerosol cans—bug sprays, air fresheners, or other such units—from the vicinity of the grill.

2. If using canned heat, empty the contents of a small can into a cup made from aluminum foil. Then place it in the fire box, heap charcoal over it in a mound, and ignite. Allow it to burn through and then spread coals over the area desired.

3. Cylindrical fire cans filled with charcoal are available at most hardware stores. Stuff the base with newspaper and place the can in the center of the fire box. When the newspaper is lit, it ignites the briquettes. After it is burning well, add a number of untreated briquettes to nearly reach the top and allow to burn. Next, carefully remove the can and rake the coals over the area desired.

Transporting Equipment

Barbecue and grill equipment must be carefully packed for transport to and from your commissary. Heavy padded canvas tarpaulins should be used for cover and protection because soot and odors from the equipment can be transferred to other equipment.

Preparing barbecue and grill equipment for return to the commissary or rental agency is a time-consuming and dirty job. All coal and ashes must be removed from the fire boxes and disposed of properly. Furthermore, the equipment must be absolutely cold before handling. Numerous layers of soaking wet newspapers can be placed on grills to cool them down, and additional water can be poured over them to speed up the process. Access to a hose is very helpful.

To clean pots, skillets, and wire grills, soap-moistened abrasive pads are a great aid. However, after returning to the commissary, you should again thoroughly clean all equipment, steaming it, if possible. Then, and only then, can you inspect and repack it for future use.

In catering barbecues, as with other types of parties, proper sanitation and refrigeration must not be overlooked. All work and serving areas should be inspected, and must be scrupulously clean. While flying and creeping insects may not be bothersome in the barbecuing area, since smoke and heat will drive them away, they could be a source of great annoyance in the service areas. If you must use an insect repellent, do it very carefully; spray it as close to the ground as possible and do not spray it near food.

If the truck you are using does not have refrigeration facilities, keep all foods in portable foam or fiberglass coolers, using canned freezing pellets or dry ice to retain the desired temperature.

Unless proper refrigeration and refrigerated serving facilities are available, it would be inadvisable to serve any of the following foods at a warm-weather barbecue: egg and milk mixtures, custards, eclairs, cream puffs, and cream-filled cakes. These items are particularly sensitive to spoilage.

Immediately destroy any leftover foods. Do not give foods to guests or to your client unless you planned this as part of your special service and had made arrangements for the extra food to be stored properly, cooked with the intention of being sent home, and properly packaged to maintain safe temperatures. Strict adherence to this procedure will not only enhance your reputation, but will also protect you from the danger of illness resulting from possible food contamination.

WEDDINGS

Despite the more casual attitude toward marriage today, it is estimated that 8 out of 10 couples still prefer formal weddings. Many of these couples and their parents will be seeking your services.

In discussing plans with prospective clients, you must determine the location of the affair, the time of service, number of guests expected, food preferences, and general arrangements, as well as be prepared to answer any questions concerning etiquette and protocol. You should then prepare and submit a proposal for the menu and desired services for the client's approval (Figure 9-13).

Although a social caterer is usually not involved in the selection of a florist, orchestra, or photographer for a wedding, your client may ask for your recommendations. It would certainly be advantageous to suggest people you know and with whom you will be able to work smoothly.

Some establishments (such as hotels and clubs) may permit only an "approved" florist, orchestra, or photographer to work in their facility. Their reasoning is usually based on past experience—poor performance, abuse of house rules, lack of cooperation. You should be aware of such conditions before making any recommendations to your client.

Music

If music is to be used in a public hall, hotel, or similar establishment, union musicians may be employed. The union may also determine the size of the orchestra for the occasion. Rules vary, so check with the local musicians' union before hiring any orchestra or musical group.

Successful Catering Inc.
Hyde Park, N.Y. 12538
914-555-1212

Account Representative:	Bernard Splaver
Client:	Mr. and Mrs. Dieter Doppelfeld
Address:	26 Horseshoe Lane Hyde Park, N.Y. 12538
Telephone:	914-555-1212
Function:	Wedding
Date:	June 15, 1990
Time:	3:00 PM—Reception 4:30 PM—Dinner Guests leave by 8:30 PM
Location:	The Vanderbilt Mansion Route 9 Hyde Park, N.Y.
Number of Guests:	125–150
Linens:	White tablecloths topped by ecru lace cloths on all tables; white cloth napkins
Gratuities:	Included in price
Table Cards:	Handwritten in Spencerian script (guest list to be supplied 7 days before event)
Service:	American service Service staff in black and white
Music:	Orchestra arranged by client; we will coordinate food-service with band leader
Matches/Cocktail Napkins:	Supplied by client
Price:	$_____
Contract Deposit:	Signed contract due by January 15, 1990 with a $_____ deposit

Figure 9-13a. Wedding Menu Proposal.

The music is an important and integral part of the wedding and reception. The leader announces the "grand entrance" of the newlyweds, their first dance together, and then the first dance of the newly married couple with their parents. The protocol of a religious ceremony before, during, or after the meal; the cutting of the cake; and the music associated with this ritual are also the orchestra leader's responsibility.

Lively and entertaining music contributes immeasurably to the total enjoyment of the affair. It is essential, however, that the orchestra leader coordinate the musical selections with the meal service. Dance music should not be played during the service of a food course. The musical selections to be featured during the meal should be planned with the client.

Unless specifically requested by the client, you are not required to serve food to the orchestra. However, if you can afford the expense, it can be a good-will gesture to provide a snack during one of their breaks.

Reception Menu
Reception 3:00–4:30 PM

Ice Carving
Wine Rack filled with Champagne

Carving Station
Smoked Turkey Served on Herb Biscuits
Gravlax Served on Cocktail-Size Pumpernickel

Cold Hors d'Oeuvres
Deluxe Crudités with 2 Dips
Jumbo Shrimp Canapes on Jalapeno Corn Bread
with Avocado Cream
Beetjuice Pickled Eggs Stuffed with Herb Spread
Heartshaped Melon Carving with Fresh Fruit
New Potatoes with Caviar and Sour Cream

Hot Hors d'Oeuvres
Eggplant Roll-ups
Codfish Cakes with West Indian Pumpkin
Steamed Chinese Dumplings
Spanikopitas • Stuffed Grape Leaves

Beverages (2 bar setups)
Champagne
Chardonnay • Cabernet Sauvignon
Sparkling Mineral Water
Fresh Orange Juice
Cola, Ginger Ale, Iced Tea

Dinner Menu
Dinner 4:30 PM

Dinner Beverage
Champagne Toast
Continued service of wines

Appetizer
Cold Poached Salmon with Asparagus

Entrée
Blackened Beef with Corn and Pepper Sauce

Salad
Mixed Green Salad with Caper Dressing

Dessert
Wedding Cake
6 tiers on 4 sets of columns
Yellow Cake with Dark Chocolate Filling
All White Decoration
Served with Frozen Vanilla Yogurt

Figure 9-13b. Wedding Menu.

Flowers

Flowers for the wedding and reception are the responsibility of the client. However, you should discuss with the client and the florist the flowers to be used on the buffet and head table.

A skilled florist will be able to tint flowers to match or harmonize with the bride's color scheme. The florist will provide wedding canopies and aisle markers, construct reception and head table backgrounds, and decoratively arrange plants and flowers.

All of the constructed pieces and floral decorations must be removed by the florist following the function or at a time determined by the florist and the caterer. The area must be cleaned to the complete satisfaction of the supervisor of the premises. If a client-engaged florist neglects to properly clean up, all related cleaning costs will probably be added to the client's bill.

Photographer or Videographer

A good photographer—skilled in spotting and in capturing on film those special moments so precious at weddings—should be employed to record the highlights of the affair. An expert photographer works without being too conspicuous or obtrusive. He or she can pick out suitable backgrounds for posed shots and is knowledgeable about wedding customs and religious protocol.

Be sure the photographer supplies you with several good pictures of your part of the function: the buffet table, the bride and groom cutting the cake, the head table, and similar activities. These can be invaluable sales promotion tools.

Menu

If your client wishes a printed menu, you must provide a correct and clearly written menu for the printer. Formal menus have often been written in French; however, today English is not only acceptable but preferable for English-speaking clientele. The menu tells people what they will get to eat and therefore should use meaningful language that draws a clear picture of what is to be served. Although the menu is the poetic link between the kitchen and the guest and should be artfully written, it should be precise enough to be clearly understood by the guests. Foreign words should be avoided whenever they can be replaced by suitable English words. Oftentimes, foreign words are only used to add meaningless embellishment and do little more than confuse the guests.

Wedding Cake

The wedding cake is not only the focal point of the buffet or dessert table, but the cutting of it may be one of the highlights of the affair. It is important that you work out the details of the cutting ceremony with the client and the photographer so there will not be any last-minute confusion to spoil the event.

Although there are many wedding cake designs, traditionally, a wedding cake is always a tiered cake. The tiers are arranged either one on top of the other or separated by inverted plastic or glass champagne glasses, or by plastic or floral columns.

Posed photos of the bride and groom cutting the cake may be taken without disturbing the side of the cake that guests see, or affecting the delicately balanced top layers on a tiered cake. Before the photographer actually takes the picture, the caterer should cut two pieces of cake from the rear of the bottom layer, and place them on a small plate. Conceal these until the bridal cake-cutting pose is photographed. Then photographs of the bride and groom sharing the pieces of cake may be taken. Your staff will then take over the cutting and serving of the cake.

Cutting the Cake

It is customary to use the wedding cake as the main dessert item for the wedding menu. It is served by itself, or topped with ice cream, vanilla custard, or fresh fruit.

It is also customary that pieces of the cake be bagged or boxed, then given to the guests to take home as a memento. Special bags with grease-resistant liners, appropriately decorated, are available in stores selling party goods.

Traditionally, the top layer of the cake and the ornament are not cut, but are removed, boxed, and given to the newlyweds to be saved for their first anniversary celebration. The exposed second tier is then sliced and served before cutting into the next lower tier. The tiers may be cut in a variety of ways to obtain the number of portions needed (Figure 9-14).

Decorating a Head Table

The head table is the focal point of the entire dining room. Not only should it be distinguished in appearance from the other tables, but, whenever possible, it should be elevated on either a platform or a dais.

Prefabricated platforms are available and can be built in as many "steps" or rows as you desire. These are often worthwhile investments for on-site establishments, such as hotels and public banquet halls. Before purchasing any of these collapsible platforms, however, be certain to make provisions for storage. And remember, when elevated arrangements are requested, you are entitled to an additional charge for setup, use, and breakdown.

If a dais is needed but the facility in which you are serving does not have one, you should be able to supply it. Homemade ones are easy to build, store, and transport, and can be set up by just two people (Figure 9-15). This equipment also represents a plus factor in terms of the services you can offer. And by charging a fee for use and transportation, your construction costs will be self-liquidating; you may, in fact, even show a profit on your investment.

Head Table Construction

Five portable (4- by 6-foot) platform sections will hold two 8-foot by 30-inch tables end to end, seating from 8 to 10 persons, with sufficient space behind chairs so that staff have room to serve comfortably.

These portable platform sections should be hooked together for safety (see Figure 9-15) and be covered with removable rugs or painted a glossy black, probably the most practical color. Keep in mind that neither the chairs nor the tables should extend to the very edge of the platform.

As a safety feature, for crowd control, and for aesthetic value, place two upright stanchions, at least 36 inches high and screwed into flanges bolted to the floor, at the front ends of the platform (Figure 9-16). A plumber can build these in short order.

Brass pipe, chrome, or even plain black pipe (painted gold, aluminum, or any other desired color) are also effective, but they should be capped with the same metal as the base. Insert screw eyes into each stanchion to hold decorative gold rope or ribbons (available from fabric and trimming stores).

Head tables should always be draped or skirted. To serve as a base for the skirts, a "silence cloth," similar to a lightweight blanket, should be positioned first to cover the entire table. This cloth reduces service noise and acts as an anchor for table drapes. Today draping has been made easy with pre-folded clip-on drapes that are fastened with plastic clips.

The front of the head table can be garlanded with ferns, smilax, lemon, or huckleberry leaves, or natural string smilax, all of which can be obtained from your florist. Natural string smilax is the most elegant.

Napkins can add interest and beauty to the head and guest tables, particularly when they are folded into interesting shapes (see Figure 9-17). The colors should match or be complementary to the overall color scheme.

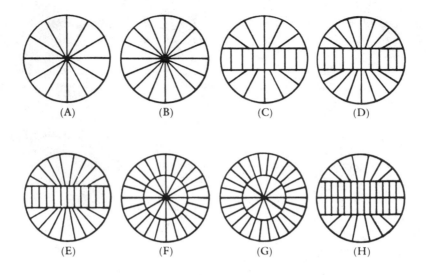

Cutting guide for tiered wedding cake. (A) 8-in., 2-layer cake; yield: 12 servings. (B) 9-in., 2-layer cake; yield: 16 servings. (C) 10-in., 2-layer cake; yield: 20 servings. (D) 11-in., 2-layer cake; yield: 26 servings (E) 12-in., 2-layer cake; yield: 30 servings. (F) 12-in., 2-layer cake; yield: 36 servings. (G) 13-in., 2-layer cake; yield: 36 servings. (H) 14-in., 2-layer cake; yield: 40 servings.

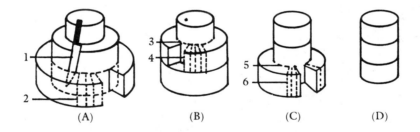

Cutting tiered cakes. (A) Cut vertically through bottom layer at edge of 2nd layer as indicated by dotted line No. 1; then cut out wedges as shown by 2. (B) Follow same procedure with middle layer; cut vertically through 2nd layer at edge of top layer as indicated by dotted line No. 3; then cut wedges as shown by 4. (C) When entire 2nd layer has been served, cut along dotted line 5; cut another row of wedges as shown by 6. (D) Remaining tiers may be cut as desired.

Figure 9-14. Cutting Guide for Tiered Cakes. (Reprinted with permission from the American Institute of Baking (Chicago), "With a Bakery Food—It's Easy.")

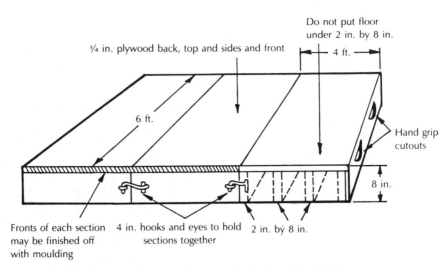

Do not put floor under 2 in. by 8 in.

¼ in. plywood back, top and sides and front

4 ft.

6 ft.

Hand grip cutouts

8 in.

Fronts of each section may be finished off with moulding

4 in. hooks and eyes to hold sections together

2 in. by 8 in.

Figure 9-15. Homemade Portable Risers for Dais or Head Table.

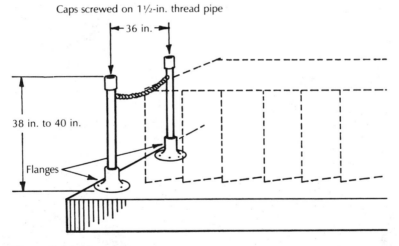

Caps screwed on 1½-in. thread pipe

36 in.

38 in. to 40 in.

Flanges

Figure 9-16. Stanchions.

Cat Tail

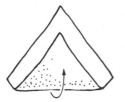

1. Fold into a triangle leaving a border.

2. Fold bottom up one inch.

3. Flip napkin over— roll from left, tuck in.

4. Stand napkin on plate.

Trillium

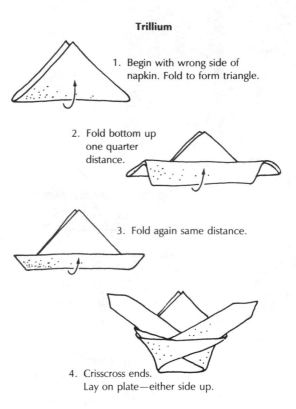

1. Begin with wrong side of napkin. Fold to form triangle.

2. Fold bottom up one quarter distance.

3. Fold again same distance.

4. Crisscross ends. Lay on plate—either side up.

Siamese Cat Tail

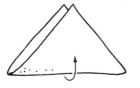

1. Fold napkin into a triangle.

2. Roll both ends to center.

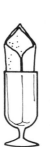

3. Place napkin in glass.

Shooting Star

1. Fold bottom up to form triangle.

2. Fold points 1 and 2 to top point.

3. Flip over to form a triangle.

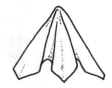

4. Stand on end.

Figure 9-17. Napkin Designs.

SIGNATURE ITEMS

Any event that you cater, be it a simple barbecue or a lavish wedding, will be made more distinctive and memorable if you develop an unusual food offering or a surprise presentation. Your business will then become identified with this signature item. It should, if possible, be an exclusive recipe developed and not easily duplicated (for example, pecan diamonds or a special chocolate). Or, it could be the service of an extra fancy item (for example, the offer to pour brandy in a guest's coffee as a house treat), or a generous dish of fancy cookies accompanying the dessert.

The signature item can be presented during any part of the meal, but it must be visually and tastefully impressive. Memorable signature items can be the deciding factors when catering contracts are awarded. The following are some examples:

Complimentary cheese and fruit tray
Butter roses on butter plates
Freshly baked herb biscuits
Small ice cream cones filled with savory canapé spreads
Canister of penny candies with dessert
Whole spiced figs as a table relish
Second helpings of the entrée offered to guests from a silver platter
An assortment of antipasti arranged on a lazy susan on each table
Mineral water for each table
Center table arrangement of provolone cheese, whole tomatoes, green peppers, celery hearts, and sesame bread sticks
Takeout soft ice cream in cups at dining-room exit
Logo-decorated take-home boxes of candy
Chocolate-covered stem strawberries presented after dessert

SPECIAL EFFECTS

Some clients may want a little more artifice and dazzle to make their parties memorable extravaganzas. The following is a list of items that can be rented or purchased from many metropolitan agencies:

Helium-filled balloons and balloon sculptures
Neon sculpture
Laser lights
Hot dog stands with red, white, and blue umbrellas
Hand-painted or plain canopies
Huge papier-mâché animals
Silverplated place mats
Candy-striped ice cream wagons
Grand pianos
Tents (from 12 feet square to 50 by 200 feet)
Heaters for tents
Palm trees, yucca trees, ficus trees, exotic plants and flowers
Terra-cotta urns and vases
Clear glass cubes for seating or decoration
Boughs of flowers in vases of molded ice
Antique hay wagons
Split-rail fences
Victorian gazebos
Vintage cars
Pennants
Pom-poms
Football bleachers
Lucite pillars with crystal bowls of flowers on top
Banquettes
Disco floors and lights
Mirrored balls
Sound systems
Soap-bubble machine

Many special linen items are also available. For example:

Gold or silver lamé
Batik prints
Paisley prints
White eyelet
Taffeta
Moiré
Mohair cloths
Solid-colored cloths with hand-painted borders, topped with white linen cloths

You can also consider such special party entertainment as:

Astrologers or palm readers
Belly dancers

Big screen television showing current video taping of the event
Caricaturists
Children's entertainment—puppets, clowns
Disc jockey
Handwriting analyst
Hypnotist
Magic, ESP
Mechanical robots
Mimes
Mobile discotheque
Rollerskate disco
Video games

·10·

Kosher Catering

THE MEANING OF KOSHER

The Hebrew word *kosher* means fit or proper relative to Jewish dietary laws. The kosher designation means that a given product is permitted and acceptable to those adhering to the Jewish dietary laws, and conforms to strict kosher standards. These dietary laws are Biblical in origin, resulting in regulations that have been interpreted, refined, and expanded by rabbis over the centuries. So complex and extensive is the rabbinic legislation that those considering setting up a kosher catering operation are strongly urged to first consult a local rabbinic authority for guidance. The intention of this chapter is not to give specific details about setting up a kosher kitchen, but to explain the fundamentals of kosher law and provide insight into its practical

application. The laws concerning the preparation, selection, and service of food (even though they were delivered to Moses more than 3000 years ago) are deeply woven into Jewish religious and family life and remain virtually unchanged today. They still govern, to differing degrees, the eating habits of many Jewish families.

Use of the word *kosher* is not simply a matter of maintaining rigid standards of food preparation and service. It requires constant rabbinic certification and supervision. Chefs need not keep kosher themselves (or be Jewish, for that matter) but all preparations must be supervised by an authorized rabbi or his representative, a *mashgiach* (kosher supervisor), who is on the premises at all times to oversee that strict standards are constantly maintained. Losing kosher certification will irreparably harm a caterer's reputation in the Jewish community and destroy his or her business.

The expression "kosher style" is misleading and deceptive. Kosher doesn't define an ethnic

This chapter was edited by Rabbi Dr. Joshua Shuchatowitz, President of Planning Resources, Inc.

way of cooking or certain tastes; after all, Jews live in all parts of the world with a wide variety of culinary backgrounds. Kosher is a religious criterion, and is applicable whether the food is Eastern European or Ethiopian. Either a food is kosher or it is not; either a kitchen is kosher or it is not. Many Jewish clients who do not keep kosher themselves, however, may want to develop a so-called "kosher-style" menu that does not overtly violate kosher tradition out of deference to relatives and guests, or simply out of custom. Therefore, although they may have hired a nonkosher caterer and know that nonkosher foods will be used, they may request that basic traditions be observed, such as omitting pork or shellfish and avoiding dairy-based sauces served on meat or poultry dishes. Proper care must be taken to ensure that the guests are not led to believe that the food is kosher.

KOSHER FOODS

There are two main components of kosher dietary laws; the first concerns what foods are considered kosher and the second stipulates how these foods can be combined. Kosher food may be rendered nonkosher for a variety of reasons, such as the improper slaughter or processing of meat from an acceptable species, the mixing of meat and dairy ingredients, the use of ingredients derived from nonkosher sources, or the preparation with utensils or equipment previously used for nonkosher food.

Meat

The only mammals permitted are those that chew their cud and are cloven-hoofed. These include cattle, deer, sheep, and goats. Pork and pork products (such as lard) are prohibited.

The cuts of meat from the hindquarters are not permitted because the sciatic nerve, which runs through the hindquarter, is forbidden. In Europe (as in Israel today) butchers remove this nerve. This procedure is too time consuming and labor intensive for the American meat industry and very few butchers possess the required skills. Hindquarters are sold to nonkosher butchers.

Glatt kosher meat comes from an animal whose lungs have been checked and found to be free of any adhesions. Lately, *glatt kosher* has come to be used more broadly by consumers to mean kosher without any question, and the term can be applied to any kosher product.

Animals meant for kosher markets must be slaughtered in a proscribed humane and painless way and immediately drained of all blood, and then soaked in cold water and salted by the kosher butcher before the meat can be used. This koshering process does not impair the taste or quality, and it is a misconception that kosher meat has "several strikes against it" for the caterer. Koshered and aged meat can be just as tender as nonkosher meat; the cuts available are more limited, however, since only the forequarters can be used. The caterer will usually receive the meat from the Kosher Provision Company ready for immediate use.

Cheese

All cheeses require kosher certification. Rennet, processed from the stomachs of unweaned calves, is used in the production of cheese as a curdling and coagulating ingredient, and is also used in the production of sour cream, buttermilk, and some varieties of yogurt and yogurt-type desserts. The use of this nonkosher coagulant renders the product nonkosher.

Wine

All wines, brandies, and liqueurs containing a grape component must be prepared under strict rabbinic supervision. Any grape variety is permissible, and special yeasts for fermentation may be used.

Kosher wine producers such as Gan Eden, Weinstock, and Hagafan have helped to change the stereotype of syrupy Jewish holiday wines. Gan Eden, a young winery in Sonoma County, California, has already received 27 gold medals in major competitions for their kosher chardonnays, gamays, and chenin blancs.

Liquor

Bourbon, rye, tequila, scotch (straight or blended), and *grain* vodka (unflavored) are not of a grape origin and are therefore exempt from kosher certification.

The following products do contain wine and therefore require kosher certification: Champagne, sherry, cognac, vermouth, brandy, and sangria.

Kosher for Passover

Kosher for Passover means that, in addition to meeting all of the year-round kosher requirements, a food product meets special Passover dietary laws, which prohibit the use of fermented grain products and similar substances during the entire Passover holiday. Many products which are kosher year round require special additional supervision for Passover use.

KOSHER FOOD PREPARATION

Jewish law lists three classes of food: meat and meat by-products, milk and all dairy products, and *pareve* foods, which are neither meat nor dairy and include products like grains, cereals, fish, eggs, sugars, fruits, vegetables, vegetable oils and shortenings, and seasonings, encompassing the whole gamut of herbs, spices, and flavorings (as long as no part of either a meat or dairy product is incorporated in their manufacture). Food items from the first two classes (meat and dairy) can never be combined in the same dishes or served at the same meal. Pareve foods can be mixed with both meat and dairy. Fish, although pareve, may not be cooked together with meat, but the same pots may be used at different times. Fish may be served before a meat course, but it is customary not to serve fish and meat together on the same plate.

Obviously, with these restrictions, menu planning can be very limited. If you are using meat as the main menu item, the rest of the meal cannot contain any dairy product. Desserts, cakes, pastries, breads, and other items must all be prepared without the use of milk, butter, or cream. On the other hand, if you are serving a meatless menu, such as a fish or vegetarian specialty, you are permitted to use dairy products in any course, including dessert. (Since many commercial pastries include lard as a shortening, any cake, cookie, pie, or cracker must be purchased from a kosher bakery or certified as kosher.) The use of pareve foods is the easiest way to expand or fill in a menu otherwise restricted to using foods of one class.

These situations are obvious ones but more complex problems are encountered when you prepare, for example, a dish such as creamed turkey. The sauce for the creamed turkey must be made with either chicken fat or vegetable shortening, flour, turkey stock, and nondairy creamer since the use of cream, milk, or butter is prohibited. On the other hand, vegetable soup for a dairy meal cannot contain meat stock, but must rely on vegetable stock and seasonings for flavor.

To cover these criteria, many caterers have devised special recipes or rely on special commercial products. Other caterers prepare all dishes as they normally would be prepared, and if any one of the required ingredients is not available due to kosher limitations, that particular dish is not served. The sentiment is that there are hundreds of other dishes from which to choose. Therefore, while kosher laws exclude many foods and combinations of foods, there is still room for imagination in meeting the challenge of planning pleasing menus. The emergence of dairy, meat and seafood substitutes has also led to a whole new era in kosher food development. It is now the accepted custom to serve coffee whiteners (of pareve vegetable origin), whipped toppings, and ersatz ice cream. Of course, you must make certain that these substitutes carry a symbol of kosher certification.

Since Jewish dietary law prohibits the preparation of dairy and meat foods in the same dishes, many caterers plan and serve only one type of menu (meat, for example). However, caterers and foodservice operators serving three meals a day must, of course, prepare and serve both dairy and meat meals. Under these circumstances, they must have two separate, completely equipped kitchens or, at least, one large kitchen with a double set of ranges, ovens, broilers, fryers, cookers, and mixing bowls, as well as two complete sets of china and silver, since meat and dairy products may not be prepared or served in the same pots or dishes or with the same utensils.

The following items require special cleaning or preparation if they were used for nonkosher events: ovens, stoves, broilers and griddle, kettles, steamtables and worktables, fryolators, coffee urns, sinks, refrigerators and freezers, ice machines, pots and pans, rolling racks, shelving, storage, slicers, grinders, mixers, dishwashers, floors, storerooms.

While some hotels and catering halls do their own kosher catering, most have outside kosher caterers come in. The following equipment must be especially set aside for kosher preparation and service and cannot be koshered:

1. A complete set of dishes
2. Cooking pots and utensils
3. Knives and cutting boards

All hotel silver, stainless steel, glassware, chafing dishes, and so forth can be koshered for a kosher party under the supervision of a qualified rabbi.

KOSHER AND NONKOSHER OPERATIONS

Up to this point, only the operation of a strictly kosher establishment has been discussed. If you wish to serve kosher and nonkosher food, you will find that a great deal more planning is required. Usually, a completely separate kitchen with storage space and a complete array of equipment and utensils for kosher service would be required since the scouring process involved in converting a nonkosher item to a kosher one is impractical on a routine basis.

Although foodstuffs and items for dry storage can be stored with nonkosher foods, meat must be held under separate refrigeration. With all these inconveniences, it would seem that operating a combination kosher and nonkosher establishment is impractical. However, large operations, such as hotels, report that kosher catering can be profitable enough to justify the expense since the kosher event generates extra income during slack periods.

Hotel, motel, and club managers with attractive dining facilities often make them available for kosher affairs. The caterer koincludes the kitchen and prepares the food, using all of his or her own kosher dishes, equipment, and experienced personnel. Servers are provided by the facility, which is then reimbursed by a percentage of the gross, a per guest charge, or a separate kitchen and dining area charge (any arrangement equitable to both parties). As a result, the facility's operator not only retains the bar operation, clothes-checking, and parking facilities, but receives added revenue.

The profit margin for kosher foodservice will be comparable to that of a nonkosher operation, providing all other factors are equal. Although the cost of food and preparation will be 15%–20% higher, the selling price will also be correspondingly higher. After amortization of initial startup costs, you may expect somewhat higher profit margins.

SELECTING A MENU

For years the word kosher was synonymous with thick pastrami sandwiches, huge chunks of brisket, matzoh balls swimming in pots of chicken soup, and other heavy Eastern European fare. It is not that kosher laws preclude a more ambitious or lighter style of food, it's simply that the more tradition-bound never felt the urge to innovate.

When it comes to shaping the direction of American kosher cooking, it appears that the growing number of kosher restaurants and caterers are leading the way, challenging the traditions of the past. An increasing number of kosher cooks, responding to a more sophisticated audience, are now experimenting with ingredients and cooking techniques once thought off-limits. This new kosher cuisine includes dishes like vegetable tempura, linguini primavera, Chinese pot-stickers, beef carpaccio, seaweed-wrapped sushi, and venison. A growing number of trendy kosher restaurants from Los Angeles to Boston are offering lighter and more eclectic and elegant alternatives to traditional foods like gefilte fish, stuffed cabbage, and blintzes. Progressive kosher restaurants are serving such fare as Cajun blackened snapper and spinach-filled crepes; Italian specialties like linguine puttanesca; traditional French dishes such as sweetbreads, fish soup with rouille, and pommes de terre lyonnaise; and an eclectic variety, including chicken rolled in pecans with black trumpet mushrooms, mahi-mahi, artichokes à la romana, brook trout with lemon juice and capers, and rotelle with smoked salmon, leeks, and cream. No ethnic cuisine is exempt from kosher preparation; kosher Indian restaurants serve dishes such as rava masal dosai (wheat crepes filled with potatoes, onions, and nuts) and gobhi masala curry (cauliflower curry).

In sum, simply prepare all dishes as they would normally be prepared. If any of the required ingredients is not available due to kosher limitations, do not serve the item. Avoid menu items requiring cream sauces—there are hundreds of other dishes from which to choose. And, if you can't do it right, don't do it! Figures 10-1 through 10-9 illustrate a range of kosher menus, from the traditional to the trendy.

"Every single other cuisine has evolved in recent years; why shouldn't kosher cuisine?" asks Helen Nash, author of *Kosher Cuisine*. "What is happening to kosher cuisine is what has happened to cuisines around the world. It is a cross-fertilization of ideas."

First Course
Vegetable Paté
Pita Bread Crisps

•

Salad
Arugula, Radicchio, Endive and Enoki Mushrooms
Served with a Mustard Vinaigrette

•

Entrée
Served Plated to the Tables
Choose Either One of the Options

Option 1
Teriyaki Grilled Salmon Steaks over Mesquite
or
Mesquite Grilled Tuna Served with Salsa
Parslied New Potatoes
Miniature Vegetables

Option 2
Honey Mustard Glazed Rack of Lamb
Rosemary Roasted New Potatoes
Asparagus Bundles

•

Dessert
Crepes Filled with White and
Dark Chocolate Mousse
Served with Bittersweet Fudge Sauce
Coffee and Tea

Figure 10-1. Benefit Dance Menu.

Hors d'Oeuvres	Dinner

Hors d'Oeuvres

Cold

Special decorated "Canapes Russe"

Hot

Franks in Blankets
Potato Knishes
Liver Knishes
Kasha Knishes
Miniature Potato Pancakes
Stuffed Peppers
Fish Balls

Chafing Dishes

Chinese Prime Peppered Steak
Beef Stroganoff
Hungarian Stuffed Cabbage
Swedish Meat Balls
Barbecued Chicken
Veal Scallopine à la Marsala

Decorated Form Molds

Chopped Chicken Liver
Fruit-Filled Gelatin Mold

Swedish Table

Smoked White Fish
Nova Scotia Salmon
Assorted Imported Herrings
Gefilte Fish

Fancy Decorated Platters

Sliced Tongue, carved and decorated
Sliced Turkey, carved and decorated
Potato Salad, garni
Cole Slaw, garni
Waldorf Salad
Celery, Olives, Radishes and Pickles

Carving Table
Our Chef will carve from his table

Glazed Hot Corned Brisket of Beef
Lean Hot Roumanian Pastrami

Polynesian Fruit Display

An excellent variety of fresh fruit in season,
attractively displayed

Dinner

Tropical Whole Pineapple in Kirsch
Diced Pineapple Marinated in Kirsch
*(Plate to be decorated with galax leaves and small fruits such
as cherries, green and red grapes, plums, peaches)*

Iced Hearts of Celery
Colossal Ripe and Green Olives
Radish Roses
Sweet Gherkins
Spiced Watermelon Rinds

Salted Jumbo Peanuts and Almonds

Chicken Consommé Double with Mandels
Mock Cheese Straws

Baked Fillet of Sole with Supreme Sauce
Parisienne Potatoes

Roast Breast of Capon on Tongue, under glass
Mushroom Sauce
Wild Rice Croquettes

Cranberry and Orange Relish
in Orange Baskets en Parade
*(Orange baskets to be decorated with white ribbon
and orange blossoms)*

Kishka
(To be passed on silver platters)

Kentucky Limestone Lettuce with Hearts of Palm
Artichoke Bottoms, Pimiento Strips,
Vinaigrette Dressing

Pastry Swans, filled with mock ice cream
Brandied Peach Sauce

Petits Fours Glacé

Black Coffee or Tea with Lemon

Four-Tier Wedding Cake
*To be all white with pale pink sugar ribbons and flowers. White
gardenias to be placed between first and second tiers. Upper
tier to have sugar swans.*

Figure 10-2. Traditional Kosher Wedding Menu.

Reception

During the reception we will serve the following selection of cold canapes to be displayed on buffet tables and hot hors d'oeuvres to be passed by waiters, Butler Style:

Cold
Farmer-Style Crudités
(Presented in Large Wicker Baskets with Assorted Dips)
Homos, Tahini
Babaganoush, Beans Purée
Guacamole
Eggplant Caviar with Pita Bread
Taramousalata
Stuffed Grape Leaves, Stuffed Bell Peppers,
Stuffed Tomatoes and Stuffed Eggplant
Poached Mahch with Citronette (lemon vinaigrette)

Hot
Assorted Small Meatballs
(Veal, Lamb and Beef)
Phyllo Pastry Rolls filled with Tuna, Chicken, Lamb
and Vegetables
Artichoke Bottoms à la Grecque
Sautéed Chicken Liver and Scallions
Bell Pepper, Tomato and Eggplant Fried
Chicken Brochettes, Veal Liver Brochettes, Duck
Breast Brochettes and Vegetable Brochettes
Deep-Fried Mahch

Dinner

Marinated Black Bass and Norwegian Salmon
Citronette of Coriander

Roast Rack of Lamb
with Sweet Garlic Sauce

Vegetarian Platters
of Assorted Pastas and Vegetables

Ratatouille
Roasted Potatoes with Tarragon

Salad of Field Greens and Fresh Herbs
Raspberry Vinaigrette

Baskets of Special Breads on All Tables

Special Dessert Buffet
Fresh Fruit
Assorted Cake
Pies
Special Petits Fours
Homemade Cookies
Coffee, Tea, or Decaffeinated Coffee

Figure 10-3. Black Tie Kosher Dinner Dance Menu Prepared and Served at Elegant Nonkosher Restaurant.

Menu 1
Spinach Leaves with Orange Sections
and Blanched Almonds
Vinaigrette

Breast of Chicken Wellington

Honey Glazed Carrots and Broccoli

Challah and Assorted Rolls
Margarine

Tuille filled with Fresh Fruit
Whipped Topping

Brewed Regular and Decaffeinated Coffee
Herbal Teas

Menu 2
Gazpacho Soup

Breast of Chicken with Wild Rice and
Pistachio Nut Fillings
Madeira Sauce

Snowpeas with Red Pepper
Baked Tomato with Fresh Herbs

Challah and Assorted Rolls
Margarine

Apple Strudel with Whipped Topping

Brewed Regular and Decaffeinated Coffee
Herbal Teas

Figure 10-4. Hotel Dinner Menus.

Reception

Chinese Station
Veal Lo Mein
Chicken with Walnuts
Fried Rice
Tempura dishes
Steak Kew
Mu Shu Pancakes

Cold Table
Eggplant Salad
Petcha
Chopped Liver Molds
Party Breads
Crackers
Decorated Fresh Fruit Platters

Carving Station
Baked Sugar Cured Corned Beef
Turkey
Pastrami
Sliced Steak

Middle Eastern Station
Kibeh
Lahamagine
Sweet Rice
Green Rice
Falafel
Tehina
Chumus
Pita Bread

Served from Chafing Dishes
Chicken Hawaiian, Creole Rice
Beef Stroganoff, Toasted Egg Barley
Miniature Shishkabobs and Chickenkabobs
Tongue Polonaise, Noodle Squares
Southern Fried Chicken Tidbits
Pasta Primavera
Swedish Meatballs
Fish Canneloni, Newburg Sauce

Dinner

Kaluabeh of Salmon, Watercress Sauce
(Fresh Fruit Alternate)

Salad with Sliced Beefsteak Tomatoes,
Bibb Lettuce, Asparagus Spears,
Radicchio, Alfalfa Sprouts
Dijon Mustard Dressing

Filet of Veal
Wild Mushroom and Madeira Wine Sauce

Wild Rice with Pine Nuts
Snow Peas with Red Pepper
Dilled Baby Carrots

Baked Alaska, Hot Cherries Jubilee
Mixed Petits Fours and Miniature Pastries
White Grapes

Brewed Decaffeinated Coffee, Mocha, Tea

Basket of assorted hard rolls and bread sticks
on every table

Figure 10-5. Jewish Day School Dinner Dance Menu.

Hors d'Oeuvres

Passed Butler Service

Indonesian Chicken Sate with Peanut Sauce

Peccadillo Empanadas

Apple Beignets

Kyoto Beef Rolls

California Tuna Sushi Rolls

Potato Skins

Asparagus Wrapped with Smoked Salmon

Asparagus Puffs

Sole in Ale Butter served with

Apricot Horseradish Sauce

Potato Latkes with Applesauce

Sesame Chicken Fingers served with

Honey Mustard Dip

Fish Wonton Butterflies

Miniature Reubens

Confit of Onion in Feuillete

*And Served During Cocktail Hour
from Multiple Buffet Stations*

Southwestern U.S.A. Station

Marinated and Grilled Beef and Chicken Rolled in a
Flour Tortilla

Served with Guacamole, Shredded Lettuce, Salsa,
Chopped Tomatoes, Onions and Refried Beans

Chili

Lower East Side Station

Sliced Nova Scotia Smoked Salmon

Served with the classic accompaniments of

Mini Bagels, Black Bread Triangles, Capers, Lemons,
Dill, Tomatoes and Onions

Miniature Stuffed Cabbage, Chopped Liver

Carved Romanian Pastrami and Corned Beef

Franks with all the Trimmings

Sliced Derma with Gravy

Pickles, Sauerkraut, Cole Slaw

and Russian Dressing

Dinner

First Course

Choose either one of the following

Smoked Whitefish Mousse with Scallions

or

Cold Poached Salmon

and

Baskets of Breads and Rolls

Salad

Spring Salade

Radicchio Cup filled with

Arugula and Enoki Mushrooms

Served on a Bed of Shredded Greens finished with a
Balsamic Vinaigrette

Entrée

*Served Plated to the Tables
Second Offerings French Served*

Glazed Rack of Lamb

Rosemary Roasted Potatoes

Sauté of Miniature Vegetables

Dessert

Milles Feuilles

Filled with White Chocolate Mousse

Garnished with Fresh Berries

Assortment of Miniature Pastries, Tarts and Cookies

Demitasse and Tea

Figure 10-6. Charity Ball Menu.

Reception
Selection of Hot and Cold Hors d'Oeuvres
All Hors d'Oeuvres Passed
Fresh Vegetable Crudités
Assorted Pasta Skewers
Smoked Salmon Rosettes with Garni
Ribeye on French Garlic Bread
Brandied Duck
Potato Pancakes
Knishes—Meat and Kasha
Stuffed Mushrooms
Sesame Chicken
Salmon Caviar in New Potatoes
Fried Kreplach

Buffet Dinner Menu
Presented First Course
Salad of Belgian Endive and Mache with Walnuts and
Julienne of Apples
Vinaigrette Dressing

Red Snapper Provencale (light)
Rack of Lamb—carved in room
Curried Chicken with Assorted Condiments
Pilaf of Rice
Medley of Baby Vegetables
Bundle of Haricots Verts or Asparagus
Barley, Brown Rice and Grain Combination

Fresh Fruit Display
In a Carved Watermelon Shell
Presented on a Large Glass Mirror

Seated Dessert
Special Chocolate Delice
Platter per Table
Chocolate Dipped Fruit
To include:
Orange and Grapefruit Sections and Strawberries

Tray per Table
Mandelbrot, Small Pieces of Strudel, Lace Cookies,
and Almond Cookies
Coffee, Tea, or Freshly Brewed
Decaffeinated Coffee

Figure 10-7. Black Tie Award Dinner Menu.

Carved Grapefruit filled with Seasonal Fruit
Poached Salmon with Lime Sauce
Bibb Lettuce, Belgian Endive with Slivered Almonds
and Fanned Strawberry
Basil Vinaigrette or Honey Mustard
Champagne Sorbet in Lime Cup with Lemon Twist
Veal Chop Wellington with Natural Juices
Vegetable Sticks with Leek Tie topped
with Carrot Puree
Asparagus Tips

Baked Kishka with Sauce
Rolls and Margarine Roses
Chocolate Mousse
Layer Sheet Cake inscribed "Mazel Tov"
Apple Kugel with Raspberry Sauce
Fancy Cookies
Coffee, Tea, Sanka
Nondairy Creamer

Figure 10-8. Bar Mitzvah Reception Menu.

Sliced Seasonal Fruits and Berries

Crudités Assortment
(Carrot, Celery, Broccoli and Cauliflower Buds,
Zucchini, Yellow Squash,
Mushrooms, Green Peppers)

Russian Dressing

Sides of Smoked Salmon served with Rye and
Pumpernickel Tartines, Chopped Egg,
Onion and Capers

Mini Brochettes of Red Snapper in Spicy Sauce

Beef and Mushroom Turnovers

Spinach Wrapped in Phyllo Dough

Glazed Corned Beef and Pastrami
Miniature Rye, Pumpernickel and
Sesame Split Rolls
Mustard and Horseradish

Vegetable Tempura
(Broccoli, Carrots, Mushrooms,
Zucchini, Sweet Potatoes)

Rotini and Penne with Tomato Basil Sauce and
Pesto Sauce

Figure 10-9. Hotel Catered Reception Menu.

FURTHER INFORMATION

The following books, magazines, and newsletters will provide additional information for those interested in kosher catering.

The Classic Cuisine of the Italian Jews, Edda Seri Machlin, Giro Press, 1981.

Kosher Cuisine, Helen Nash, Random House, 1984.

Helen Nash's Kosher Kitchen, Helen Nash, Random House, 1988.

How to Run a Traditional Jewish Household, Blu Greenberg, Simon & Schuster, 1983.

The Kosher Gourmet Magazine, 21 West 28th St., 12th Floor, New York, NY 10018.

Kashrus, P.O. Box 17305, Milwaukee, WI 53217, published bimonthly.

The Jewish Homemaker, Incorporating the Kosher Food Guide, O.K. Laboratories, 1372 Carroll Street, Brooklyn, NY 11213, bimonthly.

The OU Kashrus Directory, Orthodox Union, Kashrus Division, 45 West 36 Street, New York, NY 10018, annually and Passover.

The Kof-K Guide to Kashrus, Kosher Supervision Service, 1444 Queen Anne Road, Teaneck, NJ 07666, quarterly.

Kashrus Kurrents, Baltimore Vaad HaKashrus, 7504 Seven Mile Lane, Baltimore, MD 21208.

·11·

Wine and Bar Service

In an increasingly competitive catering market, it is becoming more and more important that caterers be able to give advice on the purchasing, service, and consumption of all alcoholic beverages. Everybody is now very much aware of the need for a mature and responsible attitude toward social drinking, and nobody wants a special event ruined by one person's excessive use of wine, beer, or spirits.

As a result of increased social awareness about the risks posed by alcohol consumption, clients frequently look to those in the service industry to provide assistance and guidance on the types and quantities of beverages to offer. Don't be surprised when your clients look relieved and happy to hear that they do not need a full bar. They are likely to feel very comfortable learning that many guests will be satisfied with a couple of wine choices, beer, and perhaps a liqueur.

LICENSES AND THE LAW

All service of alcoholic beverages requires a license. Licensing requirements can be very demanding and also very different in each state. You should check with your state, town, and city authorities to learn everything possible in connection with the service of alcohol in your locality. Although a private function in an individual's home *may not* require a license, it is always advisable to obtain a license for your own and your customer's protection.

All states now have very strict legislation about the service of alcohol to persons under 21, or to those who are intoxicated. In all instances, it is prudent to make available wines, beers, and spirits to those who may legally have them, but to insist that *you* maintain control over the service.

If you hold the license, you must provide servers for the alcoholic beverages, for your own protection. The servers are not always required by law to be 21 years old or more, but it obviously would be wise for you to require it. They should be professional in their behavior and appearance at all times, and they should be instructed in how much to serve to each individual. Under no circumstances should they be drinking alcohol while on duty.

You should encourage your wait staff and bar staff to take an alcohol awareness program. Such programs are available through state and police authorities, or through professional organizations such as the National Restaurant Association. Evidence of this type of training often can reduce your liability insurance premiums.

GLASSWARE

You may choose to own, lease, or rent glassware. Whatever your choice, make sure that you have a selection that allows you to use the most appropriate glassware, while still giving consideration to cost, practicality, and appearance. Technological advances have now made it possible for mass-produced glassware to be tough and resistant, yet fine enough to enhance the beverage. Glasses are also inexpensive enough to make plastic obsolete at most catered functions. You must also ensure that you will have enough clean glassware and that you have resources for steaming in the event the glasses have to be cleaned at the last minute.

As for glass type, you can get away with an all-purpose 8-ounce wine glass, but your events will be more impressive with the appropriate glass for the wines, beers, spirits, and liqueurs. The following suggestions will help:

> Sparkling wine: narrow tulip or flute glass
> Blush or white wine: tall, wide tulip, 8 or 10 ounces
> Red wine: tall wide bowl or goblet, 8 or 10 ounces

BASIC BAR EQUIPMENT

Bar strainer	Measuring spoon
Bar towels	Mixing glass or
Bottle opener	shaker
Can opener	Mixing or stirring
Corkscrew	spoons
Ice container with	One-ounce jigger
tongs or scoop	Paring knife
Large pitchers	Wastebasket
	Zester

Fortified wine: small wine glass or pony
Beer: Pilsner glass or sleeve

For the service of most spirits and mixed drinks, a selection of the following will suffice:

> Highball glasses (10 ounces)
> Rock or footed rock glasses (5–6 ounces)
> Martini or small wine glasses
> Snifters or pony glasses

TEMPERATURE

It is very important that you have the means of chilling wine and beer to the desirable temperature *and* of maintaining it at that temperature during the service. Most red wines can be served at room temperature, although this sometimes results in the wine being served too warm. The ideal temperature for red wine is 65°F. White wines are generally chilled to 50°F. Ideally, light white wines and very sweet white wines should be served *very* chilled, more like 43° to 45°F. For ease of opening and for better presentation, sparkling wines must also be very chilled. The gas inside the wine is less likely to explode at cold temperatures.

Beers should be kept chilled; most people prefer their beer ice cold. Most spirits and liqueurs are served at room temperature, but the mixers and juices will need refrigeration.

TIMING

One of the most wasteful errors at catered events is to open *all* of the bottles of wine ahead of time. Undoubtedly it helps to have some bottles ready to pour, but if they are all opened, all too often some will remain unused and will be wasted.

If wine is to be served with a meal, be sure to coordinate the service of wine and food. Try to pour the designated wines just before or just after the appropriate dish is served.

PORTIONS

The regular size for a bottle of wine or spirits is 750 ml, which is approximately equal to 25 ounces. Using a traditional portion size of 1½ ounces for spirits, you can count on getting 16 pours from a 750 ml bottle. The number of pours from a wine bottle will depend on the portion size. The serving size for most dinner wines is 4, 5, or 6 ounces, depending on the glass size and the wishes of your client. In any event, the wine will look and taste better if you fill the glasses no more than half full. For sparkling wines, a 4-ounce pour in a flute or tulip glass is sufficient.

ADVISING THE CLIENT

For caterers who are licensed to sell, there is no need to carry an inventory of wines, beers, and spirits. You purchase products as needed and keep anything from a previous function that is left over. You should be ready, however, to offer advice on type, quality, variety, and price for *all* of the following products:

Sparkling wine
White wine
Blush wine
Red wine
Beer (bottled or on tap)
Gin
Vodka
Scotch
Bourbon
American and Canadian blended whiskeys
Rum
Liqueurs
Mixers
Juices

Fewer people these days require a full bar. They are more interested in making a wise selection that will offer something for everybody without stretching their budget, such as the following:

Reception:	Choice of beer or sparkling wine
Meal:	Choice of white or blush wine
After the meal:	Choice of Cognac or liqueur

In this scenario, you would handle only six products, and yet still offer an adequate selection.

If you employ a trained and reliable bartender, that person will have useful suggestions on premixed products, syrups, and gas cylinders. You can also ask your beer or liquor distributor for assistance.

Before and after service, make sure that you and your client agree on inventory quantities of *each* product for invoicing purposes.

Quantities

It is simple to calculate how much of any product to have on hand. First you need to know the length of time that the bar will be open. Use the following table as a guide:

Hours bar open	*Average number of drinks per person*
1	2½ to 3
2	4 to 4½
3	5 to 5½
4	5½ to 6

Use the following formula: (number of guests × average number of drinks per person) × ounces per drink = total ounces needed. Divide the total ounces needed by the bottle size to be used, and you will have the total quantity to be purchased.

For example, for a 2-hour bar with 60 people in attendance, the total quantity of spirits needed would be: (60 × 4) × 1½ = 360 ounces divided by 25 = approximately 14 bottles. You would then need to apportion the spirits based on the client's preference, such as: 3 vodka, 3 gin, 4 rum, 2 Scotch, 1 bourbon, and 1 blended whiskey.

The same formula works with wine. If wine is served with dinner, you can count on two bottles of wine per course per table of ten. That is approximately one glass per person per course.

Some clients may wish to offer only a limited open bar, and instead spend the money on serving wine or beer with dinner. It will be up to the client to decide whether wine is served with only one course or throughout the entire meal.

When offering a choice of wines, assume a ratio of 4 white to 1 red since so many people prefer white wines. Again, your client may decide to serve only one wine with a dish, based on your suggestions. If blush wines are offered as well, think of them as a white wine for your calculations.

For quantities of soda and juices, take the total number of bottles of spirits and multiply by 3. Then you will need to match the sodas and juices according to the way you have apportioned the spirits. And don't forget the ice: approximately 2 to 3 pounds per person.

In all instances, it is wise to allow a safety margin of 10 percent on top of all your calculated quantities to cover any extra guests or heavy drinkers.

Suggesting Wines

A good familiarity with one or two dozen wines available from your local distributors or retailers should put you in a position to make useful suggestions to your clients. You don't need to be an expert. However, your clients will be impressed and very grateful for your assistance. There are many helpful books on wine, but basically you need to rely on your own good judgment and expertise. Taste various wines with your own dishes, and decide which wines you could suggest with each.

Ideally, you should work toward developing a very short wine selection that offers a range of:

Colors:	White, blush, red
Styles:	Sparkling, full-bodied and strong, light-bodied and simple, dry, semi-dry, and sweet
Countries:	American, French, Italian
Prices:	Inexpensive, mid-range, expensive

In many instances, price may be the most important criterion, and you should work toward having low, medium, and high-priced selections. One possibility would be to carry price and food matching information on two or three wines in each of the following categories:

Blush:	White Zinfandel
White:	Chardonnay, Riesling, Sauvignon Blanc
Red:	Beaujolais Villages, Merlot, Cabernet Sauvignon
Sparkling:	Spanish, California, French

As for selecting wines with food, the old rules of white wine for fish and white meat are always applicable, but your clients will appreciate unusual suggestions. Many light red wines, such as Beaujolais Villages, make excellent accompaniments to fish, and some heavy Chardonnays will easily stand up to simple preparations of beef. Always bear in mind that the popularity of a wine's color may be a stronger influence than adhering to old rules. With the current, and seemingly endless, popularity of blush wines like White Zinfandel, it would be an oversight not to include one among your recommendations.

Most of all, bear in mind that the wine selections need to be appropriate, not only for any food served, but also for the age groups involved (older people have traditionally liked sweeter wines) and for the occasion.

PRICING WINES

Restaurants have traditionally operated on a markup of two and a half times over wholesale. Caterers can often work on a lower markup. You will find that it is to your advantage to put a higher markup on low-cost items and a lower markup on high-cost items. For example, a wine that costs $5 per bottle wholesale will be acceptable if priced at $13 or $15. A wine that costs $10 will be more acceptable if priced at $20.

·12·

Menu Making and Food Presentation

THE MECHANICS OF MENU MAKING

There are two basic goals to consider when planning menus: satisfying the customer and making a profit. Meeting these two objectives is paramount to success and can be achieved if you give careful attention to the following:

1. Needs of the customer
2. Eating and dining trends
3. Market conditions and product availability
4. Food combinations
5. Capacity and versatility of kitchen
6. Skill and capability of service staff
7. Costs and profits

Customer Needs

Although your business as a caterer is to sell food, you should never forget that you are a service organization. Giving the customer what they want, when and where they want it, at the price they specify, while still producing a profit for your company, is your goal.

The more you know about your clients, the better chance you have of meeting their goals and yours. Your clients are really buying peace of mind, and they are relying on you to understand and fulfill their needs.

The most important concern in most clients' minds is to have a function that is unique and successful. It is therefore important that you communicate competence and confidence, as well as a desire to create something special, fresh, and custom-designed for your client. No affair is routine. Regardless of how many weddings or bar mitzvahs, fund-raisers or business luncheons you've done, each function and each client should be approached with excitement and an eye toward personal client satisfaction.

You need to be conscious of who your clients are and what they wish to accomplish through a catered event. Be perceptive and attentive to the details that provide insight into your client's style and needs. Your first meeting or telephone conversation is your opportunity to check each other out. Listen carefully; although some clients know exactly what they want, many more will have only a vague idea and will rely on you to make suggestions. This is a prime opportunity to show them you are capable of giving them that personal touch and carrying out their requirements.

Consider the following questions as you begin to gather the information necessary to satisfy your client's desires:

1. What is the occasion?
2. What time of the day will the function be held?
3. How many guests will be expected?
4. What is the general make-up of the guest list?
5. What is the general age of the guests?
6. What type of food does your client have in mind? (Encourage your clients to tell you their favorite dishes.)
7. Are there any special services required to adhere to religious or other dietary restrictions?
8. Will the affair be inside or outdoors?
9. What cooking equipment (if any) is available?
10. How much is budgeted for the affair? (Be aware that very few prospective clients will ever answer this question straightforwardly. More than likely, they will ask you to give them a range of prices; therefore, be prepared with several menus and price categories.)

In addition to the answers to these questions, much can be learned about your clients through perceptive and conscious observation. Did your client call you from the office or house? How did they hear about you? Who will the guests be? Where will the affair be held? How do they talk about the food? Are they knowledgeable about food? Of course, meeting the client and seeing the site of the event will give you even more clues. Occupation and economic status affect people's ways of dining and entertaining. Nationality or ethnic background can give important clues to food preferences. Is the client's style formal and structured, or more laid-back and casual? You can never know too much about your clients' likes and dislikes. Encourage them to tell you about parties they enjoyed. If you are sensitive to your clients' concerns and earn their trust, making the sale and developing the right menu will be simpler and easier.

Eating and Dining Trends

Food preferences are as subject to fads and fashion as are clothes, language, and hairstyles. It is important for caterers to be aware of this and to understand the significance of trends. Being in fashion gives people a sense of identity. There is also a certain prestige associated with being part of the "in crowd," the trendsetters, what's often thought of as "society." Most trends start out as fads, short-lived but enthusiastic protests against what is customary. For example, Cajun blackened red fish can be viewed as a protest against America's customarily bland diet. Although the Cajun craze has died down (except in New Orleans), it has sparked a trend toward spicier food nationwide. Our menus are also being influenced by Mexican, Indian, Thai, Caribbean, and African cuisines mainly because of their characteristic spicy ingredients, as well as the pizzazz and flavor introduced by Cajun cooking.

Another more recent example of the evolution of fad to trend to custom is today's concern for nutrition. The tofu and brown rice fad of the 1960s has evolved into the fashionable perception of nutrition of the 1980s and 1990s where it is trendy to talk about oat bran muffins, cholesterol levels, and the newest low-calorie, low-sodium, low-fat, low-cholesterol product on the market, whether it be canola oil or the low-calorie version of Twinkies "with fresh fruit." There is strong indication that healthful foods will be commonplace by the year 2000, with all

(Above) Watermelon swans filled with fresh fruit and displayed on a large mirror for buffet service (dry ice creates the mist).

(Below, clockwise, left to right) A variety of meat and poultry dishes presented country style: Rotisserie hens, baked ham, rack of lamb, roasted turkey, charcuterie platter, crown roast of veal, strip steaks of beef, barbecued spareribs, sausage and peppers, corned beef, strip loin of beef, and roasted quail.

(Above) Fresh manicotti with meat sauce.

(Below, left to right) Tray of cold hors d'oeuvres, all served on a chaud froid base: Red pepper mousse on endive, herbed crepes with creamed goat cheese, blue-cheese-coated grapes with chopped pistachios, tahini-filled dates, and seafood salad on cucumber rounds.

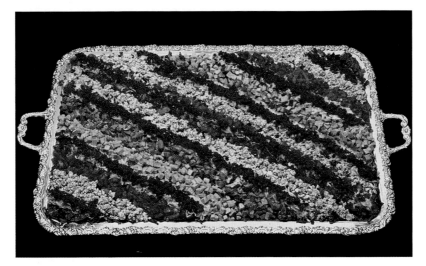

(Above) Cobb salad served on a silver tray with alternating rows of turkey, avocado, tomato, blue cheese, bacon, and marinated cabbage on a chiffonade of romaine lettuce.

(Below) Poached salmon with pasta shell and seafood salad and slices of spinach terrine with crabmeat.

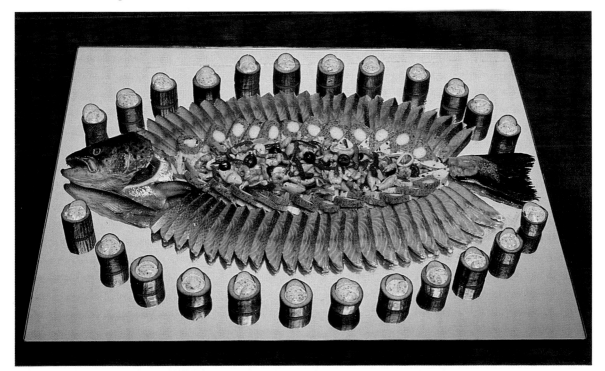

(Above) Osso bucco (veal shank) with vegetable medley and fried polenta.

(Below) Shrimp cocktail served in a scallop shell with fresh pink grapefruit segments and a citrus dressing.

menu selections being developed around sound nutritional guidelines.

Fads, fashion, and customs all play an important role in menu development. As the caterer, you can enhance your client's image and sense of style by your presentation. Although it is important to be aware of fads, to study trends and understand custom, never forget the importance of serving food that simply tastes good.

Market Conditions

Caterers must have a keen sense of product availability and market conditions. For example, why feature fruits and vegetables that are out of season and therefore expensive, when seasonal foods will suffice?

Develop new menus seasonally and always have an alternative plan should a product become unavailable or priced out of your budget. Fresh seafood is particularly susceptible to market availability, and a planned substitute is sensible. From the very beginning your client should be made aware of possible substitutions. In addition to the cost factor, serving products in season has the benefit of adding to the spirit that traditionally ushers in the new season—asparagus and lamb in spring, strawberries and corn in summer, pumpkin and game in fall, and chestnuts and dried beans in winter. Although most products are available all year round, the smart caterer will take advantage of seasonal foods and offer them enthusiastically.

It also is important to develop a good relationship with your purveyors. It is better to stick with a few suppliers whom you trust and who provide accurate market condition information than to shop only for the lowest price. Dependable service is worth a few extra pennies per pound.

Food Combinations

Although tastes change and particular dishes fall in and out of style, the basic rules of combining food remain constant. The flavors you plan for the menu should be complementary while supplying variety. A successful menu will match rich with lean, spicy with bland, smoky (salty) with sweet, and sweet with sour.

Ingredients

It is also important not to repeat ingredients on the menu. It would be incorrect to serve mushroom soup, for example, followed by an entrée served with a mushroom sauce, or to serve a chicken galantine as an appetizer when roast capon is planned for the entrée. Nor should potatoes be served as a starch for an entrée that is preceded by coquilles St. Jacques (scallops garnished with duchesse potatoes). Don't serve ice cream for dessert if the main course includes a rich cream sauce.

Cooking Method and Style of Preparation

Do not duplicate cooking methods or style of preparation within the same menu. For example, do not choose chocolate mousse for dessert if the appetizer is salmon mousse, nor a poached pear for dessert if the entrée is poached chicken breast. Quiche would not be followed by a pie or a dessert cooked en croûte (in crust). Banana fritters would not be appropriate on the same menu as goujonnette of flounder fried in beer batter, and smoked salmon would be incorrect as an appetizer for a smoked turkey entrée.

Color

Color is always important in menu planning since it gives clues as to freshness, naturalness, moistness, and proper cooking procedures. Plan variety in color without giving a "circus effect" that may come across as unnatural.

You may have learned basic principles of color harmony in an art class or seen them illustrated on a color wheel in the paint department of hardware stores. There are three primary colors (red, yellow, and blue), and three secondary colors (orange, green, and purple).

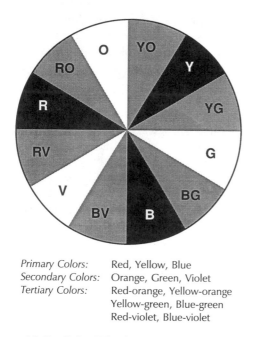

Primary Colors: Red, Yellow, Blue
Secondary Colors: Orange, Green, Violet
Tertiary Colors: Red-orange, Yellow-orange
                         Yellow-green, Blue-green
                         Red-violet, Blue-violet

Figure 12-1. Color Wheel.

These colors are opposite each other on a color wheel, as shown in Figure 12-1. Opposite colors will appear more intense when placed side by side than when presented by themselves. Food examples illustrating this principle are red tomatoes served with dark green watercress, purple grapes accompanying cheddar cheese, or fresh blueberries served with orange segments. Each food color will be intensified by being served in combination with the other. A more subtle effect can be achieved by arranging foods whose colors adjoin on the color wheel—for example, cantaloupe and watermelon balls, asparagus with hollandaise, or poached purple figs on blueberry coulis. It is critical in your planning, however, that in choosing color combinations you also select foods that taste good together.

Color contrast plays an important part, not only on each plate that is served, but also among the courses. Tomato soup followed by salmon, roast beef, and raspberries for dessert is obvi-ously too much red. Less obvious, but in the same vein, would be scallop terrine, poached suprême of chicken, and white chocolate ice cream.

Texture

Texture should be planned since food is appreciated more when served with a contrasting consistency. A flaky *fleuron* or puff pastry, for example, heightens the smoothness of a seafood mousse. A less traditional combination might be to serve the mousse in a fried wonton wrapper shell. Although overused, peas and carrots are an excellent example of texture, shape, and color contrast (square, crunchy orange carrots, side by side with round, soft green peas). Perhaps snow peas and tomato concasse would be more interesting, or oblique cut carrots and baby lima beans. Salsas or other relishes present an interesting texture contrast to broiled fish, while bacon bits and chopped chives bring out the smoothness of cream of potato soup.

Capacity and Versatility of the Kitchen

Menu makers, especially in the catering industry, are often influenced by the newest cookbooks, current food magazines, and celebrity chef videos, as well they should be. It is critical, however, that the inspiration of these wonderful outside sources does not result in menus that are beyond the capacity of your kitchen. Do you have the proper equipment? Will the menu you write include good distribution of work throughout the kitchen, with proper consideration for the available space and equipment? Remember, chances are you will be working out of a makeshift kitchen and serving food in places that were not designed for food service. Your chef ought to be included in menu development since his or her ability should determine what you feature. Selling a concept that cannot be duplicated by your food production staff will not only lead to client dissatisfaction, but will also frustrate and demotivate your crew.

Skills and Capability of Service Staff

How well will your menu hold up under the conditions of service? Did you sell a delicate salmon mousse that will be served before guests enter a tent on a hot August afternoon? Was the client able to convince you to serve a flambéed dessert even though your service staff has never flambéed a dessert before? And will anyone notice the flames anyway in such climate and setting? Can you acquire the equipment necessary for the dramatic effect you had in mind? If your staff and equipment are not up to par, or if the presentation is just too much work, the menu you planned may be a disaster. Know your service capabilities.

Cost and Profits

Creative menus and satisfied clients are important objectives for all caterers. However, this has to be accomplished within a budget that will cover your costs and provide a profit.

A successful caterer cannot function without up-to-date cost information. It is critical that you balance the most costly and sometimes extravagant ingredients with less expensive products. A balance is also important in considering the labor intensity of the preparation. If the entree preparation involves boning, marinating, and stuffing, then you should plan an appetizer and dessert that are simple to prepare so you can keep the cost competitive. It is also advisable to investigate what the going rate is in your community for catered affairs similar to yours. Do not be afraid to call your competitor and ask for price quotes.

It is important to keep your prices competitive with what your community is willing to pay. Even if you use more expensive ingredients and have planned more labor-intensive menus,

the critical question is, do you have a market for your food and service?

Figures 12-2 through 12-11 are complete menus that were designed to meet the factors discussed. The menus were planned for versatility and divided into ethnic categories; each category contains luncheon or light dinner menus, elaborate or full dinner menus, and buffet menus.

Full nutritional recipes are also included. Nutrition is and will continue to be a tremendous challenge to caterers. There is a tremendous demand for nutritionally balanced meals that taste and look delicious.

Menu 1
Scotch Eggs
Coconut Beer-battered Shrimp

Chicken Breast New Hampshire
Lamb Shoulder Pontchartrain

Pontchartrain Vegetables
Dirty Rice

Spicy Kokonda Fish Salad
Marinated Greek Salad

Fresh Fruit Cobbler
with Wild Turkey Bourbon Sauce

◆

Menu 2
Fried Squid with Spicy Tomato Sauce
Charred Beef with Garlic Herb Mayonnaise

Grilled Chicken with Black Beans and Salsa
Catfish with Crab Meat and Corn Bread Topping

Steamed Spinach
Stir-fried Vegetables

Cucumber and Sour Cream
Romaine, Orange, and Red Onion Salad
with Tarragon

Applesauce Bread Pudding
Ginger Mousse

Figure 12-2. American Buffet Menus.

Menu 1
Choose one

Corn Crepe with Asparagus Tips
and Smoked Salmon

or

Ham Bone and Collard Green Soup

Roast Turkey Oklahoma
Glazed Carrots and Snow Peas
Rice Pilaf
Chocolate Bread Pudding

◆

Menu 2
Choose one

Cajun Style BBQ Shrimp

or

American Bounty Vegetable Soup

Shaker Stuffed Flank Steak
Julienned Mixed Vegetables
Barley Pilaf
Orange Yogurt Cream

Figure 12-3. American Luncheon or Light Dinner Menu.

Menu 1
Choose one

Ravioli with Three Cheeses and Escarole

or

Celery Soup Terano Style

Mixed Greens with Vinaigrette
Roast Stuffed Pork Loin with Garlic
Zucchini with Tomatoes
Carrot Flan
Gelato and Florentine Cookies

◆

Menu 2
Choose one

Tartlet with Fontina Cheese and Onion

or

Genoa Vegetable Soup

Mixed Greens with Mustard Vinaigrette
Roast Stuffed Spring Chicken with Garlic Sauce
Spinach Soufflé
Fresh Fruit and Sherbert

Figure 12-4. Italian Luncheon or Light Dinner Menus.

Menu 1

Black Bean Crepe with Tomato Coulis
Clear Chicken Broth with Fennel Ravioli
Charred Tuna Ceviche with Guacamole
Veal Medallions with Pineapple and Green
Peppercorns
Grilled Vegetables
Wild Rice Patties
Vermont Maple Mousse

◆

Menu 2

Goat Cheese in Filo Dough
Philadelphia Pepper Pot
Smoke Roasted Bluefish with Horseradish Cream
Fillet Steak Star of Texas
Broccoli
Vegetable Flan
Glazed Carrots
Apple Flan

Figure 12-5. American Full Dinner Menus.

Menu 1

Ravioli
Rice Croquettes with a Seafood Filling
Ligurian Rabbit Stew
Stuffed Swordfish
Sautéed Greens with Prosciutto
Baked Semolina Dumplings
Mixed Greens
Platter of Miniature Italian Pastries

◆

Menu 2

Pizzetta
Scallops with Pepper
Braised Veal Shank Milan Style
Turkey Scallops Sautéed in Green Pepper Sauce
Eggplant with Fontina and Sundried Tomatoes
Fettucini with Broccoli and Pine Nuts
Mixed Salad
Fresh Fruit Tartlets

Figure 12-6. Italian Buffet Menus.

Menu 1	Menu 2
Eggplant, Fontina Cheese, and Sundried Tomatoes with Tomato Sauce	Polenta Croquettes Filled with Fontina and Prosciutto
Ravioli with Walnut Sauce	Broiled Shrimp with Garlic
Cream of Porcini Mushroom Soup	Cream of Chestnut Soup
Sea Bass with Vegetables	Ravioli with Lobster Filling
Beef Tenderloin with Spicy Tomato Sauce	Veal Scallopini alla Milanese
Zucchini with Peppers	Stuffed Swiss Chard
Glazed Carrots	Glazed Beets with Caraway
Mixed Green Salad	Risotto
Fresh Fruit with Zabaglione	Mixed Greens
	Sweet Ricotta Crepes

Figure 12-7. Italian Full Dinner Menus.

Cold Table	*Hot Hors d'Oeuvres*
Carving Station (Choose 2)	*Choose 5 (passed Russian style)*
BBQ Beef Brisket	Anise Chicken Wings
Gravlax (Marinated Salmon)	Coconut Beer Shrimp
Smoke Roasted Tenderloin	Codfish Cakes with Indian Pumpkin
Smoked Salmon Filet	Dal Puvi—Split Pea Stuffed Bread
Smoked Turkey Breast	Eggplant Rollups
Sugar Glazed Ham	Fondue Soufflé Balls
◆	Mexican Chicken Wings
Buffet Table	Saté on Skewers
Choose 5	Shrimp Toast
Canapé Variety	Spanikopitas
Caribbean Sausage with Tomatoes	Steamed Chinese Dumplings
Cheese Variety	Stuffed Grape Leaves
Crudités (raw vegetables) with Dips	◆
Fresh Fruit in Melon Carving	*Sweet Table*
Guacamole with Tortilla Triangle	*Choose 3*
Hummus with Pita Bread	Chocolate-covered Strawberries
Lettuce Bites (Thai)	Chocolate Truffles
New Potatoes with Sour Cream and Caviar	Linzer Cookies
Pickled Shrimp	Macaroons
Salmon Mousse on Cucumber Slices	Pecan Diamonds
Stuffed Snow Peas	Petits Fours

Figure 12-8. Cocktail Reception Menu.

Luncheon or Simple Dinner
Choose one
Black Bean Cakes with Salsa and Sour Cream
or
Carrot and Ginger Soup
Choose one
Grilled Swordfish with Lentil Ragout
or
BBQ Chicken Breast with Red Bliss Potatoes and
Pommery Mustard
Asparagus with Lemon Glaze
Mixed Green Salad with Low-fat Vinaigrette
Apple Strudel and St. Andrew's Glacé

◆

Full Dinner Menu
Smoked Duck Salad
Wild Mushroom Wonton Soup
Poached Salmon with Asparagus
Blackened Beef with Corn and Pepper Sauce
Mixed Green Salad with Creamy Dressing
Low-fat Bavarian with Fresh Fruit in Filo Cup

◆

Buffet Menu
Grilled Sweet Peppers in Balsamic Vinaigrette
Chicken Roulade
Lobster, Scallop and Shrimp Newburg
Veal, Pork or Turkey Medallions with Red Onion
Confit
Broccoli with Lemon Glaze
Chocolate Bread Pudding
or
Strawberry Torte

Figure 12-9. Nutritional Menus.

Luncheon or Simple Dinner
Choose one
Spring Roll
or
Hot and Sour Soup
Roast Chicken with Lemon Grass
Broccoli in Garlic Sauce
Steamed Rice
Poached Gingered Pears

◆

Full Dinner
Steamed Dim Sum Dumplings
Paper Wrapped Chicken
Miso Soup
Sweet and Sour Fish
Beef with Red Onions and Peanuts
Green Beans with Ginger
Steamed Rice
Spun Apples

◆

Buffet Menu
Goyza
Shrimp Toast
Beef Saté
BBQ Spareribs
Aromatic Chicken
Rainbow Garden Vegetables
Hot and Spicy Eggplant
Stir-fried Rice
Assorted Chinese Pastries
or
Ginger Custard

Figure 12-10. Asian Menus.

The menus suggested under the nutritional category are composed of recipes that follow the recommended dietary guidelines with 45% of calories coming from complex carbohydrates, 10% from simple carbohydrates, 15% protein, 10% polyunsaturated fat, and 10% monounsat-

urated fat. This nutritional data is supplied for the nutritional recipes included in the recipe section (identified by an asterisk). A full menu of appetizer, soup, salad, entrée, and dessert will total less than 1,000 calories.

It is up to you and your client to decide what

Luncheon or Simple Menu

Choose one

Spanikopita

or

Gazpacho

Swiss Style Shredded Veal

Glazed Carrots

Steamed Spinach

Spaetzle

Wine Gelée

◆

Full Dinner

Hummus with Raw Vegetables

Scotch Broth

Coulibiac of Salmon

Roast Pork Loin with Prunes

Glazed Beets with Caraway

Savoyard Potatoes

Mixed Green Salad

Orange Custard

◆

Buffet

Moutabel

Mashy Warak

Paella

Beef in Curry

Mashy Cousa

Boiled Rice

Pickled Cucumber

Mexican Corn Salad

Baklava

Plättar

Figure 12-11. International Menus.

menu would best fit the occasion, whether it be a wedding, a business affair, a dinner dance, or a fashion show. Having made that critical decision, your own ingenuity and expertise will determine the degree of success you will be able to attain.

FOOD PRESENTATION

Tray and Platter Design

For any menu, a good tray or platter presentation should have a focal point, that is, an area to which the eye is automatically drawn. Successful designs have strong and clean lines with a clear sense of direction and a focal point; see examples in Figure 12-12. In Figure 12-13 example A has very strong lines that set a definite direction. Example B contains smooth, consistent curves that also meet the criteria. Example C, although composed of different curves, still shows a general direction of movement.

When preparing a tray or platter, it is necessary to properly mold, cook, slice, face, and sequence the food.

Molding—Forcemeats should be rolled tightly for a smooth, round shape. Roulades should be rolled tightly and allowed to rest for at least an hour before roasting or poaching. Forcemeats should be packed firmly into the terrines or pâté mold to obtain smooth edging and slicing texture (Figure 12-14).

Cooking—Proper cooking is essential since undercooked products offer no structure for slicing, and overcooked products crumble and leave a tough surface when sliced.

Slicing—A sharp knife is essential for slicing. Without this tool, all your work is compromised. Remember to let the blade do the slicing. Do not use force or push the blade down through the item; rather, use a sawing motion with light pressure to obtain a smooth finish on the face of the slice. Proper *mise en place* is important when setting up your work station (Figure 12-15).

Facing—When slicing a roast, pâté, galantine or other large item, each slice should be laid with the "outside" face up (see Figure 12-16A). This will ensure that any pattern on the face of the gross piece (the uncut portion left on the tray to provide height and a focal point) is displayed

Platter setup with straight and curved lines

Platter with straight lines, a centerpiece with a salad cascading from it

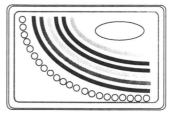

Platter setup with curved lines, a centerpiece and individual garnish

Modern straight line setup

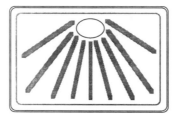

Straight line setup with a centerpiece, the lines radiating from the centerpiece

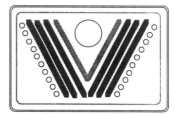

Straight line setup with lines on the bias

Figure 12-12. Platter Setups.

A   B   C

Figure 12-13. Basic Platter Designs.

on the presentation face of the slice. The pattern could be an inlay in a pâté or simply the fat pattern in a roast beef or baked ham. If the slice is placed with the "outside" face down (see Figure 12-16B), there is a reversal of the pattern on the face as compared to the gross piece. When shingling a line of slices, the rhythm of the line will be disrupted if one or more of the slices are reversed (Figure 12-17).

Sequencing—The line of slices should be displayed in the same order in which they were sliced. This will ensure the consistent progression of the pattern in the item. The natural marbling in a piece of meat or the diminishing size of a whole fish or turkey breast sets up a visible pattern that can be easily disrupted by omitting a slice or causing a change in sequence (Figure 12-18).

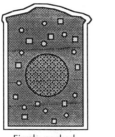

Firmly packed
pâté en croute

Loosely packed
pâté en croute

Figure 12-14. Pâté en Croute.

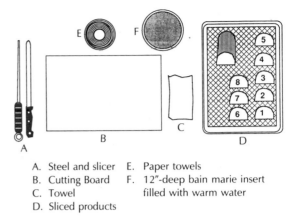

A. Steel and slicer   E. Paper towels
B. Cutting Board   F. 12"-deep bain marie insert
C. Towel   filled with warm water
D. Sliced products

Figure 12-15. Proper *Mise en Place*.

A. *Correct*: Slice with outside face up

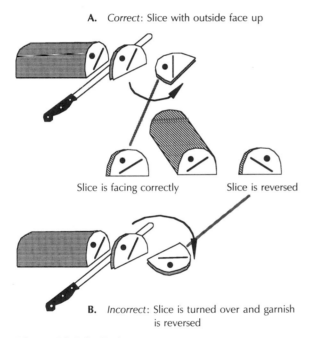

Slice is facing correctly   Slice is reversed

Consistent facing   Reversal

Figure 12-17. Shingling.

B. *Incorrect*: Slice is turned over and garnish
is reversed

Figure 12-16. Facing.

Height—Height is another factor in a presentation. Height can be achieved in the following ways:

1. Gross piece or unsliced roast or galantine (displayed on a platter) (Figure 12-19).
2. Use of rack of bones upon which sliced meat is stacked.
3. Whole pieces of fruit (Figure 12-20).

Correct sequencing   Skip in sequencing

Figure 12-18. Sequencing.

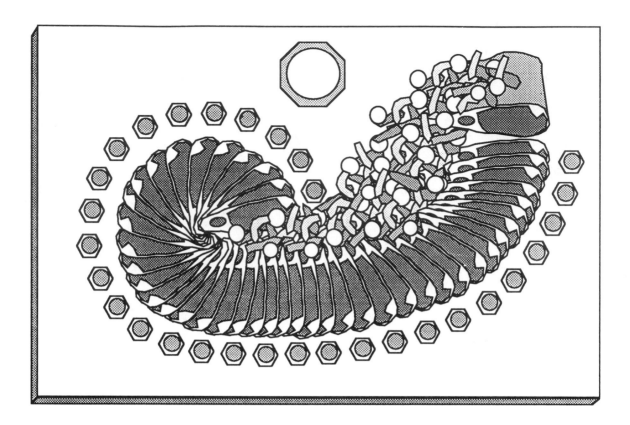

Roast strip loin cooked medium rare, pressed to keep shape during cooling, sliced ⅛" thick. Keep one quarter of the roast unsliced for a head piece.

Cucumbers of daikon radishes shaped with a cutter, hollowed out, and filled with a mayonnaise-based herb or horseradish sauce.

Assorted vegetables in different shapes. Marinate in basic vinaigrette dressing and drain well before placing on the platter.

A butternut squash hollowed out and used to hold vegetable flower decorations or cold sauce.

Figure 12-19. Roast Strip Loin Platter with Vegetables and Herb Sauce.

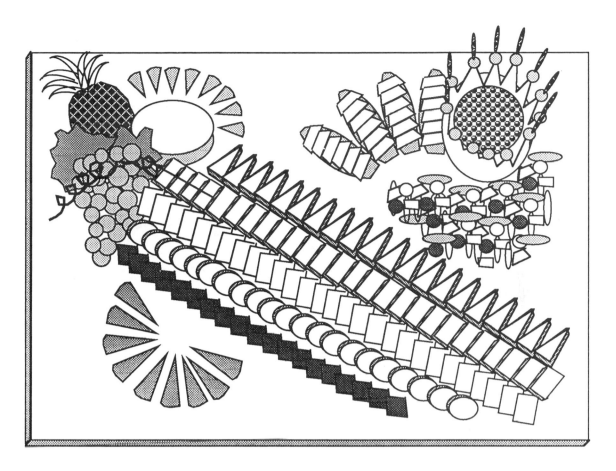

Centerpieces are made up of fruit and some whole cheeses, and are used for both display and eating. The grapes are rolled in cheese and then in chopped nuts. The leaves are made of dough. Hollowed-out melon holds fruit salad.

Pineapple cut in quarters, then sliced and arranged back in the skin.

Various types of cheese, cut in attractive shapes, lined up for easy service.

Crackers or French bread to accompany the cheese.

Figure 12-20. Fruit and Cheese Platter.

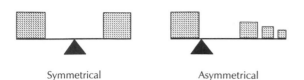

Symmetrical   Asymmetrical

Figure 12-21. Symmetrical and Asymmetrical Balance.

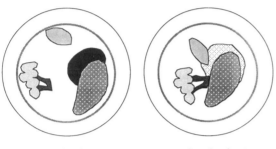

A. No focal point   B. Clear focal point

Figure 12-22. Examples of Plate Presentation.

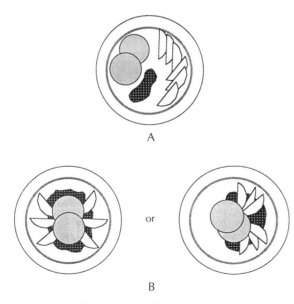

A

or

B

Figure 12-23. Example of Balance and Focal Points in Plate Presentation.

4. Functional containers (hollowed out acorn squash filled with a sauce or salad).

Plate Design

Plate presentations have the same requirements as tray and platter displays, but because they are confined to a smaller surface, balance and unity become paramount. Balance can be achieved either symmetrically or asymmetrically (Figure 12-21). Food items are given visual weight by their color (dark food appears heavier than light foods), size (large items look heavier than smaller items), and texture (rough-textured items appear heavier than smooth-textured items). It is also important that the layout be cohesive. Since elegance typically flows from simplicity, the fewer areas of focus in the presentation, the better. For example, note the difference in configuration in Figures 12-22A and 12-22B.

In Figure 12-22A, the food components are distributed to all parts of the plate. The plate may be filled but the presentation is not unified. In Figure 12-22B, the components are arranged to appear as a single offering that works well together. The feeling should be one of presenting a delicious combination of food working together, not just three separate components that happen to be on the same plate. Note in Figure 12-23A that these haphazard arrangements have no unifying focal point. Figure 12-23B illustrates the same food components arranged in two different ways with a focal point. Also note the different types of balance illustrated.

PRIORITIES IN FOOD PREPARATION AND SERVICE

Taste

The single most important goal of preparing foods is to make them taste good. Taste is affected by proper seasoning, execution of basic

GUIDELINES FOR PLATE PRESENTATION

Survey Market
Consider the taste of the market, the type of customer, the type of service personnel, the dining room decor, the lighting.

Improve Techniques
Maximize the natural attractiveness of food through proper preparation.

Manage Materials
Use special tableware for food that is unattractive by nature (creamed chicken, chili, or lamb stew, for example).
Use plates effectively.
Learn to use what you have to do what you want.

Plan Variety
Be selective in the choice of foods. Strive to create contrasts produced by simple combinations of natural materials.

Limit Garnishes
Strive for very simple visual statements—light, elegant touches instead of massive, complex construction. Be neat
Enhance food presentation with garnishes (keep in mind that too much garnish distracts from the food itself).
Make sure that the garnish complements the flavor of the food as well as its appearance.
Make sure the guest can easily recognize what the food is.

Ensure Unity
Unify the dish so that the parts express a whole (no competition between items).
Incorporate an element of surprise.
Keep it simple.

cooking fundamentals, consistency (viscosity), and freshness and quality of the product.

Presentation

The appearance of food comes second only to taste. Factors that affect presentation are portion sizes, proper food placement or arrangement, composition (avoid repetition of same colors and methods of preparation), and execution of basic fundamentals (properly and uniformly cut meats, vegetables, etc.).

Degree of Doneness/Proper Cooking

Red meats should be cooked as ordered: rare, medium rare, and so forth. White meats, fish, and poultry should be fully cooked but still juicy. Braised and stewed items should be fully cooked until tender, but not dried out. Green vegetables should be cooked until bright, and potato purées should not be lumpy or gluey.

Temperature

Hot foods should be served on hot plates and cold foods served on cold plates.

Nonfunctional Garnishes

Always avoid the use of nonfunctional garnishes on plates and platters. A nonfunctional garnish is any item, edible or inedible, that does not contribute to the taste or texture of a dish.

A good way to avoid using a nonfunctional garnish is to ask yourself, "What purpose does this serve?" If the only answer you can come up with is "provides color," chances are you have a nonfunctional garnish. These are examples of nonfunctional garnishes:

1. A wedge or slice of orange placed on plate of eggs (scrambled, fried, or an omelet).
2. A wedge or crown of lemon on a dish that has a sauce served with it.
3. Leaves of lettuce that are used as underliners for hot food on hot plates (and cold plates on occasion).
4. The traditional sprig of parsley or watercress. (There are times, however, when watercress is appropriate. For example, watercress can be used on a plate that contains a simple grilled or roasted item.)
5. Orange, lemon, or lime "baskets."
6. Tomato roses and apple birds.
7. Paper or foil frills (booties).
8. A radish or carrot flower served with hot roast beef.

The point here is to ensure that the garnish is not merely a crutch for a presentation offering no intrinsic contrasts. A little forethought can avoid the dullness of a meal composed of foods that are cooked the same way (such as all fried foods), that are the same color (such as poached flounder, mashed potatoes and creamed celery), or that are the same shape (such as stuffed chicken breast, stuffed baked potato, and braised endive). You can easily achieve contrast in color and texture by serving two vegetables—one green and one another color. Vegetables also can be puréed and mixed with a custard to achieve contrast in texture.

Why, then, would there be a need for an additional garnish? Functional garnishes can add contrasts in color, texture, taste, and design that help make a meal unique and memorable. However, they should be considered an integral part of the presentation. Thoughtful chefs design their dishes, including garnishes, with contrasts in mind from the start. The most important thing is to choose and prepare all components properly. If you need color on the plate, maybe you're not preparing the food correctly. Overcooked beans are grey instead of bright green; overcooked meat is grey rather than pinkish. Get away from the traditional sprig of parsley and the overworked orange slice or spiced apple ring. They don't usually fit the food being presented and are merely slapped on the plate at the last minute to add color, but nothing more. Color alone doesn't justify a garnish's existence. If it is nonedible or doesn't contribute to the texture or taste of the dish, it shouldn't be there.

This does not mean that there is no place for your favorite vegetable flower cuts such as radish roses and carrot blossoms. These artistic creations add excitement and variety to crudité (raw vegetable) trays or to bowls of potato salad at picnics and buffets (see vegetable carving illustrations, pages 187–188).

Recipes

Hors d'Oeuvres
Appetizers
Soups
Entrées
Vegetables
Potatoes, Pasta, Grains
Salads
Desserts

·Hors d'Oeuvres·

Canapés
Canapé Spread
Caribbean Sausage
Cheese Soufflé Balls
Chicken Wings with Anise
Chicken Wings Mexican Style
Codfish Cakes with Pumpkin
Crudités
Dal Puri
Eggplant Roll-ups
Gyoza (steamed dumplings)
Guacamole
Hummus
Lettuce Bites
Mashy Warak (stuffed grape leaves)
Moutabel (roasted eggplant dip)
New Potatoes with Caviar
Paper-wrapped Chicken
Salmon Mousse
Saté (meat on skewers)
Shao Mai (steamed meat and shrimp dumplings)
Shrimp in Coconut Beer Batter with Dipping Sauce
Shrimp Toast
Shrimp, Pickled
Spanikopita
Spring Rolls
Stuffed Snow Peas

CANAPÉS

A canapé is a small open-face sandwich made from a crouton, which is a piece of bread that has been fried in fat or brushed with clarified butter and toasted in the oven. Canapé spread (two parts cream cheese and one part butter, seasoned with mustard, horseradish, or other flavoring) is put on the bread, followed by the topping. This important layer of fat keeps the bread from becoming soggy. The following canapés are but a few of the many possibilities.

LIVER PÂTÉ CANAPÉ

Rye bread (toasted round or triangle)
Canapé spread
Liver pâté
Truffle slice

Liver Pâté

STEAK TARTARE CANAPÉ

Rye bread (toasted round or square)
Anchovy canapé spread
Steak tartare
Chopped egg, onion, and parsley

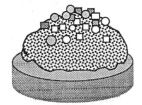

Steak Tartare

SMOKED SHRIMP CANAPÉ

Whole wheat bread (toasted round or triangle)
Pimento canapé spread
Small smoked shrimp
Watercress sprig
Horseradish cream cheese (piped on with a pastry bag)

Smoked Shrimp

ROAST BEEF CANAPÉ

Whole wheat bread (toasted triangle or round)
Anchovy canapé spread
Thinly sliced rare roast beef
Crisp fried onions
Fresh grated horseradish
Chopped parsley

Roast Beef

CANAPÉS
(continued)

SHRIMP SPREAD CANAPÉ

Whole wheat bread (toasted triangle
or round)
Flavored canapé spread
Shrimp spread
Dill sprig
Small lemon segment

Shrimp Spread

PICKLED HERRING CANAPÉ

White bread (toasted square or triangle)
Flavored canapé spread
Pickled herring, drained
Chopped onion
Capers
Chopped parsley

Pickled Herring

SMOKED SALMON CANAPÉ

White bread (toasted round or square)
Flavored canapé spread
Smoked salmon
Chopped hard-cooked egg
Dill sprig

Smoked Salmon

SARDINE CANAPÉ

White bread (toasted round or triangle)
Flavored canapé spread
Sardine
Pimento
Green herb butter (piped on with a
pastry bag)

Sardine

CAVIAR CANAPÉ

Whole wheat (toasted round or square)
Flavored canapé spread
Piped border of cream cheese
Caviar
Chopped hard-cooked egg and parsley

Caviar

HAM CANAPÉ

Whole wheat bread (toasted round
or triangle)
Mustard canapé spread
Sliced ham or ham spread
Sliced cornichons
Dot of mustard

Ham and Cornichon

CANAPÉ SPREAD
YIELD: 3 pounds

2 pounds cream cheese, softened
1 pound butter, softened
   additional flavorings as desired

Combine cheese and butter and cream together. Store, refrigerated.
Soften before using.

CARIBBEAN SAUSAGE
YIELD: 10–12 servings

1 pound lean ground beef, preferably ground round
4 ounces lean, boneless ham, coarsely chopped
½ pound raw shrimp, shelled, deveined and coarsely chopped
1 medium onion, coarsely chopped
1 fresh hot red or green pepper, seeded and chopped
   salt and freshly ground pepper, to taste
2 eggs
2½ cups saltine crackers, approximately
½ cup tiny frozen peas, defrosted
1 egg, well beaten, for coating
1 onion, sliced
1 bay leaf

1. Put the ground beef, ham, shrimp, onion, garlic, and hot pepper
   through the finest blade of a meat grinder, or chop everything as
   fine as possible and combine. Season to taste with salt and
   pepper.
2. Add the 2 eggs, one at a time, mixing thoroughly.
3. Coarsely crumble enough saltine crackers to make about 1½
   cups, then crush with a rolling pin. Beat the crackers, half a cup
   at a time, into the meat mixture with a wooden spoon, until the
   (continued)

CARIBBEAN SAUSAGE
(continued)

texture is smooth. It should not be sloppy, but firm enough to hold its shape. Use only the amount of cracker crumbs necessary.

4. Last, fold in the peas as gently as possible. Shape the mixture into a roll about 10 inches long and about 3 inches in diameter.
5. Cover a piece of waxed paper generously with more cracker crumbs. Roll the sausage in the crumbs so that it is thickly coated all over. Roll it in the beaten egg, then roll it again in more cracker crumbs to coat thickly.
6. Center the sausage on a double thickness of cheesecloth. Wrap the cheesecloth lengthwise over the sausage to enclose it completely. Tie the ends securely with kitchen string. (In the old days, the sausage would have been sewn into a kitchen cloth, but cheesecloth does just as well.)
7. Place the sausage in a heavy, covered casserole large enough to hold it comfortably. Add the sliced onion and the bay leaf, and enough water to cover the sausage by about 2 inches. Bring to a boil, reduce the heat to a simmer, cover and cook for about an hour, or until the sausage is firm to the touch and reaches an internal temperature of 155°F.
8. Lift out of the casserole by the cheesecloth ends and allow to cool. Remove the cheesecloth and place the sausage on a large platter. The cracker crumbs and beaten egg will have formed an attractive outside coating. Cut into ½-inch slices and serve cold.

CHEESE SOUFFLÉ BALLS
YIELD: approximately 25 pieces

3 cups grated cheddar cheese
2 tablespoons flour
¾ teaspoon salt
4 egg whites, beaten until stiff
  flour for dredging
1 cup egg wash (1 egg, 1 cup milk)
  bread crumbs for dredging
  oil for deep-fat frying

1. Combine cheese, flour, and salt. Fold in beaten egg whites.
2. Roll the cheese mixture into approximately 25 balls and chill.
3. Dredge in flour and shake off excess.
4. Dip in egg wash and roll in bread crumbs.
5. Heat oil to 375°F and deep-fat fry until golden brown. Drain on absorbent paper. (These may be reheated in the oven.)

CHICKEN WINGS WITH ANISE
YIELD: 25 wings

 2 scallions, sliced, including the green
½ cup soy sauce
 1 cup water
½ cup dry sherry
 2 pieces star anise, crushed
 4 whole cloves
 1 teaspoon sesame oil
¼ cup light brown sugar
25 chicken wings, trimmed

1. Combine all ingredients and simmer, covered, for 30 minutes.
2. Remove cover and simmer 15 minutes longer, basting occasionally.

CHICKEN WINGS MEXICAN STYLE
YIELD: 25 wings

SPICE MIX
 1 teaspoon cumin powder
¼ teaspoon cayenne pepper
 1 teaspoon thyme
½ teaspoon garlic powder
½ teaspoon onion powder
½ teaspoon salt
 1 teaspoon flour
25 chicken wings
 2 tablespoons oil
 2 tablespoons butter
 1 clove garlic, minced
 1 jalapeño pepper, seeded and minced
½ cup light beer

1. Combine ingredients in spice mix and rub on chicken wings. Let rest for 15 minutes.
2. Sauté wings in oil and butter until lightly browned. Drain excess fat.
3. Add garlic, jalapeño, and beer and simmer until liquid has turned to a glaze.

CODFISH CAKES WITH PUMPKIN
YIELD: 25 small cakes

1 pound salt cod
1 pound pumpkin or hubbard squash
1 teaspoon butter
2 eggs, beaten
  salt and pepper to taste
2 cups bread crumbs
  oil for frying

1. Soak fish in water for 2–4 hours, depending upon saltiness.
2. Drain fish and place in a pot. Cover with fresh water and gently simmer for 15 minutes. Drain.
3. Remove bones, shred fish, and reserve.
4. Cook pumpkin in salted boiling water until tender. Drain, purée, and mix with butter.
5. Mix fish, pumpkin, eggs, and 1 cup of the bread crumbs and season with salt and pepper. Divide into 25 portions and shape into small cakes.
6. Roll cakes in remaining bread crumbs and brown in oil. Drain on absorbent paper.

CRUDITÉS

Crudités are a selection of raw vegetables served with various flavored dips. The dips must be thick enough to cling to the vegetables. The vegetable selection can contain the following:

    carrot sticks
    celery sticks
    pepper strips
    cauliflower flowerettes
    broccoli flowerettes
    zucchini sticks
    radishes
    cherry tomatoes
    cucumbers
    pickled vegetables

Cauliflower and broccoli are better if blanched in boiling water for 30 seconds.

The dips are made from a base of mayonnaise, cream cheese, yogurt, or sour cream mixed with the desired flavoring ingredients. Several suggestions follow.

CURRIED MAYONNAISE

Sauté minced onions, apples, and curry powder, chill and mix with mayonnaise.

CHEESE DIP

Mix cream cheese with puréed cheese and flavor with wine.

DILL-FLAVORED YOGURT

Mix chopped dill and scallions with yogurt.

ONION DIP

Mix crispy fried onions and glace de viande with sour cream.

ORIENTAL

Mix soy sauce, sherry, minced ginger, and garlic with mayonnaise and garnish with sliced scallions.

Crudité platters can be made more elaborate by cutting vegetables into flowers, fans, or other fancy shapes. Following are instructions for some basic designs.

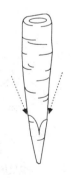

1. To make petals, cut carrots at an angle as illustrated and twist flower to remove. Continue process.

1. Trim top and bottom of scallion.

2. Cut very thin slices into the scallion.

3. Soak in water 1–2 hours and ends will curl.

2. Each flower should have 4 or 5 petals. Flowers can be stored in cold water for future use.

CRUDITÉS
(continued)

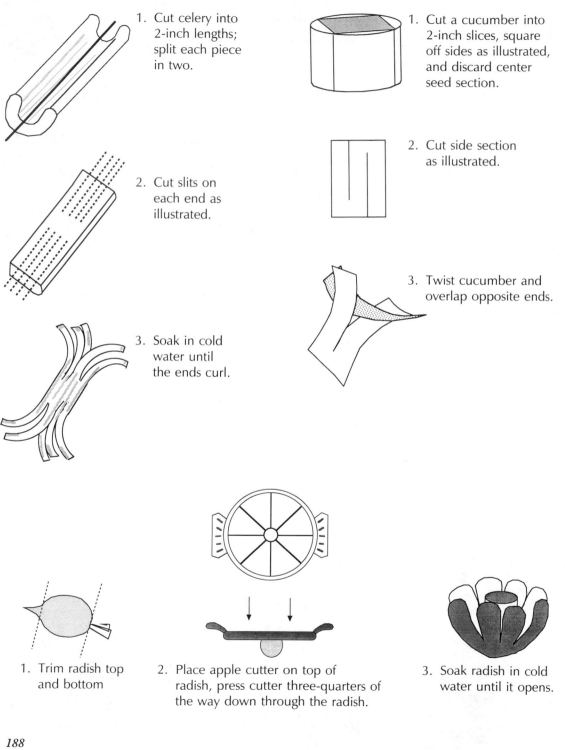

1. Cut celery into 2-inch lengths; split each piece in two.

2. Cut slits on each end as illustrated.

3. Soak in cold water until the ends curl.

1. Cut a cucumber into 2-inch slices, square off sides as illustrated, and discard center seed section.

2. Cut side section as illustrated.

3. Twist cucumber and overlap opposite ends.

1. Trim radish top and bottom

2. Place apple cutter on top of radish, press cutter three-quarters of the way down through the radish.

3. Soak radish in cold water until it opens.

DAL PURI
YIELD: 8 rolls

PEA FILLING
- 1 cup green split peas, soaked overnight
- 2 tablespoons garam masala (curry powder)
- 2 teaspoons ground cumin
- salt and pepper to taste
- 4 ounces minced onion
- 2 cloves garlic, minced

DOUGH
- 4 cups all-purpose flour
- 2 teaspoons baking powder
- 1 teaspoon salt
- 1 cup water
- 2 tablespoons oil
- oil or butter for frying

1. Place peas in a pot and cover with water. Add masala and simmer, covered, until tender.
2. Add remaining filling ingredients and mix well. Mixture should be fairly dry.
3. To make the dough, combine flour and baking powder. In a separate bowl, mix salt, oil, water.
4. Combine flour and water mixtures and mix until a smooth but stiff dough is formed. Let rest 1 hour, covered.
5. Divide dough into 8 balls and roll each out lightly. Let rest 10 minutes.
6. Place an equal amount of split pea mixture on each piece of dough, moisten edges, and draw dough around filling. Seal firmly.
7. Carefully roll out dough with filling inside ¼ inch thick. Brush with oil.
8. Cook on a hot greased griddle until lightly browned and puffy (about 10 minutes). Brush griddle with oil or butter as needed.

EGGPLANT ROLL-UPS

YIELD: approximately 25 slices

4 eggplants
  flour, for dredging
1 cup egg wash (1 egg, 1 cup milk)
4 cups Italian seasoned bread crumbs
1 cup olive oil
25 slices prosciutto
25 slices mozzarella cheese
1 quart tomato sauce

1. Peel eggplant and cut lengthwise in thin slices.
2. Dredge slices in flour, shake off excess, and dip in egg wash.
3. Dredge slices in bread crumbs. Brown in olive oil and drain on absorbent paper. Cool.
4. Layer a slice of ham and cheese on each eggplant slice. Roll up jelly-roll style and fasten with a toothpick.
5. Slice crosswise and reheat under broiler. Serve on a pool of warm tomato sauce.

GYOZA (STEAMED DUMPLINGS)

YIELD: 25 servings, 4 each

DOUGH
8 cups flour
2½ cups water

FILLING
2 pounds ground pork
1 pound shrimp, shelled, deveined, and chopped
1 pound cabbage, chopped
1 tablespoon minced ginger
½ cup minced scallions
¼ cup soy sauce
  salt and pepper, to taste
¼ cup sesame oil
½ cup egg wash (1 egg, ½ cup water)

1. To make dough, combine flour and water and knead until smooth.
2. Wrap dough and let rest 30 minutes. Divide dough into ½-ounce pieces and roll into 5-inch circles.
3. To make the filling, combine all ingredients and mix well.
4. Place 1 teaspoon of stuffing in the center of each piece of dough. Brush the edges with egg wash, fold over, and seal edges.
5. Place in a steamer and steam until filling is done and dough is cooked, approximately 12 minutes.

GUACAMOLE
YIELD: 1 pound

2 ripe avocados
1–2 green chili peppers, seeded and minced
2 tablespoons lime juice
1½ teaspoons salt
2 tomatoes, skinned and seeded
½ ounce minced onion
  ground cumin, to taste
  chopped cilantro, to taste
  chili powder, to taste

1. Remove the peel and pits from the avocados and mash with a fork until almost smooth.
2. Add remaining ingredients and mix well.

HUMMUS
YIELD: 4 cups

4–6 cloves garlic, mashed to a paste
2 pounds chickpeas, cooked and puréed
1 cup tahini (sesame paste)
¼ cup lemon juice
1 tablespoon ground cumin
¼ cup olive oil

1. Combine all ingredients in a food processor and process until smooth.
2. Adjust consistency with water if necessary.

LETTUCE BITES
YIELD: 25 servings

SAUCE
½ cup fish sauce (nam pla)
½ cup palm sugar or brown sugar
¼ cup tamarind liquid (see note)
1 teaspoon shrimp paste
¼ cup dry roasted peanuts, coarsely ground

GARNISHES
1 cup flaked coconut
1 cup chopped red onion
1 cup peeled, chopped ginger
1 cup coarsely chopped serrano or Thai chilies
1 cup coarsely chopped lime (including peel)
1 cup dried shrimp
1 cup dry roasted peanuts, chopped
4 heads limestone or Boston lettuce, washed, separated into leaves

(continued)

LETTUCE BITES
(continued)

1. For the sauce, combine all ingredients except peanuts in a saucepan and heat until ingredients melt. Boil 1 minute, remove from heat and add peanuts.
2. Toast coconut in a dry sauté pan until crisp and golden brown, stirring constantly. Remove from heat and cool.
3. Place all garnish ingredients and sauce in small bowls.
4. Place lettuce leaves in a pile on a platter and arrange bowls around the platter.
5. To eat, fill a lettuce leaf with a little bit of each ingredient and fold into little packages.

Note: Tamarind liquid is made by soaking 2 ounces of tamarind paste in ½ cup of water.

MASHY WARAK (STUFFED GRAPE LEAVES)
YIELD: 25 servings, 3 rolls each

FILLING

12	ounces minced onions
1	tablespoon minced garlic
4	ounces scallions, finely diced
½	cup olive oil
¾	cup chopped parsley
2	tablespoons chopped dill
2	tablespoons chopped mint
¼	cup lemon juice
1	tablespoon turmeric
1	tablespoon oregano
1	tablespoon ground cumin
1	tablespoon ground coriander
1	tablespoon fennel seeds, crushed
1	teaspoon cinnamon
3	ounces ginger, minced
6	ounces pine nuts, toasted
6	eggs, beaten
12	ounces rice, half-cooked and drained
3	pounds lamb, ground
	salt and pepper, to taste
75	grape leaves, soaked in water
1½	quarts lamb stock

SAUCE
  2 cups olive oil
  2 tablespoons chopped mint
  1 tablespoon chopped oregano
  3 ounces lemon juice

1. To make the filling, sauté onions, garlic, scallions and parsley in oil; let cool.
2. Combine all remaining filling ingredients (except grape leaves and stock), and mix well.
3. Divide filling among grape leaves, fold in ends of grape leaves, and roll up as you would an egg roll.
4. Place folded grape leaves in a pan seamside down, add stock, and cover. Bake in a 350°F oven for 1 hour.
5. To make the sauce, combine all ingredients and brush sauce over finished grape leaves.

MOUTABEL (ROASTED EGGPLANT DIP)

YIELD: 25 servings, 2½ ounces each

  8 eggplants (medium size)
  2 cups lemon juice
  2 cups tahini
  8 cloves garlic
  3 tablespoons salt
  3 tablespoons olive oil
     Tabasco sauce, to taste
  3 tablespoons chopped parsley
     olive oil, for garnish
 13 rounds pita bread, cut in quarters
 25 red peppers, cut into strips
 25 green peppers, cut into strips

1. Char eggplant skin under broiler or on electric flat-top.
2. When eggplant is soft, cool and remove skin and seeds under running water.
3. Purée eggplant pulp in food processor.
4. Purée lemon juice, tahini, garlic, salt, olive oil and Tabasco sauce, and combine with eggplant.
5. Mound eggplant purée on a dish and sprinkle with parsley and oil. Serve with pita bread and pepper strips on the side.

NEW POTATOES WITH CAVIAR
YIELD: 26 pieces

13 red bliss potatoes, uniform size
    oil
1 cup sour cream
8 ounces caviar

1. Rub potatoes with oil and bake in a 350°F oven until soft.
2. Remove potatoes from oven and cut in half. Trim the bottom of each half so that it can sit on a tray without rolling.
3. Scoop out the center with an apple corer, small spoon, or Parisienne scoop.
4. Fill each potato with a teaspoon of sour cream and top with caviar.

PAPER-WRAPPED CHICKEN
YIELD: 25 servings

FILLING
1 pound chicken breast, shredded
½ bunch scallions, chopped
1 ounce soy sauce
2 tablespoons sesame oil
½ tablespoon salt
½ teaspoon white pepper
25 sheets rice paper, 4″ square
½ cup egg wash
    oil for deep-fat frying

1. Mix all filling ingredients together.
2. Dip rice paper in room-temperature water and drain.
3. Place 1 tablespoon of chicken mixture in the center of each piece of rice paper.
4. Brush edges of paper with egg wash.
5. Fold paper over filling into a triangle shape.
6. Deep-fry at 350°F until golden brown.

SALMON MOUSSE
YIELD: 1¾ pounds

1 pound salmon (canned or cooked fresh)
1½ tablespoons unflavored gelatin
½ cup fish stock or juice from the can
¼ cup white wine
1 teaspoon salt
Tabasco sauce, to taste
1 tablespoon chopped dill
½ cup sour cream
½ cup heavy cream, whipped

1. Remove all bones and skin from salmon and purée in a food processor until smooth.
2. Combine gelatin, stock, and wine in a small heat-proof bowl and place in a water bath over low heat until gelatin is melted.
3. Combine salmon, salt, Tabasco sauce, dill, sour cream and melted gelatin mixture.
4. Fold in cream. Pour into a mold and allow to set overnight, refrigerated.

SATÉ (MEAT ON SKEWERS)

YIELD: 50 skewers

SAUCE

- ½ cup chopped onion
- ½ teaspoon minced garlic
  - chopped lemon grass
- 4 chili peppers, seeded and minced
- ½ cup oil
- ½ tablespoon chili paste
- 8 ounces chunky peanut butter
- 1 pint water
- ¼ cup sugar
- 2 limes, juice only
- 1 tablespoon salt
- 3–4 ounces soy sauce

MARINADE

- 3 stalks lemon grass
- 6 cloves garlic
- 1½ teaspoons cayenne pepper
- 3 tablespoons curry powder
- 1 tablespoon honey
- 1–1½ teaspoons fish sauce (nam pla)
- ½ cup oil
- 3 pounds boneless beef, pork, and/or chicken

1. To make the sauce, sauté onion, garlic, lemon grass, and chili peppers in oil.
2. Add remaining sauce ingredients and simmer until sauce just starts to separate.
3. Reserve. Stir before using, adding water if necessary.
4. Combine all ingredients for the marinade and purée in a food processor until smooth.
5. Slice meat into strips 2 inches wide and 5 inches long (you should have approximately 50 strips) and combine with marinade. Refrigerate for 2 hours.
6. Thread meat on skewers, and broil until done. Serve with sauce.

SHAO MAI (STEAMED MEAT AND SHRIMP DUMPLINGS)

YIELD: 25 pieces

DIPPING SAUCE

- ¼ cup soy sauce
- 1 tablespoon grated ginger
- 1 teaspoon minced garlic
- ¼ cup sherry
- ¼ cup water
- 2 scallions, sliced

STUFFING

- 6 ounces shrimp, shelled and minced
- ¼ cup water chestnuts, minced
- ¾ pound ground pork
- 1 egg white, beaten
- 1 tablespoon sherry
- 1 tablespoon cornstarch
- 2 tablespoons soy sauce
- 2 tablespoons minced shallots
- 1 tablespoon sesame oil
- 1 teaspoon ground ginger
- ½ teaspoon sugar
- ¼ teaspoon pepper

25 shao mai wrappers (wonton skins)
½ cup grated carrot

1. To make the dipping sauce, combine all ingredients and mix well. Reserve.
2. To make the shao mai, combine all stuffing ingredients and mix well.
3. Divide stuffing into 25 equal portions and place one portion on top of each wrapper. Draw up edges to form a pocket.
4. Place shao mai in an oiled or parchment-lined bamboo steamer. Sprinkle with carrot.
5. Steam 10–15 minutes. Serve with dipping sauce.

SHRIMP IN COCONUT BEER BATTER

YIELD: 50 shrimp

50 shrimp (21/25 size, peeled and deveined)

SEASONING MIX
½ tablespoon cayenne pepper
1 teaspoon salt
1 teaspoon black pepper
2 teaspoons garlic powder
2 teaspoons oregano

BATTER
2 eggs, beaten
1¼ cups all-purpose flour
12 ounces beer
1 tablespoon baking powder
 flour, for dredging
4 cups grated fresh coconut, dried in oven
 oil for deep-fat frying

1. Combine all ingredients for seasoning mix in a small bowl.
2. Season shrimp with one-fourth of seasoning mix.
3. Combine remaining seasoning mix with the flour.
4. To make batter, mix eggs and beer; add seasoned flour and baking powder. Mix just to combine ingredients.
5. Dredge shrimp in additional flour, then dip in batter.
6. Roll in coconut and deep-fat fry at 365°F until golden brown. Drain on absorbent paper. Serve with Sweet and Tangy Dipping Sauce (recipe follows).

SWEET AND TANGY DIPPING SAUCE

YIELD: 2½ cups

1 18-ounce jar of orange marmalade (approximately 1⅔ cups)
5 tablespoons brown mustard
5 tablespoons prepared horseradish

Combine all ingredients and mix well.

SHRIMP TOAST
YIELD: 25 servings, 4 each

3 pounds shrimp (shelled, deveined, and chopped fine)
2 tablespoons lard, melted
1 tablespoon scallions, whites only, minced
1 tablespoon minced ginger
8 ounces water chestnuts, chopped fine
3 egg whites, whipped stiff
2 tablespoons sesame oil
2 tablespoons salt
1
½ cup cornstarch
1 tablespoon baking powder
25 slices white bread
½ cup sesame seeds
  oil for deep-fat frying

1. Combine all ingredients for the shrimp spread and mix well.
2. Spread shrimp mixture on white bread and cut into triangles.
3. Sprinkle with sesame seeds.
4. Deep-fry at 375°F until golden brown.

SHRIMP, PICKLED
YIELD: 2 pounds

2 pounds shrimp (16/20 size)
1 tablespoon pickling spice
1 tablespoon Dijon mustard
1 teaspoon prepared horseradish
½ teaspoon salt
¼ teaspoon celery salt
¼ teaspoon turmeric
½ cup white vinegar
1 cup oil

1. Cook, peel, and devein shrimp.
2. Combine all remaining ingredients for marinade except oil and bring to a boil. Remove from heat and gradually mix in oil.
3. Pour marinade over shrimp and chill overnight.

SPANIKOPITA
YIELD: 25 servings

6 ounces diced onions
¼ cup olive oil
2½ pounds spinach, cooked and chopped
½ pound feta cheese, rinsed
3 eggs, beaten
2 boxes filo dough
   clarified butter

1. Sauté onions in olive oil, but do not brown.
2. Stir in spinach and simmer until the moisture evaporates.
3. Crumble in the feta cheese, add the eggs, and mix well.
4. Lay out one sheet of filo dough and brush with clarified butter. Add a second sheet and butter as well. Cut into 6 even strips vertically.
5. Place a tablespoon of spinach mixture at one end and fold the adjacent corner over the filling to form a triangle. Continue folding, keeping the triangle shape (as if you were folding a flag).
6. Brush with butter and bake in a 350°F oven until golden brown.

SPRING ROLLS
YIELD: 25 servings, 2 each

¼ cup oil
2 tablespoons minced ginger
1 cup minced scallions
3 pounds pork butt, ground
2 pounds shrimp, peeled and chopped
15 ounces canned bamboo shoots (shredded)
1½ ounces black fungus, soaked and rough cut
1½ pounds Chinese cabbage, shredded
1 pound bean sprouts
1 pound mushrooms, sliced thin
1 cup scallions, green part only, sliced thin
1 tablespoon soy sauce
1 tablespoon sesame oil
1 tablespoon salt
½ tablespoon white pepper
¼ cup cornstarch
¼ cup water
50 spring roll wrappers
½ cup egg wash or flour water paste
   oil for deep-fat frying

1. Stir-fry ginger, scallions, and pork in oil.
2. Add shrimp, bamboo shoots and fungus, and stir-fry.
3. Add cabbage, bean sprouts, mushrooms and scallions, and stir-fry.
4. Add soy sauce, sesame oil, salt, and pepper.
5. Mix cornstarch with water until a smooth paste is formed. When vegetables are tender, drain liquid and mix with cornstarch paste.
6. Add cornstarch mixture back to vegetables and bring to a boil. Remove from the heat and cool.
7. Place 1 heaping tablespoon of the vegetable mixture on a spring roll wrapper and fold ends in.
8. Roll up egg roll and secure end with egg wash or flour paste.
9. Deep-fat fry at 375°F until golden brown.

STUFFED SNOW PEAS
YIELD: 25 peas

25 snow peas, uniform size
12 ounces cream cheese, softened
 6 ounces butter, softened
 ¾ cup tomato salsa, puréed (see Salsa Crudos, page 208)

1. Trim ends of snow peas and split along straight edge.
2. Combine cream cheese, butter, and salsa and cream together.
3. Pipe mixture into peas.

·APPETIZERS·

Charred Beef with Garlic Herb Mayonnaise
*Chicken Roulade with Red Pepper Coulis
Polenta Croquettes with Fontina and Prosciutto
*Smoked Duck Salad with Raspberry Vinaigrette
*Black Bean Cakes with Salsa
Black Bean Crepes with Tomato Coulis
Goat Cheese in Filo Dough with Onion Sauce
*Grilled Peppers with Balsamic Vinaigrette
Pizzetta Napoletana
Ravioli with Three Cheeses and Escarole
Tartlets with Fontina Cheese and Onions
Corn Crepes with Asparagus Tips and Smoked Salmon
Gravlax
Ravioli with Lobster Filling
Rice Croquettes with Seafood Filling
Shrimp, Barbecued Cajun-style
Shrimp, Broiled with Garlic
Smoked Fish Cure (stove-top method)
Squid, Fried with Spicy Tomato Sauce

*Starred recipes meet recommended dietary guidelines for calories, carbohydrates,
 protein, and fat. See Chapter 12 for complete nutritional menus.

CHARRED BEEF WITH GARLIC HERB MAYONNAISE

YIELD: 25 portions, 4 ounces each

4½	pounds beef tenderloin, trimmed and cold
2	tablespoons oil
12	shallots, minced
7½	ounces cider vinegar
1½	cups white wine
12	egg yolks
3	ounces water
1¼	quarts olive oil
⅓	cup chopped herbs (combination of basil, oregano, parsley, and chives)
2	teaspoons garlic, mashed to a paste
⅓	cup spinach purée
	salt, to taste
	ground black pepper, to taste
12	scallions, sliced paper-thin on bias

1. Rub raw beef tenderloin with oil and sear in a hot pan until very brown. Chill.
2. To make the mayonnaise, combine shallots, vinegar, and white wine and reduce over high heat by one half. Chill.
3. Place shallot reduction in a stainless steel bowl and add yolks and water.
4. Slowly add olive oil, whisking eggs constantly during the addition.
5. Add herbs, garlic and spinach and season with salt.
6. Slice beef into 50 very thin slices.
7. Arrange 2 slices on each plate and cover with plastic wrap. Using the back of the spoon, spread the beef out on the plate and remove plastic wrap.
8. Sprinkle with black pepper and garnish with herb mayonnaise and scallions.

CHICKEN ROULADE WITH RED PEPPER COULIS
YIELD: 25 servings

12 ounces chicken, ground
3 egg whites, beaten
4 ounces heavy cream
2 pounds chicken breast
1 tablespoon unflavored gelatin
2 red peppers, roasted, peeled and diced
2 green peppers, roasted, peeled and diced
2 yellow peppers, roasted, peeled and diced
1 ounce shallots, minced
1 clove garlic, minced
1 pinch thyme
1 pinch basil
1 pinch chervil
1 quart Red Pepper Coulis (recipe follows)
10 ounces zucchini, skin on and sliced fine
10 ounces yellow squash, skin on and sliced fine
3 ounces Balsamic Vinaigrette (page 212)

1. Purée chicken meat in a food processor until smooth, add egg whites, and pulse in heavy cream (do not let meat get warm during processing).
2. Combine peppers, shallots, garlic, and herbs and add to chicken-cream mixture.
3. Flatten chicken breasts, sprinkle with gelatin, fill with chicken mixture.
4. Roll chicken around forcemeat and wrap in plastic wrap. Poach in water until internal temperature reaches 145°F. Cool.
5. Slice and arrange on a plate with coulis. Garnish with squash that has been tossed with vinaigrette.

CALORIES: 130; PROTEIN: 13.5 gm; FAT: 5.4 gm; CARBOHYDRATE: 5.9 gm; SODIUM: 140 mg.; CHOLESTEROL: 40 mg.

RED PEPPER COULIS
YIELD: 1 quart

¼ cup olive oil
1 ounce shallots, minced
1 clove garlic, minced
1 teaspoon jalapeño pepper, seeded and minced
2 ounces tomato paste
3½ pounds red peppers, roasted, seeded, and chopped
2¼ cups chicken stock
1 teaspoon salt
1¾ ounces balsamic vinegar

1. Sauté shallots, garlic, and jalapeño pepper in oil.
2. Add tomato paste and sauté; do not brown.
3. Add peppers and stock and simmer until peppers are tender.
4. Purée in blender.
5. Season with salt and vinegar.

POLENTA CROQUETTES WITH FONTINA AND PROSCIUTTO
YIELD: 25 servings

2½ quarts water
2 teaspoons salt
1 pound yellow cornmeal
1 pound butter
  pepper and nutmeg, to taste
8 ounces prosciutto, sliced thin
2 pounds Fontina, sliced thin
  flour, for dredging
2 cups egg wash (2 eggs, 2 cups water)
  bread crumbs
  oil for deep-fat frying
2 quarts Pizzaiola Sauce (recipe follows)

1. Combine water and salt and bring to a boil.
2. Sprinkle in cornmeal and stir or whisk constantly to prevent lumping.
3. Cook until thick. Cover and bake in a 300°F oven for 20–30 minutes.
4. Remove from heat and stir in butter. Season with pepper and nutmeg.
5. Spread half of the polenta ½ inch thick on a buttered tray.
6. Cover the polenta with half the Fontina cheese and all of the prosciutto.
7. Add the last half of the Fontina cheese and spread with the remaining polenta. Chill.
8. Cut into 25 portions. Dredge in flour and shake off excess.
9. Dip polenta in egg wash and then in bread crumbs.
10. Deep-fry at 360°F until golden brown and drain on absorbent paper.
11. Portion 1½ ounces of Pizzaiola Sauce on a plate and arrange polenta on top.

(continued)

**POLENTA CROQUETTES
WITH FONTINA AND
PROSCIUTTO**
(continued)

PIZZAIOLA SAUCE

INFUSION
 2 quarts white wine
 4 sprigs oregano
 6 leaves basil
 4 sprigs rosemary
 6 peperoncini, chopped
 1 bay leaf
 1 sprig parsley

SAUCE
 8 ounces olive oil
12 ounces onions, finely diced
 6 ounces garlic, minced
 7 pounds plum tomatoes, peeled, seeded, and diced
   salt and pepper, to taste

1. To make the infusion, reduce the wine to 1 quart, add the herbs, and allow to steep for 1–2 hours. Strain.
2. To make the sauce, sauté the onions and garlic in oil, add the tomatoes, and simmer until thick.
3. Add the strained infusion and purée in a food processor. Season and adjust consistency if necessary.

**SMOKED DUCK
SALAD WITH
RASPBERRY
VINAIGRETTE**
YIELD: 25 servings

¼ cup raspberry vinegar
 4 teaspoons minced shallots
 2 teaspoons minced garlic
   pinch of cracked black pepper
 4 pounds raw duck breast, skinned and boned
 6 cups assorted lettuces, leaves separated, rinsed, and torn
 6 cups watercress, separated, rinsed, and torn
   Raspberry Vinaigrette (recipe follows)
 6 plum tomatoes, peeled and quartered
 4 pears, thinly sliced
1⅓ cups fresh raspberries

1. For marinade, combine raspberry vinegar, shallots, garlic, and cracked pepper in a medium bowl. Add duck breasts to marinade, turning to coat evenly. Marinate for 5 minutes.
2. Preheat grill and add hickory or mesquite chips. Grill breasts for 15 minutes, turning to cook evenly.
3. Toss lettuce and watercress with raspberry vinaigrette. Divide lettuce between plates. Slice duck breast and lay on lettuce. Arrange tomato wedges and pear slices on top. Sprinkle with raspberries.

CALORIES: 150; PROTEIN: 13.2 gm; FAT: 8.7 gm; CARBOHYDRATES: 3.8 gm; SODIUM: 150 mg; CHOLESTEROL: 51 mg

RASPBERRY VINAIGRETTE

Make Balsamic Vinaigrette (page 212), substituting raspberry vinegar for the balsamic vinegar.

BLACK BEAN CAKES WITH SALSA

YIELD: 25 servings, 2½ ounces each

3	pounds dry black beans
	chicken stock
3	ounces chorizo sausage, chopped
½	ounce minced garlic
10	ounces onions, diced
3	jalapeño peppers, seeded and minced
¾	teaspoon chili powder
¾	teaspoon ground cumin
1½	teaspoons cilantro, chopped
¾	teaspoon salt
3	teaspoons lime juice
6	ounces egg white
	cornmeal
6	ounces unsalted butter
6	ounces yogurt, drained
6	ounces sour cream
	Salsa Crudos (recipe follows)

**BLACK BEAN CAKES
WITH SALSA**
(continued)

1. Check the black beans for small stones and debris. Rinse and cook in the chicken stock for approximately one hour, letting the stock reduce to dry at the end of cooking. Purée two thirds of the beans.
2. Render chorizo and sauté the garlic, onion, and peppers in the small amount of fat that accumulates.
3. Add the cumin and chili powder and sauté. Remove from heat.
4. Combine beans, sautéed sausage mixture, salt, lime juice, and egg whites and form into 25 patties.
5. Dust the patties in cornmeal and sauté in butter.
6. Combine the drained yogurt and sour cream.
7. Serve two patties per plate with sour cream mixture and salsa.

CALORIES: 160; PROTEIN: 9.5 gm; FAT: 4.6 gm; CARBOHYDRATE: 21.7 gm; SODIUM: 186 mg; CHOLESTEROL: 9 mg

SALSA CRUDOS
YIELD: 1½ pounds

  5 medium tomatoes
⅓ cup chopped onion
  2 cloves garlic, minced
2–4 jalapeño peppers, veins and some seeds removed
      juice of 1 lime
  3 tablespoons chopped cilantro (optional)

1. Peel, seed, and chop tomatoes.
2. Add remaining ingredients and mix well.
3. Let marinate at least 1 hour.

**BLACK BEAN
CREPES WITH
TOMATO COULIS**
YIELD: 25 crepes

CREPE BATTER
1¾ pints black bean cooking liquid
  6 ounces egg whites, beaten
  9 ounces milk
  1 teaspoon chopped cilantro
  1 teaspoon salt
  5 ounces flour
  5 ounces cornstarch
      vegetable spray, such as Pam®

FILLING

- 1 tablespoon oil
- 6 ounces onions, medium diced
- 6 ounces red pepper, medium diced
- 6 ounces yellow pepper, medium diced
- 2 pounds mushrooms, medium diced
- 6 ounces white wine
- 2½ cups brown sauce
- 8 ounces dried black beans, cooked, and liquid reserved
- ¼ cup chopped parsley
  arrowroot, as required

COULIS

- 2 tablespoons olive oil
- 2 tablespoons minced garlic
- 6 scallions, minced
- ¼ cup chili powder
- 8 ounces tomato paste
- 2 pounds tomatoes, peeled, seeded, and chopped
- 1 pint chicken stock
- 1 tablespoon seeded and minced serrano chile
- 1 tablespoon thyme
- 1 tablespoon basil
- 1 tablespoon oregano
- ¼ cup chopped parsley

GARNISH

- 8 ounces sour cream
- 1 ounce lime juice

1. To make the crepes, mix the black bean liquid with the egg whites, milk, cilantro, and salt.
2. Add the flour and cornstarch and mix until smooth.
3. Heat a well-seasoned sauté pan, and spray with Pam. Add 2 ounces of the crepe batter and swirl pan so batter coats evenly.
4. Lightly brown the crepe and turn and brown other side. Remove, stack, and reserve.
5. To make the filling, sauté onions, red and yellow peppers, and mushrooms in oil until tender.
6. Add the wine and reduce until almost dry. Add the brown sauce, beans, and parsley. Season and thicken with arrowroot if filling is too loose.
7. To make the coulis, sauté the garlic, scallion, and chili powder in oil.

(continued)

**BLACK BEAN
CREPES WITH
TOMATO COULIS**
(continued)

8. Add tomato paste, concasse, stock, chile, thyme, basil, and oregano and simmer until thickened.
9. Purée sauce in a food mill and add parsley. Season.
10. Place filling on crepes and roll up. Place on a tray, cover, and warm in the oven as needed.
11. Serve crepe on a 2-ounce portion of coulis and garnish with lime-flavored sour cream piped in lattice fashion.

**GOAT CHEESE IN
FILO DOUGH
WITH ONION
SAUCE**
*YIELD: 25 servings,
4 ounces each*

2¼ pounds goat cheese
24 cloves garlic, roasted and chopped very fine
12 ounces shiitake mushrooms, small dice and sautéed
⅓ cup fresh basil, roughly chopped
6 ounces spinach, blanched and roughly chopped
⅓ cup sundried tomatoes, softened and finely chopped
    salt and pepper, to taste
13 sheets filo dough
12 ounces melted butter
    Onion Sauce (recipe follows)
⅓ cup chives, cut ¾″ long, for garnish
⅓ cup tomato concasse, for garnish
⅓ cup red pepper, roasted and julienned, for garnish

1. Mix goat cheese, garlic, mushrooms, basil, spinach, and tomatoes; season with salt and pepper.
2. Brush a double layer of filo dough with butter and cut into four strips lengthwise.
3. Place a small amount of goat cheese on the end of each strip of filo.
4. Fold on the diagonal and continue to fold as you would a flag. Brush with butter.
5. Bake in a 375°F oven until golden brown.
6. To assemble, arrange 2 ounces of onion sauce on a plate. Set two filo dough triangles on top of sauce. Garnish with chives, tomato concasse, and red pepper.

ONION SAUCE

2 tablespoons butter
2¼ pounds onions, diced
12 ounces champagne vinegar
1½ pints white wine
1½ pints heavy cream
 salt, to taste

1. Sauté onions in butter until slightly colored. Add vinegar and reduce by one half.
2. Add wine and simmer 5 minutes longer; purée.
3. Add cream, and reduce to sauce consistency; season.

GRILLED PEPPERS WITH BALSAMIC VINAIGRETTE
YIELD: 25 servings

15 red peppers, roasted, peeled, and seeded
15 green peppers, roasted, peeled, and seeded
15 yellow peppers, roasted, peeled, and seeded
 1 pound tomatoes skinned, seeded, and julienned
 2 ounces shallots, minced
 1 ounce garlic, minced
 4 ounces black olives
 3 ounces capers
 1 pint Balsamic Vinaigrette (recipe follows)

1. Marinate all ingredients in vinaigrette for 1–2 hours.
2. Remove peppers and grill to order as needed. Strain remaining ingredients and reserve. Heat vinaigrette.
3. Cut peppers in strips and arrange on plate. Pour warmed vinaigrette over peppers and top with reserved tomatoes, shallots, garlic, olives, and capers.

CALORIES: 100; PROTEIN: 2.2 gm; FAT: 5.6 gm; CARBOHYDRATE: 12.7 gm; SODIUM: 150 mg; CHOLESTEROL: tr mg

**GRILLED PEPPERS
WITH BALSAMIC
VINAIGRETTE**
(continued)

BALSAMIC VINAIGRETTE
YIELD: 1½ pints

14 ounces chicken stock
½ ounce arrowroot
7 ounces balsamic vinegar
7 ounces oil
1 teaspoon salt
½ teaspoon white pepper
2 tablespoons oregano and basil

1. Heat chicken stock and thicken with arrowroot. Chill.
2. Add all remaining ingredients.

Note: This dressing can be used with other salads by varying the type of vinegar and herbs used.

CALORIES: 160; PROTEIN: 5.8 gm; FAT: 3.1 gm; CARBOHYDRATE: 27 gm; SODIUM: 65 mg; CHOLESTEROL: 10 mg

**PIZZETTA
NAPOLETANA**
YIELD: 24 servings

DOUGH
1 quart warm water
1½ tablespoons instant dry yeast
½ cup olive oil
4 pounds bread flour
4 teaspoons salt

TOPPING
3½ pounds tomatoes, peeled, seeded, and coarsely chopped
1½ tablespoons chopped fresh oregano and basil, mixed
1½ pounds mozzarella cheese, sliced ⅛″ thick
½ cup olive oil

1. To make the dough, combine water, yeast, and olive oil.
2. Mix in flour and salt and knead until dough is smooth and elastic.
3. Cover dough and let rest in a warm place for 1 hour or until the dough has doubled in volume.
4. Work dough to press out air and divide into 24 equal pieces. Allow dough to proof.

5. Roll dough into a flat circle, about 6 inches in diameter. Place on a sheet pan that has been dusted with cornmeal.
6. To assemble, sprinkle the top of the dough with tomatoes, oregano, and basil.
7. Arrange mozzarella on top of pizza and sprinkle with olive oil.
8. Bake pizza in a 400°F oven 12–15 minutes.

RAVIOLI WITH THREE CHEESES AND ESCAROLE
YIELD: 25 servings

5	pounds Basic Pasta Dough (recipe follows)
1½	pounds Fontina cheese, cubed
3	egg yolks
3	ounces white wine
6	ounces heavy cream
3	tablespoons olive oil
1½	pounds escarole, chopped
3	cloves garlic, minced
¾	cup chopped parsley
	pinch grated nutmeg
¾	teaspoon grated lemon zest
3	ounces Gorgonzola cheese
¾	cup grated Parmesan cheese
	salt and pepper, to taste
1	cup egg wash (1 egg, 1 cup water)
	Tomato Sauce (recipe follows)

1. To make the filling, in the top of a double boiler combine the Fontina, egg yolks, wine, and cream. Allow to melt and whisk until smooth.
2. Sauté the escarole in olive oil until softened. Add the garlic, parsley, nutmeg, and lemon zest.
3. Mix the Gorgonzola and Parmesan with the escarole and the melted Fontina. Whisk until smooth.
4. Roll the dough through a pasta machine to desired thickness, about ⅛ inch thick.
5. Brush one side of the dough with egg wash and lay the dough over a ravioli form. Fill each indentation with cheese filling.
6. Lay a second piece of dough across the top of the first. Roll it with a rolling pin to seal and cut into portions.
7. Cook ravioli in salted boiling water until *al dente*. Drain.
8. Portion sauce on a plate and set ravioli on top.

(continued)

**RAVIOLI WITH THREE
CHEESES AND
ESCAROLE**
(continued)

BASIC PASTA DOUGH

1¼ pounds Manitoba flour
 5 large eggs
 1 egg yolk
 2 tablespoons olive oil
 2 tablespoons cold water

1. Place the flour in a stainless steel bowl and make a well in the middle.
2. Mix eggs, yolk, oil, and water. Pour into the well in the flour.
3. Gradually work the flour into the egg mixture, kneading until the dough is smooth.
4. Cover and allow the dough to rest in the refrigerator for 1 hour.
5. Roll out to desired thickness.

TOMATO SAUCE

 6 ounces olive oil
 9 ounces onions, chopped brunoise (⅛″ dice)
 9 cloves garlic, minced
 6 ounces tomato paste
7½ pounds plum tomatoes, skinned, seeded, and coarsely ground
12 ounces chicken stock
 6 ounces white wine
 3 bunches basil, chopped
 2 bunches mint, chopped
1½ bunches marjoram, chopped
    salt and pepper, to taste

1. Sauté onions and garlic in olive oil. Add tomato paste and stir while cooking an additional 3 minutes.
2. Add remaining ingredients and simmer 30–45 minutes. Adjust seasonings.

TARTLETS WITH FONTINA CHEESE AND ONIONS

YIELD: 25 servings

CRUST

2 pounds flour
8 ounces lard
8 ounces butter
4 eggs, beaten
4 egg yolks

FILLING

4 ounces butter
4 pounds onions, sliced
2 pounds Fontina cheese, coarsely chopped
8 ounces Pecorino Romano cheese, finely grated
1 quart heavy cream
1 cup white wine
8 egg yolks, beaten
8 eggs, beaten

1. To make the dough, combine flour, lard, and butter and rub together until crumbly.
2. Add eggs and yolks and mix only until dough holds together. Chill.
3. Roll dough ⅛ inch thick and line tartlet pans. Prick dough with a fork.
4. To make the filling, sauté onions in butter until translucent. Chill.
5. Line tartlet shells with layers of onion and cheeses. The last layer should be cheese.
6. Combine cream, wine, eggs, and yolks and mix well. Season and pour over onion and cheese mixture in tartlet shells.
7. Bake in a 375°F oven until browned and custard is firm, about 20 minutes.

CORN CREPES WITH ASPARAGUS TIPS AND SMOKED SALMON

YIELD: 25 servings

CORN CREPES

2 cups fresh kernel corn
2 cups flour
8 eggs
2 cups milk
1 cup water
4 teaspoons oil
   salt and pepper, to taste

CORN SALAD

2 quarts fresh kernel corn
2 cups red and green peppers, diced
1 pint vinaigrette dressing
4 teaspoons chopped cilantro
4 teaspoons chopped parsley

75 asparagus spears, cooked
75 slices smoked salmon (approximately 6 pounds)
1 quart Hollandaise Sauce, with chives (recipe follows)

1. To make the corn crepes, mix all ingredients to form a smooth batter. Adjust consistency with more liquid or flour if necessary.
2. Preheat a well-seasoned pan and wipe it with oil.
3. Add 2 ounces of crepe batter and swirl the pan so that the batter covers the bottom of the pan.
4. Cook until golden brown, turn, and cook other side.
5. To make the corn salad, combine all ingredients and reserve.
6. To assemble, cut a slit in the crepe and roll into a cornucopia.
7. Arrange salmon on plate, fold each side in half, and place a crepe behind the salmon. Fill with corn salad.
8. Arrange the asparagus behind the corn crepe.
9. Warm the plate in the oven for 1–2 minutes.
10. Garnish salmon with Hollandaise Sauce.

HOLLANDAISE SAUCE
YIELD: 1 quart

   2 tablespoons minced shallots
   ½ cup cider vinegar
  10 crushed peppercorns
   ½ cup water
  12 egg yolks
   2 pounds butter, clarified, melted
 3–4 tablespoons lemon juice
       salt, to taste

1. Combine shallots, vinegar, and peppercorns and reduce until almost dry.
2. Remove from heat and refresh with water.
3. Add the reduction to the egg yolks and place in a stainless steel bowl.
4. Place the bowl over a pot of simmering water and whip the egg yolk mixture until soft peaks are achieved.
5. Remove bowl from heat and whip in the butter (the butter should be added very slowly in the beginning).
6. When all the butter is added, strain the sauce through cheesecloth.
7. Add lemon juice and adjust salt.
8. Hold warm for service.

GRAVLAX
YIELD: 25 servings

5 pounds salmon fillet, skin on

CURE

2½ ounces salt

5½ ounces sugar

1 tablespoon white peppercorns, crushed

2 tablespoons juniper berries, crushed

1 lemon, juice only

6 ounces onions, sliced thin

1 bunch dill, finely chopped

1. Combine salt, sugar, peppercorns, and juniper and rub on flesh side of salmon. Sprinkle with lemon juice.
2. Place onions and dill on both sides of the salmon fillet. Wrap in cheesecloth.
3. Press salmon with a weight and marinate 72 hours, refrigerated.
4. Scrape off cure and refrigerate until ready to use.
5. Serve on cocktail pumpernickel with a mustard sauce prepared by mixing brown mustard with the remaining marinade.

RAVIOLI WITH LOBSTER FILLING
YIELD: 25 servings

5 pounds Basic Pasta Dough (page 214)

1 cup egg wash (1 egg, 1 cup water)

6 1-pound lobsters, cut for sauté; save roe and tamale (see note)

½ cup olive oil

¾ cup shallots, minced

3 cloves garlic, minced

12 ounces Crimini mushrooms, cut in ⅛″ dice

3 cups tomatoes, peeled, seeded, and chopped

1½ teaspoons chopped tarragon

salt and pepper, to taste

Tomato Sauce (recipe follows)

1. Sauté lobster in olive oil until the meat firms. Remove meat from shells, dice, and reserve (save shells for sauce).
2. Add shallots and garlic to the oil and sauté until translucent.

3. Add mushrooms and tomatoes, sauté, and reduce all excess moisture.
4. Add tarragon and lobster meat, season, and chill.
5. Roll dough through pasta machine to desired thickness, about ⅛ inch.
6. Brush one side of the dough with egg wash and lay the dough over a ravioli form. Fill each indentation with lobster filling.
7. Top the ravioli with a second sheet of dough. Roll it with a rolling pin to seal and cut into portions.
8. Cook ravioli in salted boiling water until *al dente*. Drain.
9. Pool 1½ ounces of sauce on a plate and arrange ravioli on top.

Note: To prepare lobster for sautéing, separate claws and legs from body, split body and tail in half lengthwise, and cut into 2-inch pieces.

TOMATO SAUCE

    lobster shells reserved from filling
½ cup olive oil
    lobster roe and tamale reserved from filling
¾ cup shallots, minced
3 cloves garlic, minced
6 ounces brandy
3 cups white wine
3 cups canned plum tomatoes, drained (juice reserved)
1 cup tomato juice (from the can)
1½ sprigs tarragon
12 sprigs parsley
3 pints heavy cream
    salt and pepper, to taste

1. Crush lobster shells, and sauté in butter until red.
2. Add shallots and garlic; sauté until translucent. Add lobster roe and tamale, brandy, wine, tomatoes, tomato juice, and herbs; simmer 20 minutes.
3. Add heavy cream, and infuse 1–2 minutes. Strain and season.

RICE CROQUETTES WITH SEAFOOD FILLING

YIELD: 25 servings

RISOTTO

¼ cup olive oil
2 ounces shallots
1 teaspoon minced garlic
4 ounces fennel, minced
4 ounces tomatoes, peeled, seeded and chopped
½ teaspoon each fresh basil, oregano, and thyme, finely chopped
12 ounces Arborio rice
½ cup white wine
1 pint chicken stock
1 cup clam juice

SEAFOOD FILLING

1 pound lobster, cut up for sauté (see note)
2 tablespoons olive oil
2 ounces shallots, minced
1 teaspoon minced garlic
16 ounces tomatoes, peeled, seeded, and chopped
2 tablespoons chopped tarragon (pickled or fresh)
4 ounces Mascarpone cheese
4 ounces scallops
4 ounces shrimp
4 ounces squid, cleaned
1 cup fish stock (for poaching fish)
   flour, for dredging
6 ounces egg wash (1 egg, 6 ounces water)
3 cups bread crumbs
1 pint Tomato Sauce (page 214)
1 tablespoon chopped fresh Italian parsley, for garnish

1. To make the risotto, sauté shallots, garlic, fennel, tomato concasse, and herbs in olive oil. Add rice and sauté until coated with fat.
2. Add wine and stir until liquid is absorbed by the rice.
3. Gradually add the stock and clam juice, adding each addition as the previous amount is absorbed by the rice. Stir constantly.
4. When rice has absorbed all the liquid, remove from heat and refrigerate.
5. To make the seafood filling, sauté lobster in oil. Add shallots and garlic.
6. When lobster is red, remove shells and cut meat into ¼-inch pieces. Reserve.
7. Chop lobster shells in food processor and return to pan. Add tomatoes and tarragon and simmer until reduced by half. Force through a sieve to strain.
8. Reduce liquid if necessary and stir it into the Mascarpone.
9. Poach scallops, shrimp, and squid in fish stock. Remove from stock and chill. Cut into ¼-inch pieces.
10. Combine all the seafood with the Mascarpone mixture and season.
11. To assemble, portion risotto into 1-ounce servings. Make an indentation with your thumb in each portion and place 1 teaspoon of seafood mixture in the indentation.
12. Mold the risotto around the stuffing to form a ball and dredge the ball in flour, shaking off the excess.
13. Dip the ball in egg wash and roll in bread crumbs.
14. Deep-fry the risotto balls and drain on absorbent paper.
15. Portion 1½ ounces of tomato sauce on a plate and set risotto on top. Garnish with parsley.

Note: To prepare lobster for sautéing, separate claws and legs from body, split body and tail lengthwise, and cut into 2-inch pieces.

SHRIMP, BARBECUED CAJUN-STYLE

YIELD: 25 servings, 4 ounces each

96 shrimp (16/20 size)
 3 ounces butter
12 ounces onions, minced
 3 cloves garlic, mashed to a paste
12 ounces beer
 3 pints Shrimp Stock (recipe follows)
 2 tablespoons Seasoning Mix (recipe follows)
 2 tablespoons lemon juice
 2 tablespoons Worcestershire sauce
2¼ pounds unsalted butter, cut in chips
 6 ounces yellow pepper, cut in small dice and blanched
 6 ounces green pepper, cut in small dice and blanched
 6 ounces red pepper, cut in small dice and blanched
   salt, to taste
 6 cups cooked rice

1. Peel and devein shrimp and make stock from shells (see following recipe).
2. Sauté onions and garlic in butter until translucent.
3. Sprinkle onions and garlic in bottom of a shallow pan suitable for poaching.
4. Arrange shrimp in pan and add beer and shrimp stock.
5. Bring to simmer, cover with a piece of parchment paper and poach in a 360°F oven for 4–6 minutes.
6. When done, remove shrimp to a serving platter, cover, and keep warm.
7. Add seasoning mix, lemon juice and Worcestershire sauce to poaching liquid and reduce until slightly syrupy. Remove from heat.
8. Add butter, chip by chip, and swirl the pan to blend in the butter.
9. Serve sauce over shrimp accompanied by a small timbale of rice.

SHRIMP STOCK
YIELD: 3 pints

  3 ounces butter
    shrimp shells (from 16 shrimp)
  6 ounces onions, small dice
  3 ounces carrots, small dice
  3 ounces celery, small dice
  6 tablespoons tomato paste
  3 bay leaves
1½ cups white wine
  3 pints water

1. Sauté shrimp shells, onions, carrots, celery, and tomato paste in butter until mixture turns red (do not burn).
2. Add bay leaves, wine, and water and simmer 15 minutes. Strain.

SEASONING MIX
YIELD: 6 tablespoons

3 tablespoons black pepper
1 tablespoon dried rosemary
1 tablespoon dried thyme
1 tablespoon dried oregano

1. Combine all spices and grind in a blender. Store in a covered container.

SHRIMP BROILED WITH GARLIC
YIELD: 25 portions

75 shrimp (U-12 size)
 6 ounces butter, melted

STUFFING
4½ cups dry Italian bread crumbs
 12 cloves garlic, mashed
 12 ounces butter, melted
     salt and pepper, to taste
     lemon, for garnish

1. Peel the shrimp, leaving on tail. Butterfly from the inside and remove the intestinal tract.
2. Arrange shrimp cut side down on a buttered pan and brush with butter.
3. To make the stuffing, combine bread crumbs, garlic, and butter and season.
4. Place 1 tablespoon of bread crumb mixture on top of each shrimp.
5. Broil until shrimp is cooked and crumbs are crisp and brown.
6. Serve with lemon.

SMOKED FISH CURE (STOVE-TOP METHOD)
YIELD: 3 pounds cure

2 pounds kosher salt
1 pound dark brown sugar
2 tablespoons saltpeter (optional)
2 tablespoons garlic powder
2 tablespoons onion powder
1 tablespoon crushed bay leaves
2 tablespoons ground allspice
1 tablespoon ground cloves
2 tablespoons ground mace

1. To make the cure, combine all ingredients and mix well. (Extra cure can be stored in a sealed jar.)
2. Rub cure on fish or fillets. Refrigerate 2 hours for small pieces and up to 6–8 hours for larger fillets or a whole fish.
3. Carefully rinse off cure and air-dry fish 2–4 hours before smoking.
4. To smoke fish, use an aluminum foil disposable hotel pan for top and bottom.
5. Place ¼ inch of hickory chips that have been soaked in water on the bottom of the pan.
6. Make four 1-inch balls out of aluminum foil and place one in each corner of the pan.

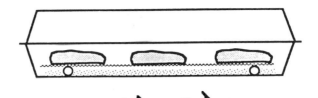

Set-up for Smoke Roasting

7. Place a wire rack on top of the foil and arrange the fish to be smoked on the rack.
8. Cover the pan with the second foil pan and secure with a weight.
9. Place the pan on the stove, turn the heat medium to high, and smoke the desired amount of time. Cooling time is approximately 15 minutes or until fish is firm to the touch. When done, allow the pan to cool slightly before opening.
10. Serve with a horseradish sauce.

Note: Use approximately 1½ pounds cure for a 5-pound fillet, which will serve 25. Suggested fish: salmon or trout. Note that five pounds of trout is about 10 trout, yielding 20 fillets or 20 portions.

SQUID, FRIED WITH SPICY TOMATO SAUCE

YIELD: 25 servings, 4 ounces each

2 tablespoons lemon juice
¼ cup Worcestershire sauce
salt, to taste
4½ pounds squid, cleaned and cut in rings
1½ cups milk
flour, for dredging
oil, for deep-fat frying
25 parsley sprigs
Spicy Tomato Sauce (recipe follows)

1. Season squid with lemon juice, Worcestershire sauce, and salt.
2. Dip squid in milk, then dredge in flour. Let rest for 10 minutes.
3. Dredge squid again in flour. Deep-fry at 375° until golden brown. Drain on absorbent paper.
4. Place tomato sauce on a plate and portion squid on top.
5. Deep-fry parsley sprigs for 45 seconds and place on top of squid.

(continued)

**SQUID, FRIED
WITH SPICY
TOMATO SAUCE**
(continued)

SPICY TOMATO SAUCE

  6 ounces olive oil
  6 cloves garlic, minced
12 ounces onions, minced
  1 tablespoon fresh basil, chopped
  1 tablespoon fresh oregano, chopped
½ teaspoon cayenne pepper
  1 tablespoon chili powder
12 ounces ham, julienned
12 ounces mushrooms, minced
1½ cups white wine
1½ quarts tomato concasse (peeled, seeded, and chopped
     tomatoes)
12 ounces tomato purée
  2 tablespoons chopped parsley
     salt and pepper, to taste

1. Sauté garlic, onions, basil, oregano, cayenne, and chili powder in oil until onions are translucent.
2. Add ham and mushrooms; sauté
3. Add wine and reduce by one half.
4. Add concasse and purée. Simmer 10 minutes (adjust consistency with stock if necessary).
5. Add parsley and season.

·Soups·

American Bounty Vegetable Soup
Borscht Moskovskaia (Russian beet soup)
*Carrot Soup with Ginger Cream
Celery Soup Teramo Style
Chicken Consomme with Fennel Ravioli
Cold Cucumber Soup with Yogurt
Cream of Chestnut Soup
Cream of Jerusalem Artichoke Soup
Cream of Porcini Mushroom Soup
Creamed Corn and Chicken Soup
Gazpacho
Genoa Vegetable Soup
Goulash Soup
Ham Bone and Collard Greens Soup
Hot and Sour Soup
Lentil Soup
Meatball Cellophane Noodle Soup
Miso Soup
Philadelphia Pepper Pot Soup
Scotch Broth
*Seafood Minestrone
Tomato Tofu Soup
*Tortilla Soup

*Starred recipes meet recommended dietary guidelines for calories, carbohydrates, protein, and fat. See Chapter 12 for complete nutritional menus.

AMERICAN BOUNTY VEGETABLE SOUP

YIELD: 25 6-ounce servings

1½ pounds beef shank, ¼" dice
6 quarts beef stock or broth
6 ounces oil or butter
6 ounces turnips, ¼" dice
6 ounces carrots, ¼" dice
6 ounces celery, ¼" dice
1½ pounds onions, ¼" dice
6 ounces leeks, cut ¼" square
6 ounces cabbage, cut ¼" square
3 cloves garlic, minced
9 ounces potatoes, ¼" dice
6 ounces lima beans or green beans
6 ounces corn, frozen
6 ounces peeled, seeded, and chopped tomatoes
   salt and pepper, to taste
3 teaspoons chopped parsley
   cheese croutons, optional

1. Combine beef shank and stock and simmer 30 minutes.
2. Sweat turnips, carrots, and celery in oil until half cooked.
3. Add onions, leeks, cabbage, and garlic and sweat 3–4 minutes longer.
4. Add beef, stock, and potatoes and simmer until beef is tender. Skim fat as it rises to the surface.
5. Add beans and corn and simmer 3–4 minutes. Add tomatoes and return to a simmer. Season.
6. Add parsley and cheese croutons before serving.

Note: The same amount of cooked beef could be substituted for beef shank; it should be added with the beans and corn.

BORSCHT MOSKOVSKAIA (RUSSIAN BEET SOUP)
YIELD: 25 6-ounce servings

2 ounces butter
1½ cups onions, finely diced
4 beets, julienned
1½ cups red wine vinegar
1 tablespoon sugar
6 tomatoes, peeled, seeded and chopped in ¼" dice
salt and pepper to taste
3 pounds beef shank
7 quarts beef stock
1½ pounds white cabbage, shredded
12 ounces boiled ham, cut into ¼" dice
16 parsley sprigs and 2 bay leaves, tied together
½ cup chopped dill
3 cups sour cream

1. Sauté onions in butter until translucent. Add beets and sauté briefly.
2. Add vinegar, sugar, tomatoes, beef, and stock and simmer very slowly until beef is almost tender, about 1 hour.
3. Add the cabbage, ham, and herb bouquet and simmer 30 minutes longer. Remove beef, parsley, and bay leaves.
4. Julienne beef and return it to soup. Degrease and adjust seasonings.
5. Garnish soup with dill and sour cream.

CARROT SOUP WITH GINGER CREAM
YIELD: 25 6-ounce servings

1 ounce butter
4 cloves garlic, minced
2 ounces ginger, minced
6 ounces celery, diced
7 ounces onions, diced
4 ounces leeks, diced
1½ gallons chicken stock
4½ pounds carrots, diced
1½ pounds sweet potatoes, diced
¼ cup white wine
2 cinnamon sticks
2 teaspoons grated nutmeg
1 teaspoon salt
2 tablespoons lime juice
12 ounces heavy cream
4 ounces carrots, cut into small dice and blanched, for garnish
ground ginger, to taste

**CARROT SOUP
WITH GINGER
CREAM**
(continued)

1. Sweat garlic, ginger, celery, onions, and leeks in butter.
2. Add stock, carrots, potatoes, white wine, cinnamon, and nutmeg and simmer until vegetables are tender.
3. Purée soup and strain through a china cap.
4. Add salt, lime juice, and half the heavy cream. Garnish with diced carrot. Reheat or serve cold.
5. Whip the remaining heavy cream and flavor it with ginger. Add a small teaspoon of cream to the soup just before serving.

CALORIES: 160; PROTEIN: 5.5 gm; FAT: 7.4 gm; CARBOHYDRATE: 18.7 gm; SODIUM: 150 mg; CHOLESTEROL: 25 mg

**CELERY SOUP
TERAMO STYLE**
YIELD: 25 6-ounce servings

5	ounces salt pork, finely chopped
2½	pounds celery, cut into medium dice
15	ounces onions, cut into medium dice
6	ounces tomato paste
5	quarts white stock
	sachet (cheesecloth bag containing 1 bay leaf, pinch of thyme, 10 peppercorns, 5 sprigs parsley)
6	ounces rice
3	teaspoons chopped parsley
1	teaspoon chopped oregano
1	teaspoon chopped basil
	salt and pepper, to taste
	grated Parmesan cheese, for garnish

1. Render salt pork until golden brown.
2. Add celery and onions. Sweat until three-quarters cooked (do not brown).
3. Add tomato paste, stock, and sachet and simmer for 20 minutes.
4. Add rice and simmer until rice is done. Remove sachet. Add herbs and season.
5. Serve with cheese on the side.

CHICKEN CONSOMME WITH FENNEL RAVIOLI

YIELD: 25 6-ounce servings

5 quarts chicken consomme
2 teaspoons salt, if needed

FILLING

2 teaspoons olive oil
3 cloves garlic, minced
1 tablespoon minced shallots
1 pound fennel, cut into small dice
1 teaspoon chervil, chopped
1 tablespoon chopped fennel leaves
½ teaspoon salt
3 tablespoons Pernod
3 ounces chicken, ground
1½ ounces heavy cream
12 ounces Basic Pasta Dough (page 214)
   fennel leaves
1 cup egg wash (1 egg, 1 cup water)
1 pound tomatoes, skinned, seeded, and julienned
   chervil leaves, for garnish

1. To prepare the filling, sauté garlic and shallots in olive oil.
2. Add fennel and cook until tender. Add Pernod and stock if necessary.
3. Add chervil, fennel leaves, and salt; cool.
4. Purée chicken in a food processor. When smooth, pulse in heavy cream.
5. Combine fennel mixture and chicken and mix well. Set aside.
6. To make ravioli, roll dough through pasta machine until the middle setting.
7. Place fennel leaves on pasta sheet, top with a second sheet of dough, and continue to roll through pasta machine until second from the thinnest setting.
8. Brush one sheet of dough with egg wash and place in a ravioli form. Fill indentations with fennel filling, and top with a second sheet of dough. Roll with a rolling pin to cut portions.
9. Cook ravioli in boiling salted water until tender; drain.
10. Serve consomme with four ravioli, tomato julienne, and chervil leaves.

CALORIES: 85; PROTEIN: 5.2 gm; FAT: 2.0 gm; CARBOHYDRATE: 10.5 gm; SODIUM: 230 mg; CHOLESTEROL: 5 mg

COLD CUCUMBER SOUP WITH YOGURT
YIELD: 25 6-ounce servings

SOUP
  - 3 ounces butter
  - 7 ounces shallots, minced
  - 3¼ pounds cucumbers, skinned, seeded, and sliced
  - 10 ounces celery root, diced
  - 1 quart stock
  - sachet (cheesecloth bag with 10 peppercorns, 5 sprigs parsley, pinch of thyme, 1 bay leaf)
  - 3 cups yogurt
  - 2 cups half-and-half
  - salt and pepper, to taste

GARNISH
  - 2 cups cucumber, cut into small dice
  - 3 tablespoons chopped dill
  - 3 tablespoons chopped parsley
  - 1½ cups cream, whipped to soft peaks

1. Sweat shallots, cucumbers, and celery root in butter until half cooked.
2. Add stock and sachet and simmer until vegetables are soft.
3. Remove sachet and purée soup in a blender until very smooth. Chill.
4. Add yogurt and half-and-half and season.
5. Add cucumber and herb garnish and serve each portion with a spoonful of whipped cream.

CREAM OF CHESTNUT SOUP
YIELD: 25 6-ounce servings

SOUP
  - 15 ounces dry chestnuts
  - 3¾ quarts water
  - 3¾ ounces butter
  - 6 ounces leeks, diced
  - 6 ounces fennel, diced
  - 12 ounces celery root, diced
  - 3¾ quarts chicken stock
  - 1½ cups dry white wine
  - 12 ounces heavy cream

GARNISH
  - 10 ounces heavy cream, whipped
  - 1¼ cups very small croutons
  - 25 sprigs fennel greens

1. Cover the chestnuts with water and bring to a boil. Remove from heat and let sit 1 hour. Remove skins.
2. Sauté leeks, fennel, and celery root in butter until tender. Add stock, chestnuts, and wine.
3. Simmer soup until chestnuts are tender, then purée soup in a food processor.
4. Add heavy cream; season.
5. Serve soup with croutons and a spoonful of whipped cream. Garnish with fennel greens.

CREAM OF JERUSALEM ARTICHOKE SOUP

YIELD: 25 6-ounce servings

5 globe artichokes
1 pint water
1 tablespoon lemon juice
3¾ quarts chicken stock
9 ounces butter
5 ounces onions, cut into medium dice
4 ounces celery, cut into medium dice
3 ounces leeks, cut into medium dice
8¾ ounces flour
28 ounces Jerusalem artichokes, peeled and sliced
  sachet (cheesecloth bag containing 3 bay leaves, pinch of thyme, 8 peppercorns, and 5 sprigs parsley)
3½ cups heavy cream
  salt, to taste
  lemon juice, to taste

1. Remove tough outer leaves from globe artichokes and reserve for later use. Trim bottoms and discard choke.
2. Dice artichoke bottoms and immerse them in water acidulated with lemon juice until ready to cook.
3. Drain globe artichoke bottoms and cook in chicken stock until fork tender. Remove, reserve, and save stock.
4. Sauté onions, celery, and leeks in butter until translucent.
5. Add flour and cook 2–3 minutes longer.
6. Whisk in chicken stock and bring to a simmer.
7. Add globe artichoke leaves and Jerusalem artichokes and simmer until leaves are tender.
8. Remove leaves and scrape pulp from leaf with a fork. Return pulp to soup and discard fibrous leaves.
9. Remove sachet and purée soup in a food processor or blender.
10. Add cream and diced globe artichoke bottoms.
11. Season with salt and lemon.

CREAM OF PORCINI MUSHROOM SOUP

YIELD: 25 6-ounce servings

7 quarts chicken stock
4 ounces dry porcini mushrooms
10 ounces mushroom trimmings (stems and scraps)
2½ ounces arrowroot
15 ounces Asti Spumante
15 egg yolks, beaten
15 ounces heavy cream
10 ounces heavy cream, whipped, for garnish

1. Combine chicken stock, porcini mushrooms, and mushroom trimmings. Reduce by one-third. Strain. Dice porcini mushrooms and reserve for garnish.
2. Combine arrowroot with 5 ounces Asti Spumante and add to soup, stirring constantly. Bring to a boil and hold hot for service.
3. For the liaison, combine egg yolks, the remaining Asti Spumante, and heavy cream.
4. Add some of the hot soup to the liaison, stirring constantly. Then add the liaison back to the soup, stirring constantly.
5. Heat soup to just under the simmer, stirring constantly; strain.
6. Add diced porcini mushrooms and season.
7. Garnish each cup of soup with a spoonful of whipped cream.

Note: This soup must not be allowed to boil or the egg yolks will cook and the soup will curdle.

CREAMED CORN AND CHICKEN SOUP

YIELD: 25 6-ounce servings

3 quarts chicken stock
2½ pounds chicken
2 tablespoons oil
1 tablespoon minced garlic
3 shallots, minced
3 scallions, minced
¾ ounce fish sauce (nam pla)
1 cup corn kernels
1 cup creamed corn
⅛ cup cornstarch
½ cup water
2 eggs, beaten
  salt and pepper, to taste
½ bunch coriander leaves

1. Simmer chicken in stock until tender. Strain and reserve stock. Remove chicken meat from bones and reserve.
2. Stir-fry garlic, shallots, and scallions in oil.
3. Add fish sauce, stock, corn kernels, and creamed corn; bring to a simmer.
4. Combine cornstarch and water and add to soup to thicken.
5. Add eggs and simmer 4–5 minutes. Season.
6. Garnish with coriander leaves.

GAZPACHO

YIELD: 25 6-ounce servings

SOUP

12	ounces onions
12	ounces green peppers
1¼	pounds cucumbers
1½	pounds tomatoes
1½	tablespoons minced garlic
	salt and pepper, to taste
	pinch of cayenne pepper, thyme, and savory
10	ounces tomato purée
½	cup wine vinegar
1	cup olive oil
3	tablespoons lemon juice
1½	pints tomato juice
	beef consomme, as needed

GARNISH

6	ounces tomatoes, peeled, seeded, and finely diced
4	ounces red peppers, finely diced
4	ounces green peppers, finely diced
6	ounces cucumbers, finely diced
4	ounces scallions, finely diced
2	cups croutons, cooked in garlic butter

1. Combine all soup ingredients except tomato juice in a food processor; process until very fine.
2. Pulse in tomato juice. Chill and season.
3. Adjust consistency with beef consomme.
4. Sprinkle garnishes before serving.

GENOA VEGETABLE SOUP
YIELD: 25 6-ounce servings

SOUP

3 ounces pancetta, cut into ¼″ dice
2 tablespoons olive oil
5 ounces onions, cut into ¼″ dice
3 ounces carrots, cut into ¼″ dice
1 ounce celery, cut into ¼″ dice
4 ounces peppers, cut into ¼″ dice
5 ounces zucchini, cut into ¼″ dice
5 ounces eggplant, cut into ¼″ dice
5 ounces potatoes, cut into ¼″ dice
7 ounces tomatoes, peeled, seeded, and chopped
5 quarts chicken or brown stock
1½ cups pasta (small soup type)
1½ cups cooked garbanzo beans
    salt and pepper, to taste

PESTO

1 teaspoon minced garlic
1 cup chopped basil
3 teaspoons pine nuts, toasted
1¾ tablespoons grated Parmesan cheese
3 tablespoons grated Romano cheese
6 tablespoons olive oil

GARNISH

    virgin olive oil
    grated Romano cheese

1. Render pancetta in olive oil; do not brown.
2. Add onions, carrots, celery, and peppers; sweat until half cooked.
3. Add zucchini and eggplant and sweat.
4. Add potatoes, tomatoes, and stock and bring to a simmer.
5. Simmer soup until vegetables are tender. Add pasta and beans.
6. To make pesto, combine all ingredients in a blender and purée.
7. Season soup with pesto.
8. To serve, portion soup and sprinkle with olive oil. Serve Romano cheese on the side.

GOULASH SOUP
YIELD: 25 6-ounce servings

4 ounces lard
2 pounds onions, medium dice
2 pounds beef shank, medium dice
2 ounces flour
4 ounces tomato paste
6 cloves minced garlic
¾ cup sweet paprika
4 bay leaves
1 tablespoon caraway seeds, crushed fine
1 tablespoon marjoram
1 gallon brown stock
2 pounds potatoes, medium dice
   salt and pepper, to taste

1. Sauté onions in lard until lightly caramelized.
2. Add beef shank and sauté. Stir in flour and cook 4–5 minutes.
3. Add tomato paste, garlic, paprika, bay leaves, caraway seeds, and marjoram and cook 2–3 minutes.
4. Add stock and simmer until meat is tender. Add potatoes and simmer until potatoes are soft.
5. Remove bay leaves and adjust seasonings. Degrease if necessary.

HAM BONE AND COLLARD GREENS SOUP
YIELD: 25 6-ounce servings

3 ham hocks (slash or score skin)
5 quarts chicken stock
5 ounces salt pork, ground
10 ounces onions, small dice
5 ounces celery, small dice
3¾ ounces flour
1½ pounds collard greens (remove tough stems)
   sachet (cheesecloth bag containing 1 bay leaf, pinch thyme, 10 peppercorns, and 5 parsley sprigs)
10 ounces heavy cream
   salt, to taste

**HAM BONE AND
COLLARD GREENS
SOUP**
(continued)

1. Combine ham hocks, sachet, and chicken stock and simmer 30 minutes.
2. In another pan, render salt pork. Add onions and celery and sauté until onions are translucent.
3. Add flour and cook 2–3 minutes longer.
4. Add stock and ham hock mixture and bring to a simmer.
5. Cut collard greens into 1-inch dice and add to soup.
6. Simmer until the collard greens are tender.
7. Remove the ham hocks, dice the meat, and return it to soup.
8. Discard sachet and add cream. Season.

Note: If collard greens are too strong, they can be blanched before adding to the soup. For a variation, substitute cabbage or mustard greens for collard greens.

**HOT AND SOUR
SOUP**
YIELD: 25 6-ounce servings

2 tablespoons oil
½ tablespoon minced ginger
¼ cup sliced scallions
8 ounces pork butt, shredded
2½ ounces bamboo shoots (canned)
¼ cup black fungus, soaked and diced
¼ cup tiger lily buds, soaked and tied in knots*
8 ounces Chinese cabbage, shredded
2½ quarts chicken stock
2 tablespoons soy sauce
1 tablespoon salt
1 cup vinegar
½ tablespoon white pepper
½ tablespoon black pepper
4 ounces cornstarch
1 cup water
2 eggs, beaten
2 tablespoons sesame oil
½ cup sliced scallions, for garnish
2 blocks bean curd, diced

1. Stir-fry ginger, scallions, and pork in oil.
2. Add bamboo shoots, black fungus, tiger lily buds, and Chinese cabbage. Stir-fry until cabbage is soft.
3. Add chicken stock and bring to a simmer. Add soy sauce, peppers, and vinegar.
4. Combine cornstarch and water and add to soup. Bring soup to a boil.

5. Add eggs slowly, stirring occasionally.
6. Finish soup with sesame oil; garnish with sliced scallions and diced tofu.

*Because lily buds are long and thin, they look more attractive tied in knots. They also fit better on a spoon.

LENTIL SOUP
YIELD: 25 6-ounce servings

2½ ounces butter
1½ cups diced onions
1 cup diced leeks
2 cloves garlic, minced
2½ ounces tomato paste
3 tablespoons vinegar
4 ounces carrots, small dice
4 ounces celery, small dice
2½ cups lentils
3¾ quarts chicken stock
1 bay leaf
1 teaspoon thyme
1 teaspoon caraway seeds
3 strips lemon peel
salt and pepper, to taste

1. Sauté onions, leeks, and garlic in butter.
2. Add tomato paste and sauté 1 minute. Add vinegar and deglaze.
3. Add carrots, celery and lentils and sauté.
4. Add stock, bay leaf, thyme, caraway seeds, and lemon peel. Simmer until lentils are tender.
5. Remove bay leaf and lemon peels and adjust seasonings.

MEATBALL CELLOPHANE NOODLE SOUP
YIELD: 25 6-ounce servings

MEATBALLS
12 ounces pork, ground
4 ounces finely chopped Chinese cabbage
¼ cup finely chopped scallions
¼ tablespoon minced ginger
1 egg, beaten
⅛ cup cornstarch
⅛ teaspoon white pepper
½ tablespoon salt
½ tablespoon sesame oil
1 tablespoon soy sauce

**MEATBALL
CELLOPHANE
NOODLE SOUP**
(continued)

SOUP STOCK

2½ quarts chicken stock
 1 package cellophane noodles, soaked and roughly chopped
 ½ ounce dried black fungus, rehydrated and chopped
 1 tablespoon salt
 ¼ tablespoon black pepper
 1 tablespoon soy sauce
 2 ounces mushrooms, sliced
 2 eggs, beaten
 5 ounces spinach, blanched and roughly chopped

1. To make the meatballs, combine all ingredients and mix well.
2. Roll meat into ¾-inch balls.
3. To make the soup, bring chicken stock to a simmer. Add noodles, fungus, salt, pepper, and soy sauce and return to a simmer.
4. Add meatballs and simmer until meatballs are cooked.
5. Add mushrooms, eggs, and spinach and simmer 2–3 minutes longer.

MISO SOUP
YIELD: 25 6-ounce servings

 2 tablespoons oil
 ¼ cup chopped scallions
 8 ounces cabbage, diced
 4 ounces miso bean paste
 2 quarts hot water
1½ packages katsuo dashi
 ¼ tablespoon black pepper
 ½ ounce dried seaweed, soaked and roughly chopped
1½ blocks bean curd, diced
 ¼ kamaboko fish cake, diced
 2 eggs (made into thin pancake, cut julienne)
 ¼ bunch watercress, roughly chopped

1. Stir-fry scallions and cabbage in oil until cabbage is soft.
2. Add miso bean paste, water and katsuo dashi and bring to a simmer.
3. Add all remaining ingredients except watercress and egg and simmer 15–20 minutes.
4. Whip egg with a fork and pour into a nonstick 12-inch sauté pan. Cook over low heat or in the oven at 225°F until egg is cooked. Roll egg like a jelly roll and slice into ⅛-inch strips.
5. Add watercress and egg just before serving.

PHILADELPHIA PEPPER POT SOUP

YIELD: 25 6-ounce servings

20 ounces honeycomb tripe
7½ quarts white veal stock
20 ounces veal shank
3 ounces butter
12 ounces onions, cut into medium dice
5 ounces celery, cut into medium dice
5 ounces carrots, cut into medium dice
sachet (cheesecloth bag containing 8 peppercorns, 5 sprigs parsley, pinch of thyme, marjoram, and sage)
20 ounces potatoes, cut into medium dice
salt and pepper, to taste
7 ounces green peppers, cut into medium dice and blanched
7 ounces red peppers, cut into medium dice and blanched
Spaetzles (recipe follows)

1. Simmer tripe and veal shank in stock until tender, approximately 1½–2 hours.
2. Remove tripe and shank. Trim fat, cut into ¼-inch dice, and reserve.
3. Sweat onions, celery, and carrots in butter.
4. Add stock, sachet, and potatoes and simmer until tender.
5. Add veal shank, tripe, and red and green peppers; season.
6. Garnish each serving with spaetzles.

SPAETZLES

3 eggs
5 ounces milk
salt, to taste
grated nutmeg, to taste
10 ounces flour, approximately

1. Beat eggs and mix with milk, salt, and nutmeg.
2. Mix in flour and whip lightly to smooth out batter.
3. Using a spaetzle machine, press mixture into a pot of boiling salted water.
4. Cook until tender.
5. Drain, rinse under cold water, and drain again.

SCOTCH BROTH
YIELD: 25 6-ounce servings

3 pounds lamb, cut into ⅓″ dice and blanched
5 quarts white stock
8 ounces barley
2 tablespoons butter
4 ounces carrots, finely diced
4 ounces turnips, finely diced
4 ounces onions, finely diced
4 ounces leeks, finely diced
4 ounces celery, finely diced
4 ounces savoy cabbage, finely diced
　salt and pepper, to taste
　chopped parsley, for garnish

1. Combine meat, stock, and barley and simmer 1 hour.
2. Sauté vegetables in butter and add to soup.
3. Simmer until vegetables are tender. Degrease, season, and garnish with parsley.

SEAFOOD MINESTRONE
YIELD: 25 6-ounce servings

1 cup white wine
50 mussels, cleaned and debearded
7 cups fish stock, approximately
2 tablespoons olive oil
6 bacon slices, chopped
9 teaspoons minced garlic
4 cups leeks, cut into small dice
1½ cups onions, cut into small dice
1 cup celery, cut into small dice
9 tablespoons tomato paste
1½ teaspoons salt
1½ teaspoons rosemary
1½ teaspoons thyme
1 teaspoon pepper
3 bay leaves
3 slices lemon
1 cup dry kidney beans, soaked
1 cup short-grain rice (Arborio is preferable)
4½ cups tomatoes, coarsely chopped
12 tablespoons raw shrimp, peeled, deveined, and chopped
　Pesto (recipe follows)

1. Combine white wine and mussels in a covered pot and steam just until shells open, about 2–3 minutes.
2. Remove mussels from shells and reserve.
3. Strain mussel liquid through cheesecloth and combine with fish stock.
4. Sauté bacon in olive oil until translucent. Add garlic, leeks, onion, and celery and sauté.
5. Add tomato paste and sauté 2–3 minutes, stirring constantly.
6. Add seasonings, lemon, beans, rice, and tomato and simmer until beans are tender (approximately 1 hour).
7. Add mussels and shrimp. Remove from heat immediately. Serve in heated bowls garnished with ½ teaspoon pesto.

PESTO
YIELD: 8 ounces

  4 ounces fresh basil
2½ ounces pine nuts, toasted
  2 tablespoons olive oil
  2 ounces Parmesan cheese, grated
  1 clove garlic, minced

Purée all ingredients in a blender, adding water if necessary to form a smooth paste.

CALORIES: 125; PROTEIN: 6.9 gm; FAT: 12.1 gm; CARBOHYDRATE: 200 gm; SODIUM: 200 mg; CHOLESTEROL: 28 mg

TOMATO TOFU SOUP
YIELD: 25 6-ounce servings

2½ quarts chicken stock
1 tablespoon katsuo dashi
1 ounce Japanese soy sauce
   salt, to taste
½ teaspoon white pepper
1 block bean curd, sliced
½ pound tomatoes, skinned, seeded, and diced
2 eggs, beaten
2½ ounces spinach, roughly chopped
1 tablespoon sesame oil

1. Bring chicken stock to a boil. Add katsuo dashi, soy sauce, salt, and pepper.
2. Add bean curd and tomato and return to a boil.
3. Add eggs slowly, stirring occasionally. Finish soup by adding spinach and sesame oil.

TORTILLA SOUP
YIELD: 25 6-ounce servings

2 ounces garlic, minced
10 corn tortillas, pulverized in a food processor
5 tablespoons chopped cilantro
1½ pounds onions (puréed in food processor)
1½ pounds fresh tomato purée
8 ounces canned tomato purée
2 tablespoons ground cumin
1 tablespoon chili powder
4 bay leaves
5 quarts chicken stock
   pinch of cayenne pepper
   Tabasco sauce, to taste
1 pound chicken breast, grilled and julienned
2 avocados, skinned, seeded, and diced
4 ounces cheddar cheese, shredded
9 tortillas, julienned

1. Sweat garlic in a small amount of chicken stock.
2. Add tortillas, cilantro, onion, and tomato purées, and bring to a simmer.
3. Add seasonings and stock and simmer until flavor is developed, about 20 minutes. Strain and adjust hotness with cayenne and Tabasco sauce.
4. Garnish each cup with chicken, avocado, cheese, and tortillas.

CALORIES: 120; PROTEIN: 10.8 gm; FAT: 5.0 gm; CARBOHYDRATE: 9.4 gm; SODIUM: 60 mg; CHOLESTEROL: 20 mg

·ENTRÉES·

Barbecued Brisket
Beef Curry
Beef Tenderloin with Spicy Tomato Sauce
Beef with Red Onions and Peanuts
*Blackened Beef with Corn and Pepper
    Sauce
Shaker Stuffed Flank Steak
Strip Steak, Star of Texas
Lamb Shoulder Pontchartrain
Ham, Glazed
Pork Loin Stuffed with Prunes and Apples
Pork Loin Stuffed and Roasted Genoa
    Style with Garlic-Flavored Juice
Pork Scaloppine with Pineapple and Green
    Peppercorns
Spareribs, Barbecued
Ligurian Rabbit Stew
Veal Scaloppine with Egg and Cheese
    Coating
Veal Scaloppine with Stuffing
Veal Shank, Braised Milan Style
Veal, Shredded Swiss-Style
Aromatic Chicken
Broiled Chicken with Black Beans and
    Salsa

*Chicken Breasts with Barbecue Sauce
Chicken Breast New Hampshire
Chicken Roasted with Lemon Grass
Cornish Hen Stuffed and Roasted with
    Garlic Sauce
Turkey Oklahoma
Turkey Medallions with Red Onion Confit
Turkey Scallops Sautéed in Green
    Peppercorn Sauce
Broiled Swordfish with Tomato-Basil
    Coulis
Catfish Topped with Crabmeat and
    Cornbread Crumbs
Coulibiac (salmon en croute)
*Grilled Swordfish with Lentil Ragout and
    Horseradish Cream
Paella "Valenciana"
*Salmon Poached with Asparagus and Basil
Sea Bass with Vegetables and Squid
*Seafood Newburg
Smoke-roasted Bluefish with Horseradish
    Sauce and Leek Compote
Stuffed Swordfish
Sweet and Sour Fish
Vatapa (spicy fish stew)

*Starred recipes meet recommended dietary guidelines for calories, carbohydrates, protein, and fat.
 See Chapter 12 for complete nutritional menus.

BARBECUED BRISKET

YIELD: 25 servings

8 pounds fresh beef brisket, trimmed
3 ounces liquid smoke
¼ cup oil
1 pound onions, finely chopped
½ cup cider vinegar
½ cup brown sugar
⅓ cup spicy mustard
¼ cup molasses
1 tablespoon hot pepper sauce
¼ cup Worcestershire sauce
1½ pints ketchup
1½ pints brown stock

1. Rub brisket with liquid smoke and allow to marinate 1 hour.
2. Sear meat on all sides in hot oil; remove.
3. Add onions and sauté until lightly browned.
4. Add remaining ingredients and bring to a simmer. Return brisket to liquid, cover, and braise in a 350°F oven until fork-tender (approximately 2½–3 hours).
5. One hour before the meat is done, remove the lid and baste the brisket with the braising liquid. Cook uncovered, basting 2 to 3 times during the final hour of cooking.

Note: The brisket may be finished on the barbecue to brown and glaze the surface.

BEEF CURRY
YIELD: 25 8-ounce servings

15 pounds beef chuck, cut into 1-inch cubes
6 tablespoons shrimp-flavored soy sauce
3 tablespoons turmeric
6 tablespoons malt vinegar
1 pound onion, chopped
10 cloves garlic, minced
5 ounces ginger, peeled and finely minced
2 tablespoons chili powder
1½ cups vegetable oil
4 bay leaves
1 cinnamon stick
12 peppercorns
5 quarts stock

1. Combine meat, soy sauce, turmeric, and vinegar and marinate 12 hours, refrigerated.
2. Sauté onion, garlic, ginger, and chili powder in oil until lightly browned.
3. Add beef, marinade, bay leaves, cinnamon, peppercorns, and stock. Simmer until meat is tender, approximately 45 minutes to 1 hour.

BEEF TENDERLOIN WITH SPICY TOMATO SAUCE
YIELD: 25 5-ounce servings

50 2½-ounce beef tenderloin medallions (approximately 8 pounds)
clarified butter

INFUSION
4 pints white wine
4 sprigs oregano
20 leaves basil
4 sprigs rosemary
6 peperoncini, chopped
2 bay leaves
4 sprigs parsley

SAUCE
1 cup olive oil
1 pound onions, finely diced
8 cloves garlic, minced
7 pounds plum tomatoes, peeled, seeded, and chopped
salt and pepper, to taste

**BEEF TENDERLOIN
WITH SPICY
TOMATO SAUCE**
(continued)

GARNISH
   2 pounds porcini and oyster mushrooms, sliced
   4 ounces butter
   4 teaspoons chopped parsley
     salt and pepper, to taste

1. To make the infusion, reduce the wine until 6 ounces remain. Add the herbs and allow to steep for 1–2 hours; strain.
2. To make the sauce, sauté the onions and garlic in oil. Add the tomatoes and simmer until thick.
3. Add the strained infusion and purée in a food processor; season (reduce consistency if necessary).
4. Sauté the beef medallions in the butter to desired degree of doneness. Portion 2 ounces of sauce on a plate and arrange 2 medallions of beef on top.
5. Sauté the mushrooms in butter and add the parsley. Season and place the mushrooms on top of the beef.

**BEEF WITH RED
ONIONS AND
PEANUTS**
YIELD: 25 4-ounce servings

6½ pounds beef top butt, trimmed and cut into 25 4-ounce steaks
   7 ounces vegetable oil
   3 ounces sesame oil
  10 cloves garlic, minced
   6 stalks lemon grass, sliced thinly
   4 pounds red onions, sliced
   8 ounces peanuts, roasted
   3 tablespoons sugar
     salt and pepper, to taste

1. Combine steaks, 3 ounces vegetable oil, and sesame oil.
2. Stir-fry garlic and lemon grass in remaining vegetable oil.
3. Add onions and stir-fry until softened.
4. Add peanuts, and sugar; season.
5. Grill or sauté steak and serve with onion-peanut mixture.

BLACKENED BEEF WITH CORN AND PEPPER SAUCE
YIELD: 25 servings

CORN AND PEPPER SAUCE

12	ears corn
¼	cup olive oil
3	cups onions, cut into medium dice
6	ounces tomato paste
1	quart red wine
½	gallon brown stock
6	bay leaves
6	sprigs thyme
3	ounces butter
3	cups finely diced green pepper
3	cups finely diced red peppers
1	tablespoon minced jalapeño pepper
12	cloves garlic, minced
9	ounces shallots, minced
1½	teaspoons turmeric
1½	teaspoons curry powder

25	tenderloin steaks, approximately 7 pounds
1	tablespoon curry powder
4	tablespoons fennel seeds
	pinch of cayenne pepper

1. Dampen corn husks and roast corn in a 375°F oven for 15 minutes.
2. Shock corn and remove kernels from the cob; reserve.
3. Grill cobs over hot coals until evenly browned; reserve.
4. Sauté onions in olive oil until golden brown.
5. Add tomato paste and sauté. Add wine and reduce to one-fourth.
6. Add stock, bay leaves, thyme, and the corn cobs; reduce until three-fourths of original volume. Strain.
7. Sauté peppers, garlic, and shallots in butter. Add corn, turmeric, curry powder, and sauce, and simmer until vegetables are tender.
8. Season tenderloin steaks with curry powder and fennel seeds and grill to desired doneness.
9. Pool corn sauce on plate and set beef on top, sliced into five pieces.

CALORIES: 260; PROTEIN: 25.8 gm; FAT: 11.6 gm; CARBOHYDRATE: 13.5 gm; SODIUM: 105 mg; CHOLESTEROL: 93 mg

SHAKER STUFFED FLANK STEAK

YIELD: 25 5-ounce servings

STUFFING

6	ounces butter
18	slices white bread, crustless, cut into ½-inch cubes
1½	pounds onions, finely diced
1	pound celery, finely diced
1	pound mushrooms, finely diced
2	tablespoons chopped parsley
1	tablespoon chopped rosemary
1	tablespoon chopped basil
1	tablespoon chopped savory
½	tablespoon chopped sage
4½	pounds ground meat (mixture of beef, veal, and pork)
6	eggs, beaten
2	tablespoons salt
	pepper, to taste

6	flank steaks (about 8 pounds) butterflied and flattened with a mallet
6	tablespoons oil
12	ounces mirepoix (6 ounces onions and 4 ounces each carrots and celery, finely diced)
⅓	cup tomato purée
1½	cups red wine
2½	quarts brown beef stock
1	tablespoon chopped tarragon
6	bay leaves
2¼	ounces arrowroot
12	ounces water
	salt, to taste

1. Sauté bread cubes in half of the butter until golden brown. Remove from pan and set aside.
2. Add the remaining butter, and sauté the onions, celery, and mushrooms until onions are translucent. Chill.
3. Combine the chilled vegetable mixture with the herbs, ground meat, and eggs. Add the bread cubes and salt and pepper.
4. Spread stuffing on flank steaks. Roll the meat like a jelly roll and tie.
5. Brown flank steaks in oil on all sides and remove.
6. Add mirepoix and tomato paste and brown lightly.
7. Add wine and reduce by half.
8. Add stock, tarragon, bay leaves, and meat, and return to a simmer, cover and braise in a 350°F oven for 1–1½ hours, or until fork tender.

9. Remove flank steaks, cover, and keep warm.
10. Degrease braising liquid and reduce to 2 cups.
11. Mix arrowroot with water, and add to the braising liquid. Bring to a simmer, season, and strain.
12. Slice flank steak into ¾-inch slices and serve with sauce.

STRIP STEAK, STAR OF TEXAS
YIELD: 25 5-ounce servings

BREAD CRUMB TOPPING
- 6 cloves garlic, mashed to a paste
- 2 tablespoons chopped parsley
- 5 cups fresh white bread crumbs
- 9 ounces butter, melted
  salt and pepper, to taste

- 25 beef strip steaks, 6 ounces each (10 pounds total)
  salt and pepper, to taste
- 6 cloves garlic, mashed to a paste
  oil
  Barbecue Sauce (recipe follows)
  Onion Stars (recipe follows)

1. To make bread crumb topping, combine all ingredients and rub together until well mixed. Set aside.
2. Season steak with salt, pepper, and garlic. Rub with oil.
3. Broil or grill steak until rare.
4. Brush steak with barbecue sauce and top with bread crumb topping.
5. Place steak on a tray with a rack and bake in a 500°F oven until crumbs are browned.
6. Garnish each steak with an onion star.

BARBECUE SAUCE

- 3 ounces oil
- 12 ounces red onions, diced
- 12 cloves garlic, mashed to a paste
- 1½ pints brown stock
- 1 pint orange juice concentrate
- 2 tablespoons Worcestershire sauce
- 6 ounces Heinz 57 sauce
- 12 ounces ketchup
  pinch celery seeds

**STRIP STEAK,
STAR OF TEXAS**
(continued)

1. Sauté onions in oil until translucent.
2. Add garlic and sauté.
3. Add remaining ingredients and simmer 15–20 minutes or until sauce is thick.

ONION STARS

  3 ounces butter
2¼ pounds onions, diced
1½ cups milk
  6 eggs, beaten
12 ounces cake flour
  6 ounces cornstarch
    pinch nutmeg
    salt and pepper

1. Sauté onions in oil until soft and golden brown. Cool slightly.
2. Add onion and milk. Purée in a blender until smooth.
3. Combine onion mixture and egg and mix in all remaining ingredients; beat until batter is smooth.
4. Preheat a star "croustada" iron in a 325°F fryer. Dip the star iron in the batter, then back in the fryer.
5. Hold the iron submerged until the batter sets (about 50 seconds). Gently shake the batter star off the iron.
6. Continue frying batter star until crisp and golden brown; drain on absorbent paper.

Note: Consistency of batter can be adjusted by the addition of more milk or flour.

**LAMB SHOULDER
PONTCHARTRAIN**
YIELD: 25 5-ounce servings

10 pounds lamb shoulder
 2 tablespoons oil
 6 ounces onions
 6 eggs, beaten
1½ cups fresh white bread crumbs
1½ cups brown stock
    pinch of rosemary
    pinch of thyme
 3 pounds ground lamb
 2 tablespoons chopped parsley
    salt and pepper, to taste

3 ounces oil
12 ounces mirepoix (6 ounces onion, 3 ounces carrot, and
   3 ounces celery, finely diced)
6 ounces tomato paste
1½ pints red wine
3 pints brown stock
   sachet (cheesecloth bag) containing 2 tablespoons rosemary,
   2 tablespoons thyme, and 20 peppercorns
6 cloves garlic, mashed
   Garlic Crumb Topping (recipe follows)
2 tablespoons arrowroot
½ cup water
   salt, to taste
   Pontchartrain Vegetables (recipe follows)

1. Cut a pocket in each lamb shoulder and flatten meat slightly with a mallet.
2. Sauté onions in 2 tablespoons oil; cool.
3. Mix eggs, bread crumbs, rosemary, and thyme with onions.
4. Add ground lamb and parsley, and mix well. Season.
5. Place stuffing in shoulders and tie with twine.
6. Sear shoulders in oil, remove, and add mirepoix. Caramelize slightly.
7. Add tomato paste and brown. Deglaze with red wine. Add brown stock and sachet.
8. Return shoulders to pan, and bring to a simmer. Cover and braise in a 350°F oven for 1 hour or until meat is fork tender.
9. Remove shoulders and discard string and sachet. Top with garlic crumb mixture and return to oven to brown crumbs.
10. Degrease braising liquid and reduce by half. Dissolve arrowroot in water and use to thicken braising liquid. Strain and season.
11. Slice lamb shoulders and arrange on plates. Nappé with 2 ounces of sauce. Serve with Pontchartrain Vegetables.

GARLIC CRUMB TOPPING

1½ cups bread crumbs
3 cloves garlic, mashed
2 tablespoons chopped parsley
2 tablespoons butter, melted

Lightly rub all ingredients together until well mixed.

(continued)

**LAMB SHOULDER
PONTCHARTRAIN**
(continued)

PONTCHARTRAIN VEGETABLES

12 ounces red beans, soaked overnight
12 ounces black beans, soaked overnight
12 slices bacon, chopped
12 ounces onions, cut into medium dice
12 ounces red pepper, cut into medium dice
 6 ounces green pepper, cut into medium dice
1½ ounces celery, cut into medium dice
 6 cloves garlic, mashed to a paste
 3 ounces butter
12 ounces zucchini, cut into medium dice
1½ pounds okra, sliced ½ inch thick and blanched
1½ pounds mushrooms, cut into medium dice
 6 scallions, sliced ½ inch thick
1½ pounds tomatoes, peeled, seeded, and chopped
1½ pints thin brown sauce
    pinch of thyme
    pinch of ground cumin
    pinch of oregano
 2 tablespoons chopped parsley
    salt and pepper, to taste

1. Simmer beans in water until tender. Drain and reserve.
2. Render bacon until half-cooked. Add onions, peppers, celery, and garlic and sweat until vegetables are three-quarters cooked. Do not brown.
3. Sauté zucchini in butter until half cooked. Add okra, mushrooms, and scallions and sauté.
4. Combine both vegetable mixtures and add tomatoes, brown sauce, spices, and beans. Simmer until vegetables are tender. Season. (If vegetable mixture becomes too thick, add brown stock.)

HAM, GLAZED
YIELD: 25 servings

10–12 pounds ham, cured, cooked, bone-in
   25 cloves
    2 ounces mustard
    2 cups brown sugar

1. Remove all skin from ham except for 3–4 inches around the shank end.
2. Trim fat, leaving approximately a ⅛-inch covering, and rub ham with mustard.

3. Score fat in a diamond pattern and stick one clove where each line crosses.
4. Pack a thin layer of brown sugar evenly all over ham.
5. Place on a rack and bake at 350°F until a rich glaze has developed (approximately 2 hours).
6. If sugar should collect and burn on the bottom of the roasting pan, add water to dissolve.

PORK LOIN STUFFED WITH PRUNES AND APPLES
YIELD: 25 servings

12 pounds boneless pork loin, well trimmed
3 apples, peeled and diced
12 prunes
salt, pepper, ground ginger to taste
12 ounces mirepoix (6 ounces onion, 3 ounces carrot, 3 ounces celery, finely diced)
1½ quarts brown stock
1 ounce cornstarch

1. Push a sharpening steel lengthwise through the pork loin, widen opening with a slicer, and stuff with apples and prunes.
2. Tie and season. Roast on a rack in a 350°F oven until internal temperature reaches 165°F, approximately 2 hours.
3. Add mirepoix half an hour before roast is done.
4. When roast is done, remove roast and deglaze pan with stock. Simmer 15 minutes.
5. Combine cornstarch and water and use to thicken stock. Return sauce to a simmer. Strain, season, and degrease.

PORK LOIN STUFFED AND ROASTED GENOA STYLE WITH GARLIC-FLAVORED JUICE
YIELD: 25 6-ounce servings

STUFFING
1½ pounds pork
1½ pounds sweet Italian sausage
3 cups white bread crumbs
6 ounces heavy cream
4 eggs, beaten

DRY PESTO
1 cup basil, chopped
2 cups parsley, chopped
1 cup pine nuts, toasted
8 cloves garlic, minced
1 cup grated Pecorino Romano cheese

PORK LOIN STUFFED AND ROASTED GENOA STYLE WITH GARLIC-FLAVORED JUICE
(continued)

PORK LOIN

- 10 pounds boneless pork loin, well trimmed and cut into 4 pieces
  salt and pepper, to taste
- 4 12″ × 12″ pieces of caul fat
- 1 pound mirepoix (8 ounces onion, 4 ounces celery, 4 ounces carrot, diced)
- 1 cup tomato paste
- 4 cloves garlic, minced
- 2 bay leaves
- 2½ quarts pork or veal stock
  salt and pepper, to taste

1. Combine the ingredients for the stuffing and mix well.
2. Combine the ingredients for the pesto and pulse in a food processor until minced.
3. Butterfly the pork loin and pound lightly with a meat mallet.
4. Spread the pesto mixture on the pork, then spread the stuffing over the pesto.
5. Roll up the pork loin, jelly-roll fashion. Wrap in caul fat and secure with butcher's twine.
6. Roast the pork in a 350°F oven until internal temperature reaches 160°F, approximately 1½ hours.
7. When the pork is done, remove and allow to rest. Pour off excess fat.
8. Add the mirepoix and tomato paste to the roasting pan and caramelize lightly.
9. Add the garlic, bay leaf, and stock and simmer until approximately 12 ounces remain. Strain and season.
10. Portion 1½ ounces of juice on a plate and arrange 2–3 slices of pork on top.

PORK SCALOPPINE WITH PINEAPPLE AND GREEN PEPPERCORNS
YIELD: 25 6-ounce servings

- 75 2-ounce pork scaloppine (approximately 12 pounds)
  salt and pepper, to taste
- 12 ounces clarified butter
- 12 shallots, minced
- 4 tablespoons green peppercorns
- 1¼ pints port wine
- 3 pints fond de veau lie (veal stock thickened with cornstarch)
- 1½ pounds unsalted butter, cut in chips
  fresh pineapples, cut into 50 ½″ rings (approximately 2 pineapples)

1. Flatten pork scaloppine with a mallet.
2. Season pork and sauté in butter. When done, arrange on a platter and keep warm.
3. Add shallots and peppercorns and sauté until shallots are translucent.
4. Add port and reduce by half.
5. Add fond de veau lie and reduce to sauce consistency.
6. Remove from heat and add butter chip by chip, swirling the pan to blend.
7. Grill pineapple slices just until hot and arrange on platter with pork.
8. Serve sauce over pork.

Note: Veal or turkey may be substituted for pork scaloppine.

SPARERIBS, BARBECUED
YIELD: 25 servings, 4 ribs each

14 racks spareribs (approximately 12 pounds)
2 cups oil for baking

SEASONING MIX
1 cup salt
4 teaspoons garlic powder
4 teaspoons white pepper

COLOR MIX
¾ cup soy sauce
¾ cup sherry

BARBECUE SAUCE
2 cups hoisin sauce
2 cups bean paste
3 cups ketchup
4 teaspoons minced ginger
4 teaspoons white pepper
½ cup minced scallions
1 cup sherry
½ cup sesame oil
2 cups sugar
1 cup honey

**SPARERIBS,
BARBECUED**
(continued)

1. Trim spareribs. Combine seasoning ingredients and rub mix on both sides of the ribs.
2. Combine color mix and paint ribs on both sides.
3. Mix barbecue sauce ingredients and cover ribs on both sides. Marinate overnight.
4. Roast on a rack in a 350°F oven for 1½ hours. Brush with oil.

LIGURIAN RABBIT STEW
YIELD: 24 8-ounce servings

12 rabbits, cut up (approximately 20 pounds)
1 cup oil
6 ounces butter
12 ounces celery, small dice
12 ounces carrots, small dice
1½ pounds onions, small dice
8 cloves garlic, minced
1½ teaspoons rosemary
2 bay leaves
1½ teaspoons thyme
1½ teaspoons black peppercorns, crushed
1½ quarts white wine
pinch of grated nutmeg
2 quarts crushed tomatoes, with juices
12 ounces pine nuts, toasted
6 cups brown sauce
salt and pepper, to taste

1. Brown rabbit on all sides in butter and oil. Remove and keep warm.
2. Add celery, carrots and onions and sauté until lightly colored. Add garlic, rosemary, bay leaves, thyme, and black peppercorns and sauté.
3. Add white wine and reduce by half.
4. Add nutmeg, rabbit, tomatoes, pine nuts, and brown sauce. Bring to a simmer.
5. Braise the rabbit, covered, in a 350°F oven until meat is fork tender, approximately ½ hour.
6. Degrease sauce, strain sauce if you like, and season.

VEAL SCALOPPINE WITH EGG AND CHEESE COATING

YIELD: 25 6-ounce servings

MILANESE SAUCE
- 1 cup glace de viande (rich veal sauce)
- 2 cups red wine
- 4 cups tomato sauce
- 4 ounces butter
- 4 ounces ham, julienned
- 4 ounces beef tongue, julienned
- 4 ounces mushrooms, julienned and sautéed in butter
- 4 teaspoons chopped parsley
  salt and pepper, to taste

- 75 2-ounce veal scaloppine (approximately 10 pounds)
  flour for dredging
- 12 eggs, beaten
- 1 cup grated Parmesan cheese
- ½ pound clarified butter
- 4 cups olive oil

1. To make the sauce, reduce the glace de viande and wine to 2 cups. Add the tomato sauce and strain.
2. Finish the sauce with the butter. Add the ham, tongue, mushrooms, and parsley. Season and set aside.
3. Combine the eggs and Parmesan cheese and mix well.
4. Dredge the veal in flour and shake off the excess.
5. Dip the veal in the egg-cheese mixture and pan-fry until golden brown in butter and oil. Drain on absorbent paper.
6. Ladle 2 ounces of sauce on a plate and place the veal on top of the sauce.

VEAL SCALOPPINE WITH STUFFING

YIELD: 25 servings

STUFFING

 1 cup olive oil
 1 cup minced shallots
 1 pound ham, chopped fine
 1 pound sweet Italian sausage, loosely packed
12 ounces spinach, blanched and roughly chopped
 8 ounces ricotta cheese
 4 ounces grated Romano cheese
 1 teaspoon grated nutmeg
 1 tablespoon chopped sage

75 2-ounce veal scaloppine (approximately 10 pounds)
    seasoned flour, for dredging
 1 cup olive oil
 1 cup clarified butter
 3 cups white wine
 5 cups very strong veal stock
 8 sage leaves

1. To make the stuffing, sauté the shallots in oil and cool.
2. Combine all the remaining stuffing ingredients and mix well.
3. Spread 1 tablespoon of stuffing on each scaloppine. Fold over and secure with a toothpick.
4. Dredge scaloppine in flour and shake off the excess.
5. Sauté in butter and oil until lightly browned on both sides. Remove to a serving platter and discard toothpick.
6. Pour excess fat from the pan and add the wine and stock. Reduce to a syrupy glace.
7. Just before serving, place scaloppine back in the pan and turn and coat with the glace.
8. Arrange the scaloppine on a plate and top with a sage leaf.

VEAL SHANK, BRAISED MILAN STYLE

YIELD: 25 servings

25 2-inch thick slices of veal shank, with bone (approximately 12 pounds)
    seasoned flour, for dredging
 2 cups oil
½ pound onions, finely diced
¼ pound celery, finely diced
¼ pound carrots, finely diced
 1 cup tomato paste
 1 cup tomatoes, peeled, seeded, and chopped
 2 cups white wine
 4 quarts brown veal stock
    salt and pepper, to taste

GREMOLATA
10 cloves garlic, minced
10 teaspoons lemon zest
½ cup chopped parsley
 8 anchovy fillets, chopped

1. Dredge the veal shanks in flour and shake off the excess.
2. Brown the veal on all sides in hot oil and remove; keep warm.
3. Discard excess oil. Add onions, celery, carrots, and tomato paste and caramelize lightly.
4. Add tomatoes and wine and reduce by half. Add stock.
5. Return veal and bring to a simmer. Cover and braise in a 350°F oven until the meat is fork tender, approximately 1¼–1½ hours.
6. When the veal is done, remove to a serving platter and keep warm.
7. Degrease sauce and adjust consistency; season.
8. Serve the veal with 2 ounces of sauce ladled over the top.
9. Combine the ingredients in the gremolata and sprinkle on top.

Note: An alternate method is to finish the sauce with the gremolata.

VEAL, SHREDDED SWISS-STYLE
YIELD: 25 5-ounce servings

8 pounds boneless veal leg, cut into narrow strips
10 ounces oil
  flour, for dredging
  salt and pepper, to taste
9 ounces shallots, minced
1 pound mushrooms, sliced
1 quart white wine
1 quart demi-glace
1 quart heavy cream
3 ounces brandy
  lemon juice, to taste
  salt and pepper, to taste

1. Season and lightly flour veal. Sauté quickly in a very hot pan using very little oil (do not overload pans).
2. Remove veal when done and reserve. Collect drippings.
3. Add more oil to the pan and sauté shallots and mushrooms.
4. Add wine and reduce by half. Remove mushrooms and shallots and add to veal.
5. Add demi-glace, heavy cream, and any meat juices. Reduce to sauce consistency.
6. Add brandy and lemon juice; season.
7. Return meat and mushrooms to pan and reheat. Do not boil.

AROMATIC CHICKEN
YIELD: 25 servings
(leg and thigh)

4 ounces oil
4 tablespoons minced ginger
4 tablespoons minced garlic
2 bunches scallions, sliced thin
2 ounces orange zest
1 stick cinnamon
2 tablespoons Szechuan pepper
6 star anise
2 tablespoons salt
3 ounces sugar
1 cup sherry
1½ cups soy sauce
1 quart chicken stock
25 chicken legs and thighs, disjointed (approximately 10 pounds)
1 ounce cornstarch
1 cup water

1. Stir-fry ginger, garlic, and scallions in oil until lightly browned.
2. Add orange zest, cinnamon, pepper, anise, salt, and sugar and heat briefly.
3. Add sherry, soy sauce, stock, and chicken pieces and simmer until chicken is cooked, approximately 30 minutes.
4. When chicken is done, remove and reserve. Degrease stock.
5. Combine cornstarch with water and add to stock mixture. Bring to a boil.
6. Return chicken to sauce.

BROILED CHICKEN WITH BLACK BEANS AND SALSA

YIELD: 25 5-ounce servings

25 chicken breasts, boneless, with skin and wishbone intact (approximately 10 pounds)
    salt and pepper, to taste
6 ounces oil
    Black Beans (recipe follows)
    Sour Cream with Lime (recipe follows)
    Salsa (recipe follows)

1. Season chicken with salt and pepper and rub with oil.
2. Broil in medium heat broiler until done. (Chicken can be turned at 45° angles during broiling to create grill marks.)
3. Serve chicken on black beans, garnished with sour cream and salsa.

BLACK BEANS

18 ounces black beans, soaked overnight in water
2¼ quarts chicken stock
6 slices bacon, chopped
12 ounces onion, small dice
6 ounces ham, small dice
    salt and pepper, to taste

1. Drain black beans and combine with chicken stock. Simmer until beans are almost tender, approximately 1 hour.
2. Render bacon and add onions and ham. Sauté until onions are translucent.
3. Add bacon mixture to the beans and simmer until beans are soft.
4. Remove half the beans and mash with a spoon. Return them to the whole beans and season. Adjust consistency by reducing or adding more stock.

**BROILED CHICKEN
WITH BLACK BEANS
AND SALSA**
(continued)

SOUR CREAM WITH LIME

1½ pints sour cream
  3 ounces lime juice

1. Mix sour cream and lime.
2. Fill pastry bag with small plain tube and pipe in a crisscross pattern over chicken breast.

SALSA

18 tomatoes, skinned, seeded, and cut into small dice
12 scallions, sliced
  6 ounces cucumber, small dice
  2 tablespoons horseradish
  2 tablespoons chopped cilantro
  3 serrano chili peppers, seeded and chopped fine
  2 tablespoons lime juice

Mix all ingredients together and let marinate for 1 hour or longer.

**CHICKEN
BREASTS WITH
BARBECUE
SAUCE**
YIELD: 25 servings

BARBECUE SAUCE
  2 ounces butter
1½ pounds onions, minced
  2 ounces garlic, minced
  2 ounces jalapeño peppers, minced
  3 tablespoons chili powder
20 ounces tomato paste
  1 pint coffee
20 ounces Worcestershire sauce
1¼ cups cider vinegar
1¼ cups apple cider
10 ounces brown sugar
    stock

25 chicken breasts, skinned and trimmed (approximately 12 pounds)

1. To make the sauce, sauté onion, garlic, jalapeños, and chili powder in butter.
2. Add tomato paste and sauté.
3. Add remaining sauce ingredients and simmer 30 minutes. Adjust consistency with stock if necessary.
4. Smoke-roast chicken breasts (see page 225) and serve on a pool of barbecue sauce.

CALORIES: 250; PROTEIN: 28.3 gm; FAT: 3.9 gm; CARBOHYDRATE: 25.4 gm; SODIUM: 400 mg; CHOLESTEROL: 75 mg

CHICKEN BREAST NEW HAMPSHIRE
YIELD: 25 5-ounce servings

STUFFING
3 ounces butter
12 shallots, minced
1½ pounds mushrooms, small dice
1½ cups white wine
1¾ ounces flour
12 ounces heavy cream
6 ounces ham, small dice
⅓ cup chopped parsley
pinch of poultry seasoning
salt and pepper, to taste

CHICKEN AND COATING
25 chicken breasts, boneless, with wing bone in and skin removed
flour, for dredging
10 ounces egg wash
12 cups fresh white bread crumbs
1 pound walnuts, chopped fine
oil
clarified butter

SAUCE
2 tablespoons butter
12 shallots
1½ pints white wine
10 parsley sprigs
2 bay leaves
2¼ pints chicken velouté
1½ pints chicken stock
1½ pints heavy cream
salt and pepper, to taste

**CHICKEN BREAST
NEW HAMPSHIRE**
(continued)

1. To make the stuffing, sauté shallots in butter.
2. Add mushrooms and sauté. Add wine and reduce until almost dry.
3. Add flour and cook for 2–3 minutes.
4. Add heavy cream, ham, parsley, and poultry seasoning. Bring to a boil and cook for 3–4 minutes.
5. Season and cool.
6. To make the sauce, sauté shallots in butter until lightly browned.
7. Add wine, parsley, bay leaves and reduce by half.
8. Add velouté and stock and reduce to sauce consistency. Strain.
9. To prepare the chicken, place chicken breasts between two sheets of plastic wrap and flatten with a mallet.
10. Place stuffing on chicken and roll chicken completely around stuffing. Chill.
11. Combine bread crumbs and walnuts. Lightly flour chickens. Dip breasts in egg wash and then roll in bread crumb–walnut mixture.
12. Heat oil and butter and add chicken. Brown on all sides and drain on absorbent paper.
13. Place chicken on tray and bake in 350°F oven for 15–20 minutes.
14. Slice each chicken breast into 3 pieces. Fan out on plate and serve with accompanying sauce.

**CHICKEN
ROASTED WITH
LEMON GRASS**
*YIELD: 24 servings
(½ chicken per person)*

12 chickens, about 2½ pounds each
12 stalks lemon grass, thinly sliced
24 cloves garlic, mashed
16 shallots, mashed
 8 chili peppers, seeded and sliced
 1 cup sugar
 2 tablespoons salt
 4 tablespoons fish sauce (nam pla)
   Nuoc Cham Sauce (recipe follows)

1. Combine lemon grass, garlic, shallots, chili peppers, and sugar and purée in a food processor.
2. Add salt and fish sauce and mix well.
3. Loosen skin on chicken and rub seasoning mix under the skin.
4. Tie and roast chicken in a 350°F oven for 60 minutes, or until internal temperature reaches 165°F. Baste often with drippings.
5. Cut into pieces and serve with Nuoc Cham Sauce.

NUOC CHAM SAUCE

YIELD: 2½ quarts

     8 ounces carrots, finely grated
    12 ounces daikon radish, finely grated
     2 cups sugar
    16 cloves garlic, roughly chopped
     8 chili peppers, seeded
     2 cups lime juice
     4 cups fish sauce (nam pla)
     4 cups water

1. Mix the carrot and daikon with 1 cup sugar. Let stand 15 minutes.
2. Combine the remaining sugar, garlic, chili pepper, and lime juice and purée in a food processor.
3. Add fish sauce and water and mix well.

CORNISH HEN STUFFED AND ROASTED WITH GARLIC SAUCE

YIELD: 8 servings

     2 ounces butter
     6 ounces Cornish hen and chicken livers
     2 scallions, sliced diagonally
     ½ clove garlic, minced
     3 tablespoons brandy
     ½ cup strong, reduced chicken stock
    2½ cups croutons (½″ cubes, sautéed in butter)
     1 ounce porcini mushrooms (diced fine, reconstituted by simmering in chicken stock for 5 minutes, and drained)
     6 ounces chicken breast (½″ cubes, sautéed in butter)
     1 tablespoon chopped rosemary
       salt and pepper, to taste
    16 spinach leaves, blanched
     4 1½-pound Cornish hens, boned without cutting the skin

SAUCE
     2 tablespoons minced shallot
     ½ tablespoon minced garlic
     1 pint stock (made from the caramelized bones of the Cornish hens)
     1 cup white wine
     ¼ cup Marsala wine

**CORNISH HEN STUFFED
AND ROASTED WITH
GARLIC SAUCE**
(continued)

1. To make the stuffing, sauté the livers in butter; do not overcook. Remove, dice, and cool.
2. Add the scallions and garlic to the same pan and sauté. Add brandy and chicken stock and reduce by half.
3. Combine the liver mixture, croutons, mushrooms, chicken breast, and rosemary and mix gently; season.
4. Divide the stuffing mixture into four portions and wrap each portion in spinach leaves.
5. Place the stuffing in the cavity of the Cornish hens. Place in a roasting pan.
6. Roast hens 40 minutes in a 350°F degree oven. When done, brush hens with glace de volaille, remove, and allow to rest, keeping hens warm.
7. To make the sauce, drain excess fat from the roasting pan and add the shallots and garlic. Sauté without browning.
8. Add the stock and white wine and reduce to one-third of original volume.
9. Finish the sauce with Marsala and season.
10. Pool 1½ ounces of sauce on a plate and serve half a chicken on top.

**TURKEY
OKLAHOMA**
YIELD: 25 servings

STUFFING

3	ounces clarified butter
9	ounces onions, minced
9	ounces carrots, minced
3	ounces celery, minced
4	cloves garlic, minced
12	ounces mushrooms, diced
3	ounces parsley, chopped
6	ounces white wine
6	ounces ham, diced
	salt and pepper, to taste
	poultry seasoning, to taste
3	cups croutons, toasted in oven

FORCEMEAT

2	pounds raw ground turkey
18	ounces pork fat, ground
3	teaspoons salt
3	eggs beaten
15	ounces heavy cream
	pepper, to taste
2	pieces turkey skin or caul fat, 12″ × 26″

SAUCE
>   3 ounces fat, from roasted turkey
>   3 tablespoons minced shallots
> 1½ cups white wine
>   3 pints stock (made from turkey bones)
>   arrowroot, as needed
>   salt and pepper, to taste

1. To make the stuffing, sauté onions, carrots, and celery in butter.
2. Add garlic and mushrooms and sauté until mushrooms exude liquid.
3. Add wine and reduce excess moisture. Add ham, salt, and poultry seasoning. Remove from heat.
4. Mix in croutons and chill.
5. When preparing the forcemeat, keep meats cold at all times during preparation.
6. Combine turkey, pork fat, and salt and purée in a food processor.
7. Add eggs and process until combined.
8. Add cream slowly, pulsing machine until cream is incorporated.
9. Check consistency and adjust seasonings.
10. Spread forcemeat on plastic wrap ¾ inch thick in a rectangular shape. Repeat for second roll.
11. Spread stuffing on top of forcemeat rectangles and roll jelly-roll fashion.
12. Spread turkey skin or caul fat on a table and place forcemeat rolls in center. Pull skin up around forcemeat.
13. Tie rolls with string and roast on a rack in a 325°F oven until internal temperature reaches 150°F, approximately 90 minutes.
14. When done, remove turkey and allow to rest. Pour off excess fat from roasting pan.
15. To make the sauce, add shallots to the roasting pan and sauté.
16. Deglaze with white wine, reduce, and add turkey stock.
17. Simmer 15–20 minutes. Thicken with arrowroot, strain, and season.
18. Portion 1½ ounces of sauce on a plate and place two slices of turkey on top. Each roll will yield 25 1-inch slices.

TURKEY MEDALLIONS WITH RED ONION CONFIT
YIELD: 25 6-ounce servings

RED ONION CONFIT
- 2 ounces butter
- 18 ounces red onion, julienned
- 3 ounces honey
- 4½ ounces red wine vinegar
- 10 ounces red wine
  salt and pepper, to taste

- 75 2-ounce medallions of turkey (approximately 10 pounds)
- 5 ounces sherry wine vinegar
- 6 cups veal stock, thickened with cornstarch

1. To make the confit, sweat onions in butter 2–3 minutes.
2. Add honey and cook until onions are golden brown.
3. Add vinegar and wine and reduce until almost dry; season.
4. To cook turkey, dry-sauté in a nonstick pan. When browned on both sides, remove and reserve.
5. Deglaze pan with sherry vinegar and reduce until almost dry. Add veal stock and simmer 2–3 minutes.
6. Place turkey on a plate and pool sauce around. Arrange confit along edge.

TURKEY SCALLOPS SAUTÉED IN GREEN PEPPERCORN SAUCE
YIELD: 25 6-ounce servings

SAUCE
- 4 ounces butter
- 12 scallions, white part only, minced
- 6 cloves garlic, minced
- 6 tablespoons green peppercorns
- 3 cups white wine
- 1 cup Marsala wine
- 2 cups strong turkey or chicken stock
- 5 cups heavy cream
- ½ cup scallion greens, sliced thin
- ½ cup red pepper, blanched and cut into small dice
  salt, to taste

12 eggs, beaten
 1 cup grated Parmesan cheese
75 2-ounce turkey cutlets (approximately 10 pounds)
   seasoned flour for dredging
½ pound clarified butter
 1 cup olive oil

1. To make the sauce, sauté the scallions in butter. Add garlic, green peppercorns, white wine, and Marsala and reduce to syrupy consistency.
2. Add stock and heavy cream and reduce to sauce consistency. Add scallions and red pepper; season.
3. Combine eggs and cheese and mix well.
4. Dredge turkey cutlets in flour and shake off the excess.
5. Dip turkey cutlets in egg mixture and pan-fry in butter and oil until lightly browned on both sides.
6. Pool 2 ounces of sauce on a plate and set three turkey cutlets on top of sauce.

BROILED SWORDFISH WITH TOMATO-BASIL COULIS
YIELD: 25 6-ounce servings

10 pounds swordfish
   salt, pepper, and lemon juice, to taste
12 scallions (split lengthwise in quarters)
¼ cup oil
   Tomato-Basil Coulis (recipe follows)

1. Season swordfish with salt, pepper, and lemon juice.
2. Cut slits lengthwise in swordfish. Insert scallions and push completely through swordfish. Cut into 25 6-ounce steaks.
3. Rub steaks with oil and cook on a grill for 5–7 minutes. (Turn the steaks at 45° angles during cooking to achieve grill marks.)
4. Place 2 ounces Tomato-Basil Coulis on a plate and set the swordfish on top.

(continued)

**BROILED SWORDFISH
WITH TOMATO-BASIL
COULIS**
(continued)

TOMATO-BASIL COULIS

    2 tablespoons olive oil
    2 tablespoons butter
   12 shallots, minced
    6 cloves garlic, mashed to a paste
   ⅓ cup tomato paste
    3 quarts tomatoes, peeled, seeded, and chopped
  1½ pints chicken stock
     sachet (cheesecloth bag) containing 4 bay leaves, 4 sprigs
     thyme, 20 peppercorns, 6 sprigs parsley
    3 ounces red wine vinegar
   ⅓ cup fresh basil, chopped
     salt and pepper, to taste

1. Sauté shallots, garlic, and tomato paste in oil and butter (do not burn).
2. Add tomatoes, stock, and sachet and simmer 20 minutes.
3. Remove sachet, and purée tomato mixture.
4. Add vinegar, basil, salt, and pepper.

**CATFISH TOPPED
WITH CRABMEAT
AND CORNBREAD
CRUMBS**
YIELD: 25 5-ounce servings

    3 ounces butter
    6 ounces onions minced
  1½ pounds lump crabmeat
  1½ pints béchamel sauce
   12 shallots, minced
    2 quarts fish stock
  1½ pints white wine
   12 ounces ham, julienned
   25 5-ounce catfish fillets
    3 cups cornbread crumbs
    2 cups heavy cream
    6 ounces sherry
   12 ounces butter, cut into chips
     salt, to taste

1. Sauté onions in butter until translucent. Add crabmeat and béchamel and heat to boiling. Remove from heat and chill.
2. Butter a shallow pan and sprinkle with shallots.
3. Place catfish on top of shallots and add wine, stock, and ham. Cover with buttered paper; bring to a simmer.

4. Poach catfish in 350°F oven until done; remove to warm platter.
5. Spread catfish with crabmeat mixture and sprinkle with corn-bread crumbs. Gratinée in broiler.
6. Reduce poaching liquid until slightly thickened.
7. Add heavy cream and reduce to sauce consistency.
8. Flavor heavy cream with sherry and swirl in butter chip by chip. Adjust salt.
9. Serve catfish on a bed of sauce with ham.

COULIBIAC
YIELD: 25 servings (4 rolls)

4 ounces butter
8 ounces shallots, minced
6 pounds mushrooms, thinly sliced
1 pint white wine
6 cups cooked rice
6 pounds salmon fillets
  salt and pepper, to taste
¼ cup lemon juice
4 sheets puff pastry, approximately 16″ × 11″
8 eggs, hard-cooked and coarsely chopped
3 tablespoons chopped dill
6 ounces egg wash (1 egg, ½ cup water)

1. Sauté shallots in butter until translucent. Add mushrooms and sauté until moisture is released.
2. Add wine and reduce until almost dry. Add rice, mix well and chill. Divide into four equal portions.
3. Cut salmon into wide lengthwise slices and divide into four equal portions. Season with salt, pepper, and lemon juice.
4. To assemble coulibiac, lay one sheet of puff pastry on a floured board. Spread a 9-by-5-inch rectangle in the center of the dough with half a portion of the mushroom mixture.
5. Place half a portion of the salmon slices on top of the mushrooms. Sprinkle with chopped egg and dill and cover with the remaining portion of salmon.
6. Cover the salmon with the remaining portion of mushroom mixture.
7. Brush edges of dough with egg wash. Fold the sides of the dough to enclose the filling and then fold the ends under. Repeat this process for the remaining three coulibiac.
8. Brush coulibiac with egg wash and bake in a 350°F oven until internal temperature reaches 145°F, about 30 minutes. Let rest 20 minutes before cutting. Each roll should yield six or seven slices.

GRILLED SWORDFISH WITH LENTIL RAGOUT AND HORSERADISH CREAM

YIELD: 25 4-ounce servings

SWORDFISH

25 4-ounce swordfish steaks (approximately 6½ pounds)
 3 tablespoons lime juice
 3 shallots, minced
 1 teaspoon minced garlic
   pinch of chervil

LENTIL RAGOUT

 5 ounces bacon, finely diced
 1 pound onions, finely diced
14 ounces leeks, finely diced
12 ounces carrots, finely diced
10 ounces celery, minced
 1 tablespoon minced garlic
 5 ounces tomato paste
2½ ounces sherry wine vinegar
25 ounces French lentils
1½ quarts chicken stock, approximately
   cheesecloth bag containing caraway seeds, lemon peel, 10
   peppercorns, 5 sprigs parsley, pinch thyme
 2 teaspoons salt
   white pepper, to taste
10 ounces white wine
12 ounces veal stock, thickened with cornstarch

HORSERADISH CREAM

 1 pint creme fraiche, whipped to a peak
 1 pint nonfat yogurt
 1 pound apples, peeled and grated
   grated horseradish

1. Combine swordfish with lime juice, shallots, garlic, and chervil, and marinate for 4–6 hours.
2. To make lentil ragout, render bacon. Add onions, leeks, carrots, celery, and garlic, and sauté.
3. Add tomato paste and sauté.
4. Add all remaining ragout ingredients and simmer until lentils are tender.
5. Remove cheesecloth bag and season.

6. To make the horseradish cream, combine creme fraiche, yogurt, and apples; mix well. Add horseradish to taste.
7. Drain and grill swordfish. Place on a bed of lentil ragout and nappé with sauce.

CALORIES: 301; PROTEIN: 30.0 gm; FAT: 8.5 gm; CARBOHYDRATE: 23.5 gm; SODIUM: 291 mg; CHOLESTEROL: 53 mg

PAELLA "VALENCIANA"
YIELD: 25 servings

25 chicken thighs (10 pounds)
6 ounces olive oil
10 ounces onions, minced
10 ounces chorizo sausage, sliced
6 ounces green peppers, diced
3 tablespoons minced garlic
6 cups rice (uncooked)
12 ounces canned tomatoes, chopped
9 ounces pimentoes, chopped
6 ounces green olives
1½ pounds chickpeas (garbanzo beans), cooked
1 pint clam juice
salt and pepper, to taste
1½ teaspoons ground saffron
2 quarts chicken stock, hot
3 pounds shrimp, peeled (size 16–20)
75 mussels or small clams (approximately 6 pounds)

1. Brown chickens in oil. Remove from pan, reserving oil. Roast in 350°F oven until internal temperature reaches 150°F, approximately 30 minutes. Reserve.
2. Sauté onions, chorizo, and green peppers in reserved oil.
3. Add garlic and rice and sauté.
4. Add tomatoes, pimentoes, olives, chickpeas, and clam juice and stir well. Season.
5. Distribute chicken throughout rice.
6. Infuse saffron in stock and simmer 10 minutes.
7. Add shrimp and clams and bake, covered, 10–15 minutes at 350°F. Uncover and bake 5 minutes longer.

SALMON POACHED WITH ASPARAGUS AND BASIL

YIELD: 25 3½-ounce servings

75 asparagus spears, cleaned and trimmed
50 slices salmon, 1¾ ounces each (about 7 pounds)
1½ pints white wine
1½ pints fish stock
12 shallots, minced
15 ounces fresh tomatoes, peeled, seeded, and chopped
   fresh basil chiffonade

BASIL SAUCE

1 ounce butter
4 ounces shallots, minced
1 tablespoon garlic, minced
9 ounces vermouth
3 pints fish velouté
3 tablespoons chopped basil
3 bay leaves
12 ounces heavy cream
2 teaspoons salt

1. To make sauce, sauté shallots and garlic in butter.
2. Add vermouth and reduce by half.
3. Add velouté, basil, bay leaves, and heavy cream, and simmer 15–20 minutes.
4. Strain and adjust salt.
5. To cook fish, roll two pieces of salmon around three asparagus spears. Set in pan that contains wine, fish stock, and shallots.
6. Sprinkle tomato on top of salmon and bring to a simmer.
7. Cover with parchment or waxed paper and poach in a 350°F oven until done (approximately 6–8 minutes).
8. Remove fish, cover, and keep warm.
9. Strain poaching liquid, reduce to a syrupy consistency, add basil sauce, and adjust seasonings.
10. Serve salmon with sauce over top. Sprinkle with chiffonade of basil.

CALORIES: 175; PROTEIN: 24.3 gm; FAT: 6.2 gm; CARBOHYDRATE: 5.9 gm; SODIUM: 149 mg; CHOLESTEROL: 54 mg

SEA BASS WITH VEGETABLES AND SQUID

YIELD: 25 6-ounce servings

 1 cup olive oil
12 ounces red onions, cut into 2-inch julienne strips
 4 cloves garlic, mashed to a paste
 4 cups tomatoes, skinned, seeded, and cut into 2-inch julienne strips
 6 cups zucchini, cut into 2-inch julienne strips
   salt and pepper, to taste
25 6-ounce fillets sea bass (approximately 12 pounds)
 4 ounces butter
 1 quart white wine
12 squid, cooked and sliced, tentacles cut in half
 2 teaspoons finely chopped oregano
 2 teaspoons finely chopped parsley
 2 teaspoons finely chopped basil

1. To make the topping, sauté onions and garlic in oil until translucent.
2. Add the tomatoes and zucchini and sauté briefly. Season and cool.
3. Place the sea bass in a buttered shallow pan and top each portion with ¼ cup of the vegetable mixture.
4. Add wine and bring to a simmer. Cover with a piece of parchment or wax paper and poach in a 350°F oven until done, approximately 5–8 minutes.
5. When the fish is done, remove to a serving platter, cover and keep warm.
6. Reduce poaching liquid to 6 ounces and season.
7. Place the fish on a plate and nappé with the poaching liquid. Arrange a few slices of squid on top of each portion and sprinkle with herbs.

SEAFOOD NEWBURG

YIELD: 25 3½-ounce servings

2¼ cups olive oil
2½ pounds lobster, cooked, diced, and shells reserved
2½ pounds shrimp, peeled, deveined, and shells reserved
3 ounces shallots, minced
3 ounces tomato paste
6 ounces brandy
6 quarts fish stock
1 quart evaporated skim milk
5¼ ounces arrowroot
½ cup water
6 ounces butter
2½ pounds scallops, cleaned
6 ounces sherry
¾ cup snipped chives

1. Sauté lobster and shrimp shells and shallots in oil. Add tomato paste. Sauté 2–3 minutes.
2. Add brandy and flambé. Reduce to syrupy consistency.
3. Add stock and evaporated milk and bring to a simmer.
4. Mix arrowroot with water and use to thicken stock mixture. Simmer 15–20 minutes.
5. Strain and reserve sauce.
6. Sauté scallops and shrimp in butter. Add sauce and lobster meat and heat until just hot.
7. Finish with sherry and chives.

CALORIES: 220; PROTEIN: 22.7 gm; FAT: 9.1 gm; CARBOHYDRATE: 11.3 gm; SODIUM: 330 mg; CHOLESTEROL: 114 mg

SMOKED-ROASTED BLUEFISH WITH HORSERADISH SAUCE AND LEEK COMPOTE

YIELD: 25 5-ounce servings

25 5-ounce fillets bluefish (approximately 5 pounds)
3 ounces lemon juice
   salt and pepper, to taste
8 cups hickory wood chips, soaked
   Leek Compote (recipe follows)
   Horseradish Sauce (recipe follows)

1. Season fish with lemon, salt, and pepper.
2. Spread ¼ inch of hickory chips in the bottom of a disposable foil hotel pan. (See smoke-roast diagram, page 225.)
3. Place the fish on a wire rack and set the rack on top of the hickory chips. (Do not allow fish to touch the hickory chips.)
4. Cover pans with foil or a second foil pan.

5. Place pans with fish on burner over high heat. When smoke appears, lower heat slightly.
6. Smoke fish for 5–6 minutes (reposition pans occasionally to be sure to burn all chips).
7. Remove pans from heat and let sit for 2 minutes before opening.
8. Remove fish from smoker. Remove skin and set fish on a portion of Leek Compote. Nappé with Horseradish Sauce.

LEEK COMPOTE

    6 ounces butter
    3 cloves garlic, mashed to a paste
4½ pounds leeks, sliced
    3 cups white wine
2¼ cups chicken stock
    2 tablespoons chopped parsley
1½ pounds tomatoes, peeled, seeded, and chopped
      salt, to taste

1. Sweat garlic and leeks in butter until wilted.
2. Add wine and stock and reduce until leeks are tender and liquid has almost evaporated. Stir occasionally.
3. Add parsley and tomatoes; season.

HORSERADISH SAUCE

    12 shallots, minced
     9 ounces cider vinegar
1½ pints white wine
     3 bay leaves
    20 peppercorns
1½ pints heavy cream
1½ pounds unsalted butter, cut into chips
    12 ounces horseradish, fresh or bottled
     2 tablespoons lemon juice
       salt, to taste

1. Combine shallots, vinegar, white wine, and peppercorns and reduce to 1 ounce.
2. Add heavy cream and reduce to sauce consistency.
3. Remove from heat and add butter chip by chip, swirling the pan to blend. Strain.
4. Add horseradish, lemon juice, and salt.

STUFFED SWORDFISH
YIELD: 25 6-ounce servings

STUFFING
  1 cup olive oil
  8 ounces onions, minced
  1 pound swordfish, diced
  ¾ cup brandy
  5 cups fresh bread crumbs
  1 tablespoon chopped parsley
     salt and pepper, to taste

SWORDFISH
 25 6-ounce swordfish steaks (approximately 10 pounds)
  4 basil leaves, chopped
     thyme, to taste
     lemon juice, to taste
     salt and pepper, to taste
 25 ounces mozzarella cheese, cut into 25 slices
     olive oil, as needed

1. To make the stuffing, sauté onions and diced swordfish in oil. Add brandy and cook until liquid has evaporated.
2. Add bread crumbs and parsley and mix gently. Season and chill.
3. Season swordfish slices with basil, thyme, lemon, salt, and pepper.
4. Spread each slice of swordfish with stuffing and top with a slice of mozzarella cheese.
5. Roll swordfish slices so that stuffing is enclosed and secure with twine.
6. Dip swordfish in oil and broil until done, approximately 10 minutes. Remove twine before serving.

SWEET AND SOUR FISH
YIELD: 25 6-ounce servings

FISH
  9 pounds fish, cut in strips (cod or pollock works well)
     lemon juice, to taste
     salt and pepper, to taste
     flour for dredging
     oil for deep-fat frying

BATTER
  7 cups cold water
  6 tablespoons baking powder
  8 cups flour
  ½ cup sesame oil

SWEET AND SOUR SAUCE
- ½ cup oil
- 1 pint orange juice
- 1 pint stock
- ½ cup lemon juice
- ½ cup vinegar
- 1 cup ketchup
- 2 cups sugar
- 2 ounces honey
- red food color
- ½ cup cornstarch
- 1 cup water

GARNISH
- 4 cups mixed fruit (pineapple, lychee nuts, raisins), for garnish

1. Season fish with lemon juice, salt, and pepper and set aside.
2. To make batter, blend all batter ingredients together. Do not overmix.
3. To make sauce, combine all sauce ingredients except cornstarch and water. Bring to a boil.
4. Mix cornstarch and water and add to orange juice mixture. Bring to a boil.
5. Dredge fish in flour. Dip in batter and deep-fry in 350°F oil.
6. When golden brown, drain, and serve with Sweet and Sour Sauce.
7. Garnish with mixed fruit.

VATAPA (SPICY FISH STEW)

YIELD: 25 5-ounce servings

3 quarts fish stock
4 pounds shrimp, peeled, deveined, and shells reserved
4 pounds monkfish (cut in 2" cubes)
6 ounces olive oil
1 pound onion, diced
4 cloves garlic, minced
8 jalapeño peppers, minced
1 coconut, peeled, shredded, and liquid reserved
4 ounces peanuts, chopped
4 ounces ginger, minced
4 ounces tomato paste
1 cup white wine
8 ounces roux
1½ quarts heavy cream

GARNISH
12 ounces tomatoes, peeled, seeded, and chopped
1 coconut, peeled and shredded
6 ounces peanuts
¼ cup chopped cilantro
salt and pepper, to taste

1. Add shrimp shells to fish stock and simmer 15 minutes. Strain.
2. Poach monkfish in fish stock. Drain, chill, and save stock.
3. Sauté onions, garlic, and peppers in oil.
4. Add coconut, peanuts, ginger, and tomato paste and sauté 3–4 minutes.
5. Add wine and reserved coconut juice and reduce by half.
6. Add reserved stock. Thicken with roux and simmer to sauce consistency.
7. Add heavy cream and reduce if necessary.
8. Sauté shrimp in oil (do not overcook).
9. Add shrimp and monkfish to stew and reheat.
10. Stir garnish into stew or sprinkle on top of each serving.

· VEGETABLES ·

*Asparagus with Lemon Glaze
Broccoli Polonaise
Eggplant and Fontina Cheese
Glazed Beets with Caraway
Glazed Carrots and Snow Peas
Green Beans and Ginger
Grilled Vegetables
Hot and Spicy Eggplant
Julienned Vegetables
Mashy Cousa (stuffed squash)
Rainbow Garden
Sautéed Spinach and Prosciutto
Spinach Soufflé
Steamed Spinach
Stir-fried Vegetables
Vegetable Flan
Zucchini and Peppers, Baked
Zucchini Sauté with Tomatoes and Basil

*Starred recipes meet recommended dietary guidelines for calories, carbohydrates, protein, and fat. See Chapter 12 for complete nutritional menus.

ASPARAGUS WITH LEMON GLAZE

YIELD: 25 4-ounce portions

SAUCE

1½ teaspoons grated lemon zest
12 ounces chicken stock
1½ ounces lemon juice
1½ teaspoons grated ginger
     black pepper, cracked, to taste

VEGETABLE AND GARNISH

8 pounds asparagus, cleaned and trimmed
1 ounce sesame seeds, toasted, for garnish

1. Combine all sauce ingredients and bring to a boil. Reduce to one-third and strain.
2. Cook asparagus and drain.
3. Brush with lemon glaze and sprinkle with sesame seeds.

CALORIES: 18; PROTEIN: 2.5 gm; FAT: 0.2 gm; CARBOHYDRATE: 2.8 gm; SODIUM: 26 mg; CHOLESTEROL: tr mg

BROCCOLI POLONAISE

YIELD: 25 4-ounce servings

6 heads broccoli, cleaned (10 pounds)
2 cups bread crumbs
6 ounces butter
3 eggs, hard-cooked, chopped
2 tablespoons chopped parsley
  salt and pepper, to taste

1. Place broccoli in rapidly boiling salted water. Cook until firm.
2. Drain and immediately immerse in cold water. Reserve. (To reheat, return to hot water.)
3. Sauté bread crumbs in butter until golden brown and crisp.
4. Mix crumbs with eggs and parsley; season.
5. Sprinkle crumb mixture over hot broccoli.

EGGPLANT AND FONTINA CHEESE

YIELD: 25 4-ounce servings

EGGPLANT

- 4 large eggplants
  salt
- 2 pounds Fontina cheese, sliced
- 12 ounces sun-dried tomatoes, in oil
  flour, for dredging
- 1 cup egg wash (1 cup water, 1 egg)
  dry bread crumbs
  olive oil, for frying

SAUCE

- ½ cup olive oil
- 8 ounces onions, sliced
- 4 teaspoons mashed garlic
- 8 ounces green pepper, diced
- 1 quart tomatoes, peeled, seeded, and chopped
- 1 quart tomato sauce
- 4 bay leaves
- 2 tablespoons chopped Italian parsley
- 6 leaves basil
  salt and pepper, to taste

1. To prepare the eggplant, peel and cut lengthwise in ¼-inch slices. Salt and allow to set for 1 hour. Using a cookie cutter, cut circles 1½ inches in diameter.
2. Rinse off the salt and pat dry with a paper towel.
3. Sandwich two eggplant circles with a Fontina cheese slice and sun-dried tomato.
4. Dredge in flour and shake off the excess. Dip in egg wash.
5. Roll in bread crumbs and brown in olive oil.
6. To make the sauce, sauté the onions, garlic, and green pepper in oil.
7. Add the tomatoes, tomato sauce, bay leaves, parsley, and basil and simmer 20–30 minutes. Remove the bay leaf and coarsely purée sauce in food processor. Season.
8. Portion 1½ ounces of sauce on a plate and top with the eggplant.

GLAZED BEETS WITH CARAWAY
YIELD: 25 3-ounce servings

7 pounds beets, trimmed
¾ cup sugar
½ cup vinegar
1 tablespoon caraway seeds
1 ounce cornstarch
4½ cups water
   salt and pepper, to taste

1. Cook beets in boiling water. When tender, peel and cut in uniform pieces (quarters, eighths, or slices). Reserve cooking liquid.
2. Combine 1 quart of beet cooking liquid, sugar, vinegar, caraway seeds, and beets. Bring to a simmer.
3. Combine cornstarch and water and use to thicken beet liquid. Return to a simmer and adjust seasonings.

GLAZED CARROTS AND SNOW PEAS
YIELD: 25 4-ounce servings

4 pounds carrots, cut oblique (2 uneven cuts on a diagonal)
1½ cups maple syrup
9 ounces butter
3–4 cups water
   salt, to taste
   white pepper, to taste
2½ pounds snow peas

1. Combine all ingredients except snow peas in a large, round, shallow heavy-duty pan with straight walls. Bring to a boil. Toss or stir as mixture boils. Carrots should be cooked by the time the mixture reduces to a glaze.
2. Cook snow peas in boiling salted water for 1½ minutes. Drain and immediately immerse in cold water. Drain again and add to carrots just before serving. Adjust seasoning.

GREEN BEANS AND GINGER
YIELD: 25 3-ounce servings

4 pounds green beans, trimmed
3 ounces oil
8 ounces ginger, cut in fine julienne
3 cloves garlic, minced
5 ounces lemon grass, cut in fine julienne
2 tablespoons hot bean paste
1½ pounds napa cabbage, sliced
    salt, to taste

1. Blanch beans in boiling water. Immediately immerse in cold water and reserve.
2. Stir-fry ginger, garlic, lemon grass, and green beans until hot.
3. Add hot bean paste and cabbage and stir-fry until cabbage is tender. Season.

GRILLED VEGETABLES
YIELD: 25 4-ounce servings

3 red peppers, cut in half and seeded
3 yellow peppers, cut in half and seeded
3 green peppers, cut in half and seeded
6 zucchini, split lengthwise
6 yellow squash, split lengthwise
2 large Spanish onions, cut into quarters
6 ounces oil
2 teaspoons thyme
2 serrano chilies, finely diced
6 ounces butter

1. Rub vegetables with oil and sprinkle with thyme.
2. Place on grill and mark both sides, by turning each piece half a turn when you flip them.
3. Chill and cut into bite-size pieces.
4. Sauté serrano chilies in butter until tender.
5. Add reserved vegetables and heat. Season.

HOT AND SPICY EGGPLANT
YIELD: 25 3-ounce servings

6 pounds eggplant
3 ounces oil
4 tablespoons minced ginger
4 tablespoons minced garlic
1 cup thinly sliced scallions
6 ounces green pepper, finely diced
6 ounces red pepper, finely diced
3 ounces preserved vegetables, finely diced
¼ cup hot bean paste
½ cup rice wine vinegar
¼ cup sugar
1 tablespoon salt
1 tablespoon pepper
1 cup soy sauce
1 pint chicken stock
½ cup oyster sauce
1 tablespoon cornstarch
½ cup water
2 tablespoons sesame oil

1. Peel eggplant and cut into 2-inch-long strips. Steam until half cooked. Reserve.
2. Stir-fry ginger, garlic, and scallions in oil.
3. Add peppers and preserved vegetables and stir-fry until peppers are tender.
4. Add bean paste, vinegar, sugar, salt, pepper, soy sauce, stock, and oyster sauce and bring to a simmer.
5. Combine cornstarch and water and add to stock mixture. Return to a simmer.
6. Add eggplant and simmer long enough to finish cooking eggplant and blend flavors. Add sesame oil.

JULIENNED VEGETABLES
YIELD: 25 servings

6 ounces butter
12 ounces carrots, julienned
12 ounces celery, julienned
12 ounces turnips, julienned
12 ounces leeks, julienned
12 ounces yellow squash, julienned
12 ounces zucchini, julienned
   salt and pepper, to taste

1. Sweat carrots, celery, and turnips in butter until half cooked.
2. Add leeks and sweat 2–3 minutes longer.
3. Add yellow squash and zucchini and cook until tender. Season.

MASHY COUSA (STUFFED SQUASH)
YIELD: 25 servings

25 zucchini or yellow squash, 3–4 ounces each
½ cup olive oil
12 ounces onions, minced
1 tablespoon minced garlic
4 ounces scallions, finely diced
¾ cup chopped parsley
2 tablespoons chopped dill
2 tablespoons chopped mint
¼ cup lemon juice
1 tablespoon turmeric
1 tablespoon oregano
1 tablespoon ground cumin
1 tablespoon ground coriander
1 tablespoon fennel seeds, crushed
1 teaspoon cinnamon
3 ounces ginger, minced
6 ounces pine nuts, toasted
6 eggs, beaten
3 cups cooked rice
3 pounds ground lamb
    salt and pepper, to taste
1 quart tomato sauce

1. Hollow out the center of the squash with an apple corer, leaving the end intact to hold stuffing.
2. To make the stuffing, sauté onion, garlic, scallions, and parsley in oil. Cool.
3. Combine remaining ingredients, except tomato sauce, and mix well.
4. Stuff squash and place in a pan. Top with tomato sauce.
5. Bake, covered, in a 350°F oven until squash is tender, about 40 minutes.

RAINBOW GARDEN
YIELD: 25 3-ounce servings

½ cup oil
1 pound carrots, cut into fine julienne
1½ pounds celery, cut into fine julienne
1 pound daikon, cut into fine julienne
1 pound yellow squash, cut into fine julienne
1 pound zucchini, cut into fine julienne
4 tablespoons minced ginger
4 tablespoons minced garlic
1 cup thinly sliced scallions
½ cup light soy sauce

1. Stir-fry carrots, celery, and daikon in oil until half cooked.
2. Add yellow squash and zucchini and stir-fry.
3. Add ginger, garlic, and scallions and stir-fry. Finish with soy sauce.

SAUTÉED SPINACH AND PROSCIUTTO
YIELD: 25 3-ounce servings

9 ounces olive oil
12 cloves garlic, minced
12 ounces onions, minced
4½ ounces prosciutto, finely shredded
6 pounds spinach, trimmed and washed
6 ounces Parmesan cheese, grated
salt and pepper, to taste

1. Sauté garlic and onions in olive oil.
2. Add prosciutto and spinach and sauté until spinach wilts.
3. Add cheese and season.

SPINACH SOUFFLÉ
YIELD: 25 4-ounce servings

5 pounds spinach, trimmed and cleaned
6 ounces butter
6 ounces flour
1½ pints half-and-half
pinch of grated nutmeg
salt, to taste
4 egg yolks
8 egg whites, beaten
1 cup grated Parmesan cheese

1. Cook spinach quickly in salted boiling water. Drain, immediately immerse in cold water, drain, and chop.
2. Combine butter and flour and cook 2–3 minutes. Add half-and-half and bring to a simmer, stirring constantly.
3. Simmer sauce 10 minutes. Add spinach and season with nutmeg and salt.
4. Stir a little sauce into the egg yolks to prevent curdling; then add the heated yolks to the remaining sauce. Let cool.
5. Whip egg whites to a soft peak and fold into spinach mixture.
6. Fill buttered soufflé dishes halfway and sprinkle with Parmesan cheese.
7. Bake in water bath in a 350°F oven until done, approximately 12 minutes.

STEAMED SPINACH
YIELD: 25 4-ounce servings

5½ pounds spinach, trimmed and washed
6 ounces butter
6 shallots, minced
   salt and pepper, to taste
   grated nutmeg, to taste

1. Sauté shallots in butter. Add all of the spinach, cover, and allow to steam. (Be careful not to burn spinach.)
2. When spinach is wilted and tender, season.

Note: The spinach can be cooked first and reheated in the butter and shallots.

STIR-FRIED VEGETABLES
YIELD: 25 servings

  7 ounces peanut oil
 12 ounces carrots, sliced thin
 14 ounces red pepper, sliced thin
 12 ounces celery, sliced thin
 12 ounces snow peas
 15 ounces onions, sliced
 15 ounces mushrooms, cut in quarters
 12 ounces broccoli flowerettes, blanched
  3 tablespoons minced ginger
  1 tablespoon minced garlic
  6 ounces soy sauce
  3 ounces sherry
 18 ounces stock
  3 heaping tablespoons cornstarch
    salt, to taste

1. Stir-fry carrots, red pepper, and celery in oil until half cooked.
2. Add snow peas, onion, mushrooms, and broccoli and stir-fry until the vegetables are almost done.
3. Mix ginger, garlic, soy sauce, sherry, stock, and cornstarch; stir well.
4. Add ginger mixture to vegetables and bring to a boil, stirring constantly. Adjust salt.

VEGETABLE FLAN
YIELD: 25 servings

 1½ pounds broccoli, or other vegetable
  3 ounces butter
  3 ounces onion, diced
 12 ounces heavy cream
  9 eggs, beaten
    salt and pepper, to taste
    grated nutmeg, to taste

1. Place broccoli in rapidly boiling salted water. Cook until firm.
2. Drain and immediately immerse in cold water. Drain again and reserve.
3. Sauté onions in butter until onions are translucent.
4. Combine drained broccoli and onion and purée in a food processor.
5. Mix broccoli purée with heavy cream and eggs.

6. Season and pour into buttered 2-ounce soufflé cups.
7. Bake in water bath (loosely covered with foil) in a 350°F oven until set, about 20 minutes.
8. Unmold and serve.

ZUCCHINI AND PEPPERS, BAKED
YIELD: 24 4-ounce servings

12 small zucchini
 4 yellow peppers, roasted, skinned, and seeded
 ½ cup oil
 4 cloves garlic, minced
 5 pounds tomatoes, peeled, seeded, and chopped
4–5 leaves basil
   salt and pepper, to taste
12 anchovy fillets, split lengthwise
25 slices mozzarella cheese

1. Blanch zucchini in boiling salted water. Drain and split in half.
2. Cut peppers into strips.
3. Sauté garlic in oil and add tomatoes and basil. Reduce until sauce consistency and season.
4. Top each zucchini half with tomato sauce, a pepper strip, anchovy fillet, and mozzarella slice.
5. Bake zucchini in a 350°F oven until cheese melts, approximately 12 minutes.

ZUCCHINI SAUTÉ WITH TOMATOES AND BASIL
YIELD: 25 3-ounce servings

 8 ounces butter
 6 ounces onion, minced
 5 pounds zucchini, sliced ¼″ thick
 9 tomatoes, skinned, seeded, and diced
1½ cloves garlic, minced
 3 teaspoons fresh basil, chopped
   salt and pepper, to taste

1. Sauté onions in butter until translucent.
2. Add zucchini and sauté until three-quarters done.
3. Add tomatoes, garlic, basil, and seasonings.
4. Sauté until tomatoes are hot.

POTATOES,
·PASTA, GRAINS·

Baked Semolina Dumplings
Barley Pilaf
Couscous Timbales
Dirty Rice
Fettuccine with Broccoli and Pine Nuts
Fried Rice
Grilled Polenta
Lemon Pepper Pasta
Potatoes au Gratin
Rice Pilaf
Risotto
Savoyard Potato
Spinach Spaetzle
Steamed Rice
Wild Rice Patties

BAKED SEMOLINA DUMPLINGS
YIELD: 25 servings

2½ quarts milk
6 ounces butter
1½ tablespoons salt
   pinch of grated nutmeg
22–24 ounces semolina or cream of wheat
4 egg yolks
1¾ cups grated Parmesan cheese
2 ounces butter, melted
1 cup grated Parmesan cheese, for topping

1. Combine milk, butter, salt, and nutmeg and bring to a simmer.
2. Sprinkle in the semolina, stirring constantly to prevent lumping.
3. Cook until thickened. Cover and bake in a 325°F oven for 15–20 minutes.
4. Spread gnocchi mixture ½ inch thick on a buttered tray. Refrigerate until firm.
5. Cut into desired shapes and arrange on a buttered dish. Sprinkle with cheese.
6. Bake in a 425°F oven until golden brown and hot.

BARLEY PILAF
YIELD: 25 servings

6 ounces butter
12 ounces leeks, medium dice, white part only
8 ounces celery, sliced thin
4 cups barley
7 cups brown stock
1 cup red wine
4 bay leaves
¾ cup chopped parsley
½ cup chopped chives
   salt and pepper, to taste

1. Sauté leeks and celery in butter.
2. Add barley and stir until coated with fat.
3. Add stock, wine, and bay leaves and bring to a simmer. Season.
4. Cover and bake in a 350°F oven for 35–40 minutes. Stir in parsley and chives.

COUSCOUS TIMBALES
YIELD: 25 servings

4 ounces butter
8 ounces onion, minced
5 cups couscous
2½ quarts stock, seasoned
1 ounce parsley, chopped

1. Sauté onion in butter until translucent.
2. Add couscous and sauté, stirring until coated with butter.
3. Add stock, and bring to a simmer.
4. Cover and bake in a 350°F oven until couscous has asborbed all the liquid, approximately 25 minutes.
5. Stir in parsley. Pack in a timbale mold, and unmold on plate to serve.

DIRTY RICE
YIELD: 25 servings

1 pound chicken livers
1 pound chicken giblets
4 ounces butter
8 ounces onion, minced
8 ounces celery, minced
1 ounce Cajun seasoning
1 ounce parsley, chopped
5 pounds cooked rice, hot

1. Sauté chicken livers in a small amount of butter. Chill, chop, and reserve.
2. Simmer giblets in water until tender. Drain, trim, chop, and reserve.
3. Sauté onion and celery in remaining butter.
4. Combine rice with livers, giblets, vegetables, seasoning, and parsley.

FETTUCCINE WITH BROCCOLI AND PINE NUTS
YIELD: 25 servings

  5 ounces butter
  1½ cups shallots, minced
  10 cloves garlic, minced
  2 quarts broccoli stems, chopped
  3 sprigs tarragon
  3 bay leaves
  1½ cups white wine
  1½ pints chicken stock
  6 ounces cooked chickpeas
  3 cups heavy cream
     salt and pepper, to taste
  5 pounds fettuccine
  6 cups broccoli flowerettes, blanched
  3 cups cooked chickpeas
  2¼ cups grated Asiago cheese
  1½ cups pine nuts, toasted

1. Sauté the shallots and garlic in butter; do not brown. Add broccoli stems, tarragon, bay leaves, and wine and sweat until the broccoli is tender.
2. Add the stock and 6 ounces of chickpeas. Purée in a blender.
3. Finish with heavy cream and adjust consistency; season.
4. Cook pasta in boiling water and drain. Toss with sauce, broccoli flowerettes, and 3 cups of chickpeas.
5. Arrange pasta on a plate and garnish with cheese and pine nuts.

FRIED RICE
YIELD: 25 servings

  4 ounces peanut oil
  5 eggs, beaten
  8 ounces onions, diced
  1 pound bean sprouts
  4 scallions, sliced
  1 ounce parsley, chopped
  ½ cup soy sauce
  1 pound meat or shrimp, cooked and chopped
  6 pounds cooked rice, day-old

1. Scramble eggs in 1 ounce oil. Remove, chop, and reserve.
2. Sauté the onion and bean sprouts in the remaining oil.
3. Add the scallions, parsley, soy sauce, and meat and sauté briefly.
4. Add rice and sauté, stirring constantly, until all ingredients are mixed.

GRILLED POLENTA

YIELD: 25 servings

1¼ ounces butter
1½ teaspoons garlic
2 cups skim milk
3½ cups white stock
3½ cups chicken stock
1 pound cornmeal
2 teaspoons salt
black pepper, to taste

1. Sweat garlic in butter. Add milk and stocks and bring to a simmer.
2. Slowly sprinkle in cornmeal, stirring constantly. Bring to a simmer.
3. Bake, covered, in a 350°F oven, until thick (about 45 minutes). Stir occasionally.
4. Pour into a buttered hotel pan and cool.
5. Cut into portions and grill or bake as needed.

Note: Finished polenta should be crisp on the outside and warm in the middle.

LEMON PEPPER PASTA

YIELD: 25 servings

4½ pounds semolina flour
pinch of salt
20 eggs, beaten
1½ tablespoons black pepper
1½ tablespoons grated lemon zest
butter

1. Mix all ingredients together to form a smooth dough.
2. Let the dough rest, covered, 1 hour in the refrigerator.
3. Roll through the pasta machine to the second from the thinnest setting.
4. Cut into noodles and dry 15 minutes. Cook in boiling salted water until done.
5. Drain and toss with butter.

POTATOES AU GRATIN

YIELD: 25 servings

8 pounds red bliss potatoes
3 pints skim milk
1½ teaspoons salt
1½ teaspoons minced garlic

6 ounces red onions, minced
12 ounces Parmesan cheese
¾ ounce arrowroot
3 ounces water
6 ounces white bread crumbs

1. Cut unpeeled potatoes into ⅛-inch slices. Immerse immediately in skim milk.
2. Add salt and garlic and simmer until potatoes are tender.
3. Add half the cheese. Combine arrowroot with water and use to thicken sauce. Return to a boil.
4. Pour potato mixture into a hotel pan. Top with bread crumbs and remaining cheese.
5. Bake in a 400°F oven until browned.

RICE PILAF
YIELD: 24 servings

4 ounces butter
8 ounces onion, finely chopped
4 cups rice
8 cups stock, well seasoned
1 bouquet garni (optional) of parsley, thyme, and bay leaf
2 ounces butter

1. Sauté onions in butter until translucent. Add rice and stir until coated with fat.
2. Add stock and bouquet garni. Return to a simmer.
3. Cover and bake in a 350°F oven for 18–20 minutes.
4. Remove from oven and rest 5 minutes.
5. Fluff with a fork and finish with butter.

VARIATIONS

Saffron Pilaf: Infuse 1 teaspoon saffron in stock before adding to the rice.

Risi Bisi: Add cooked peas, sautéed diced ham, and red pepper to finished pilaf.

Herb: Add fresh chopped herbs to the stock.

Nut: Add sautéed or toasted nuts to finished pilaf.

Barley: Substitute barley for rice, using the standard pilaf method. Increase stock to 11–12 cups.

RISOTTO
YIELD: 25 servings

4 ounces butter
8 ounces onions, minced
1 clove garlic, mashed to a paste
4 cups short round-grain rice
10–11 cups stock, well seasoned
4 ounces Parmesan cheese, grated
2 ounces butter

1. Sauté onions in butter until translucent.
2. Add garlic and sauté briefly.
3. Add rice and stir until coated with fat.
4. Add stock 2 cups at a time, adding each additional cup after the preceding one has been absorbed by the rice.
5. Simmer slowly, uncovered, stirring often.
6. When all liquid has been absorbed, stir in cheese and butter. Rice should remain firm and be in a creamy liquid.

SAVOYARD POTATO
YIELD: 24 servings

5 pounds potatoes, peeled and sliced
14 ounces Gruyère cheese, grated
1 clove garlic, minced
4 eggs, beaten
salt and pepper, to taste
2½ pints stock

1. Mix all ingredients except stock.
2. Shingle potatoes in a full-size hotel pan.
3. Add stock and bake 30 minutes, loosely covered, in a 350°F oven.
4. Finish baking, uncovered, until potatoes are tender, approximately 45 minutes.

SPINACH SPAETZLE
YIELD: 25 servings

2 pounds flour
8 eggs, beaten
1½ pounds spinach, cleaned, blanched, and puréed
1½ ounces Sapsago cheese, grated
milk
salt and pepper, to taste
grated nutmeg, to taste

1. Combine flour, eggs, spinach, and cheese and mix well. Adjust consistency with milk (mixture should be slightly glutenous).
2. Add seasonings. Push batter through a spaetzle press into boiling salted water.
3. Simmer spaetzle until expanded. Drain, immerse immediately in cold water, and drain well.
4. Reheat by sautéing in butter.

STEAMED RICE
YIELD: 25 servings

4 ounces butter
2½ quarts stock or water
1 tablespoon salt
5 cups rice

1. Heat stock and add butter and salt.
2. Stir in rice and place in a hotel pan. Cover with a lid.
3. Place pan in a steamer and cook until rice has absorbed all liquid.
4. Remove and let sit 10 minutes. Fluff with a fork before serving.

WILD RICE PATTIES
YIELD: 25 servings

1 ounce butter
4 ounces onion, diced
4 cups cooked white rice
4 cups cooked wild rice
3–4 cups bechamel sauce, very thick
2 teaspoons chopped parsley
salt and pepper, to taste
fresh white bread crumbs
butter, for frying

1. Combine all ingredients except for bread crumbs and mix well. Season.
2. Portion and shape into 25 patties. Dredge in bread crumbs.
3. Brown rice patties in butter.

·SALADS·

Banana Salad
Chinese Cabbage Salad
Cobb Salad
Cucumber, Onion, and Seaweed Salad
Cucumbers and Sour Cream
Kokonda Salad (African fish salad)
Marinated Greek Salad
Mexican Corn Salad
Oriental Duck Salad
Potato Salad with Apples
Romaine, Orange, and Red Onion Salad with
    Honey-Tarragon Dressing
Tabbouleh Salad
Tortellini Salad
Wurst Salad

BANANA SALAD
YIELD: 25 4-ounce servings

10 pounds bananas
1 15-ounce can coconut cream
3 tablespoons curry powder
1 cup raisins
1 pound coconut, toasted

1. Purée four bananas with the coconut cream. Add curry powder.
2. Slice the remaining bananas and mix with the raisins and coconut cream/banana mixture. Chill.
3. Garnish with toasted coconut.

CHINESE CABBAGE SALAD
YIELD: 25 1-cup servings

6 quarts Chinese cabbage, shredded
2 pounds canned pineapple, crushed and drained
3 green peppers, diced
2 quarts celery, peeled and diced
   Boston lettuce

DRESSING
1½ cups vegetable oil
6 ounces vinegar
¼ cup soy sauce
3 cloves garlic, minced

1. Combine all ingredients for dressing and mix well.
2. Add salad ingredients, mix, and marinate 1–2 hours.
3. Serve on a bed of Boston lettuce.

COBB SALAD
YIELD: 25 servings

1½ quarts French Dressing (recipe follows)
8 tomatoes, peeled, seeded, and chopped
1¼ pounds cabbage, thinly sliced into 1" strips
3 avocados, peeled, pits removed, and cut into ¼" cubes
   juice from 1 lemon
2 pounds cooked chicken, cut into ¼" cubes
2 pounds blue cheese, crumbled
1¼ pounds bacon, diced and fried crisp
   romaine lettuce, shredded

COBB SALAD
(continued)

1. Marinate tomatoes in half the French dressing. Marinate the cabbage in the remaining half.
2. Toss avocados in lemon juice.
3. Line a platter with shredded romaine lettuce. Arrange uniform piles of avocado, chicken, blue cheese and drained tomato around the platter.
4. Place drained cabbage between the chicken and blue cheese.
5. Sprinkle chopped bacon over the cabbage.

FRENCH DRESSING

1½ cups white wine vinegar
4½ cups oil
 1 teaspoon dry mustard
   salt and pepper, to taste

1. Whip seasoning into vinegar.
2. Slowly add oil and continue to whip until emulsified.

CUCUMBER, ONION, AND SEAWEED SALAD
YIELD: 25 3½-ounce servings

 6 pounds cucumbers, peeled and sliced thin
1½ pounds onion, sliced thin
 2 ounces sugar
 1 tablespoon salt
 1 teaspoon pepper
 1 pint cider vinegar
 1 cup cold water
 1 cup salad oil
 3 ounces dried seaweed, soaked in water and cut into 1″ pieces

1. Combine all ingredients except seaweed and marinate for 1–2 hours.
2. Add seaweed and gently combine.

CUCUMBERS AND SOUR CREAM

YIELD: 25 servings

7 pounds cucumbers, peeled and sliced
salt
½ cup vinegar
1½ pints sour cream
1½ pints mayonnaise
¼ cup sugar
1 cup lemon juice
salt and pepper, to taste
2 tablespoons chopped dill

1. Combine cucumbers with salt and vinegar. Allow to marinate for 30 minutes. Drain.
2. To make dressing, combine sour cream, mayonnaise, sugar, lemon juice, salt and pepper, and dill and mix well.
3. Mix cucumbers with dressing.

Note: Yogurt can be substituted for the mayonnaise and mint for the dill.

KOKONDA SALAD (AFRICAN FISH SALAD)

YIELD: 25 4-ounce servings

6 pounds firm white fish, cooked and flaked
1 cup lemon juice
4 red peppers, shredded
8 bananas, sliced
4 green peppers, shredded
1 pound grated coconut
8 tomatoes, peeled, seeded, and chopped
1 pound pineapple, cut into ½″ cubes

DRESSING
3 cups sour cream
8 green chilies, minced
1 teaspoon ground cumin
salt and pepper, to taste

1. Combine all ingredients for the salad.
2. Combine all ingredients for the dressing and mix well. Add to salad.
3. Mix gently without breaking up fish and refrigerate 1–2 hours.

MARINATED
GREEK SALAD
YIELD: 25 3½-ounce servings

1½ quarts French Dressing (see page 304)
  1 tablespoon oregano
15 tomatoes, peeled, seeded, and chopped
  3 red peppers, cut into ¼″ cubes and blanched
  4 green peppers, cut into ¼″ cubes and blanched
  5 cucumbers, peeled and cut into ¼″ cubes
  2 red onions, small dice
50 Greek olives
1½ pounds feta cheese, crumbled

1. Combine all ingredients except feta cheese and mix well.
2. Arrange on a platter and sprinkle with cheese.

MEXICAN CORN
SALAD
YIELD: 25 4-ounce servings

  1 pound corn kernels, cooked
  1 pound green peppers, small dice
  1 pound red peppers, small dice
 ¼ can green chilies, small dice
  8 ounces tomatillos, small dice
  8 ounces red onion, small dice
  8 ounces zucchini, small dice
  4 ounces black olives, pitted
 ½ cup chopped parsley
  1 pound Monterey Jack cheese, small dice
  6 tomatoes, peeled, seeded, and chopped

DRESSING
1½ cups olive oil
1½ cups vegetable oil
  1 cup lemon juice
  1 tablespoon oregano
  1 tablespoon ground cumin
    salt and pepper, to taste

1. Combine all ingredients for the salad except cheese and tomatoes.
2. Combine all ingredients for the dressing and mix well.
3. Mix salad with dressing and marinate for 1–2 hours. Drain excess dressing and add tomatoes and cheese.
4. Garnish with black olives.

ORIENTAL DUCK SALAD
YIELD: 25 3-ounce servings

3 pounds duck, cooked and shredded
1 pound scallions or leeks, shredded
8 ounces water chestnuts, sliced
8 ounces bean sprouts
8 ounces celery, cut on the bias very thin
Chinese cabbage, shredded

DRESSING

6 ounces soy sauce
6 ounces dry sherry
1½ tablespoons minced ginger
1½ cloves garlic, minced
8 ounces oil
½ cup sesame seed oil
¼ cup rice wine vinegar
¾ teaspoon mustard

1. Combine all ingredients for dressing and mix well.
2. Add salad ingredients except for Chinese cabbage and allow to marinate 1–2 hours.
3. Serve on a bed of shredded Chinese cabbage.

POTATO SALAD WITH APPLES
YIELD: 25 6-ounce servings

6 pounds red bliss potatoes, peeled and cut into ½" cubes
1 pound celery, cut into ¼" cubes
1 pound onion, cut into ¼" cubes
2 pounds apples, cut into ¼" cubes
¼ cup sesame seeds, toasted, for garnish

DRESSING

1 pint salad oil
juice from 4 lemons
½ cup cider vinegar
1 tablespoon salt
½ teaspoon pepper
½ cup sugar

1. Combine all dressing ingredients and mix together until well blended.
2. Cook potatoes in boiling salted water until tender; drain.
3. Combine warm potatoes, celery, and apples with dressing and mix gently. Chill.
4. Garnish with sesame seeds.

ROMAINE, ORANGE, AND RED ONION SALAD WITH HONEY-TARRAGON DRESSING
YIELD: 25 servings

  2 quarts French dressing (see page 304)
  4 ounces honey
  1 tablespoon tarragon
  4 heads romaine lettuce (cut into 1″ pieces)
20 navel oranges, peeled, seeded, and cut in segments
  1 pound red onion, cut into 1″ julienne

1. Combine French dressing, honey, and tarragon and mix well; reserve.
2. Combine romaine lettuce, oranges, and onions and toss with dressing just before serving.

TABBOULEH SALAD
YIELD: 25 servings

  8 ounces bulgur wheat
  2 bunches parsley, chopped
  2 bunches mint, chopped
  1 red onion, minced
  4 cucumbers, cut into ¼″ cubes
  6 tomatoes, cut into ¼″ cubes
½ cup pine nuts, for garnish
  6 ounces olive oil
  4 ounces lemon juice
  3 cloves garlic, mashed to a paste
    salt and pepper, to taste

1. Boil 1 quart of water and add bulgur. Allow to sit off the heat until doubled in size, approximately 45 minutes.
2. Drain and spread on a tray to cool.
3. Combine remaining ingredients and mix well.
4. Garnish with pine nuts.

TORTELLINI SALAD
YIELD: 25 servings

2½ pounds tortellini
8 ounces Italian Dressing (recipe follows)
3 cups Pesto (recipe follows)
1¼ pounds Genoa salami, diced
1 pound red onion, diced
8 ounces celery, diced
8 ounces red pepper, diced
8 ounces green pepper, diced
8 ounces tomatoes, peeled, seeded, and chopped

1. Cook tortellini in boiling salted water until tender. Drain and mix with Italian Dressing.
2. Add remaining ingredients and mix gently. Serve at room temperature.

ITALIAN DRESSING

¼ cup wine vinegar
½ teaspoon basil
½ teaspoon oregano
½ teaspoon minced garlic
6 ounces olive oil

1. Mix herbs and garlic in vinegar.
2. Whip in olive oil until well emulsified.

PESTO

3 cloves garlic, mashed to a paste
2 cups chopped fresh basil
½ cup chopped fresh parsley
½ cup chopped roasted pine nuts

Finely chop all ingredients or purée in a food processor.

WURST SALAD
YIELD: 25 6-ounce servings

8 pounds German sausage (knockwurst or bratwurst, skinned and sliced)
8 green peppers, julienned
8 red peppers, julienned
8 onions, thinly sliced
1 cup gherkins, julienned

DRESSING
1 quart salad oil
1½ cups cider vinegar
1½ teaspoons dry mustard
1 teaspoon paprika
1 teaspoon salt
1 teaspoon sugar
  pepper, to taste
2 cloves garlic, minced

1. Combine all salad ingredients.
2. Combine all dressing ingredients and mix well.
3. Combine salad with dressing and marinate for 1–2 hours.

·DESSERTS·

Apple Flan
Apple Strudel
Spun Apples
*Fresh Fruit Bavarian and Fruit Salsa
Fruit Cobbler with Wild Turkey Bourbon Sauce
Fruit Torte
Glazed Pineapple Madagascar
Poached Gingered Pear
Poached Pears with Rice Filling
Albert Kumin's Chocolate Truffles
Chocolate Bread Pudding
Chocolate Polenta Soufflé
Chocolate Terrine with Mint Sauce
Flan de Maranja (orange custard)
Ginger Custard
Ginger Mousse
Orange Yogurt Cream
St. Andrew's Glacé (low-fat ice cream)
Vermont Maple Mousse
Almond Macaroons
Baklava (Greek filo and nut pastry)
Dark Hard Ganache
Frangipane (petits fours)
Linzer Dough
Pecan Diamonds
Plättar (Swedish pancakes)
Wine Gelée with Fresh Fruit

*Starred recipes meet recommended dietary guidelines for calories, carbohydrates, protein, and fat. See Chapter 12 for complete nutritional menus.

APPLE FLAN
YIELD: 25 servings

10–12 green apples, peeled and cored
    8 ounces sugar
      cinnamon, to taste
    2 pounds pie crust or Sweet Pie Dough (recipe follows)
1½ pints heavy cream or half-and-half
  12 ounces beaten eggs
      vanilla, to taste
    4 ounces hazelnuts, ground
    4 ounces apricot glaze, melted

1. Cut apples into slices and toss with sugar and cinnamon.
2. Roll out pie crust and line two quiche pans. Flute and trim edges.
3. Line dough with parchment paper or foil and fill with dried beans or pie weights.
4. Prebake pie shells in a 375°F oven for 15 minutes, or until they are half cooked.
5. Remove paper and beans and line pan neatly with apple slices.
6. Mix heavy cream, eggs, and vanilla and pour over apples.
7. Bake in a 350°F oven until browned and custard is set, approximately 30 minutes.
8. Cool slightly and brush with apricot glaze.

SWEET PIE DOUGH NO. 1
YIELD: 1½ pounds

  4 ounces sugar
  8 ounces butter
12 ounces flour
½ teaspoon grated lemon zest
    vanilla, to taste
  1 egg, beaten

1. Combine sugar, butter, and flour and rub together with your hands until fine and crumbly.
2. Mix in lemon zest, vanilla, and egg. Wrap in plastic wrap and chill before using.

SWEET PIE DOUGH NO. 2
YIELD: 2 pounds

14 ounces flour
12¼ ounces butter
3 ounces sugar
1 teaspoon grated orange zest
6 hard-cooked egg yolks, chopped

Mix all ingredients together to form a dough. Wrap in plastic wrap and chill before using.

APPLE STRUDEL
YIELD: 25 servings

FILLING

5 pounds Granny Smith apples, peeled, cored, and sliced
6 ounces butter
1½ cups golden raisins
¾ cup sugar
1½ teaspoons cinnamon
pinch of grated nutmeg

15 sheets filo dough
½ pound butter, melted
powdered sugar, for dusting
Fruit Sauce, made with raspberries (recipe follows)
St. Andrew's Glacé (page 325)

1. Mix all filling ingredients together.
2. Place on a tray and bake in a 350°F oven until apples are tender, approximately 25 minutes. Cool.
3. Lay a sheet of filo dough on a piece of parchment or wax paper and brush with butter.
4. Lay a second sheet of dough on top and brush with butter. Repeat process, making 3 rolls using 5 sheets of dough for each roll.
5. Place filling on one of the long ends and roll dough up around apples, jelly-roll fashion. Tuck ends under.
6. Place on a tray seam-side down and brush with butter.
7. Bake in a 400°F oven until browned and hot, approximately 30 minutes.
8. Dust with powdered sugar and serve with Fruit Sauce and St. Andrew's Glacé.

APPLE STRUDEL
(continued)

FRUIT SAUCE
YIELD: 30 ounces

28 ounces raspberries or strawberries, frozen
2 ounces kirschwasser
6 ounces honey

Purée berries, strain, and mix with remaining ingredients.

SPUN APPLES
YIELD: 25 servings

BATTER
6 cups flour
6 eggs, beaten
4 cups water

APPLES AND SYRUP
6 cups sugar
1½ cups cold water
12 firm apples, cored, peeled, and cut into 8 wedges

1. To make batter, combine flour, eggs, and water and set aside.
2. Combine sugar and water and bring to a boil. Cook until syrup reaches 300°F.
3. Dip apple wedges in batter and deep-fry at 360°F in peanut oil until golden brown. Drain on absorbent paper.
4. Dip fried apples in syrup and coat completely. Remove and submerge in ice water. Drain and serve.

FRESH FRUIT BAVARIAN AND FRUIT SALSA
YIELD: 25 servings

1 papaya, cut into small dice
1 pint strawberries, cut into small dice
1 honeydew melon, cut into small dice
1 cantaloupe melon, cut into small dice
1 bunch mint
17 sheets filo dough
2 ounces butter
   Fruit Bavarian, poured into 25 2-ounce molds (recipe follows)

1. Cut filo into 6 equal squares and stack 4 individual squares together. Brush top layer with butter.
2. Press dough into a muffin tin and bake in a 375°F oven until crisp and golden brown, about 10 minutes.
3. Combine fruit and divide into dough cups. Garnish with mint and serve with Fruit Bavarian.

CALORIES: 160; PROTEIN: 5.8 gm; FAT: 3.1 gm; CARBOHYDRATE: 27 gm; SODIUM: 65 mg; CHOLESTEROL: 10 mg

FRUIT BAVARIAN

14 ounces fruit purée, cooked if necessary (see note)
16 ounces nonfat yogurt
 8 ounces low-fat ricotta cheese, puréed until smooth
 6 ounces maple syrup
 2 teaspoons vanilla extract
 3 ounces water
⅔ ounce unflavored gelatin
 3 ounces port wine
 6 egg whites
 2 ounces sugar

1. Combine fruit purée, yogurt, ricotta cheese, maple syrup, and vanilla extract and mix well.
2. Combine water, gelatin, and port wine and heat over a water bath until gelatin melts.
3. Combine egg whites and sugar and whip until medium stiff peaks form.
4. Add gelatin mixture to fruit mixture a little at a time. Allow to sit until almost set and fold in beaten egg whites.
5. Pour into springform pans as described above or, for a separate dessert, pour into individual dishes or molds.

Note: Papaya, pineapple, fresh figs, and kiwi must be cooked or the gelatin will not set.

FRUIT COBBLER WITH WILD TURKEY BOURBON SAUCE
YIELD: 25 servings

4 cups flour
2½ tablespoons baking powder
4 cups sugar
8 eggs, beaten
1½ pints milk
1½ teaspoons vanilla extract
1 tablespoon grated lemon zest
4 pounds fresh fruit, sliced
1 cup sugar
cinnamon and nutmeg (optional)
Wild Turkey Sauce (recipe follows)

1. Combine flour and baking powder.
2. Mix sugar, eggs, milk, vanilla, and lemon zest. Combine with flour mixture, mixing only enough to combine ingredients.
3. Toss the fruit with 4 tablespoons sugar and arrange in the bottom of a buttered ovenproof casserole.
4. Pour the cobbler batter over the fruit and bake in a 375°F oven until golden brown, about 30–40 minutes.
5. Serve with Wild Turkey Sauce.

WILD TURKEY BOURBON SAUCE

1 quart half-and-half
12 egg yolks
8 ounces sugar
2 teaspoons vanilla extract
8 ounces Wild Turkey

1. Heat half-and-half in a stainless steel bowl over a water bath.
2. Combine egg yolks and sugar and temper into the half-and-half by adding the heated half-and-half slowly to the cold yolk mixture. Heat, stirring constantly until mixture thickens (do not boil). Strain and cool.
3. Add vanilla and Wild Turkey.

FRUIT TORTE
YIELD: 2 10-inch cakes, 12 servings each

1 10-inch layer St. Andrew's Sponge Cake (recipe follows)
Simple Syrup (recipe follows)
Fruit Bavarian (page 315)
4 ounces heavy cream, whipped

1 ounce almonds, toasted
2 ounces cake crumbs
24 strawberries
3 cups Fruit Sauce, made with strawberries (page 314)

1. Split sponge cake layer in half lengthwise and place in the bottoms of two springform pans.
2. Sprinkle cake with simple syrup.
3. Fill pans with prepared bavarian. Refrigerate and allow to set for 2 hours.
4. Unmold cakes and mark 12 portions on each torte. Place a rosette of whipped cream on each portion.
5. Garnish each serving with a strawberry.
6. Cut and place on a 9-inch plate and serve with 1 ounce of Fruit Sauce.

ST. ANDREW'S SPONGE CAKE
YIELD: 2 10-inch layers

2 teaspoons cream of tartar
14 ounces powdered sugar
28 ounces egg whites
13 ounces cake flour, sifted
⅔ ounce grated lemon zest
2 ounces butter, melted
4 teaspoons vanilla extract

1. Combine cream of tartar, sugar, and egg whites and whip until medium stiff peaks form.
2. Fold in flour and lemon zest.
3. Fold in butter and vanilla.
4. Pour into two 10-inch cake pans that are greased and the bottoms lined with parchment paper.
5. Bake in a 350°F oven until center springs back when pressed and edges pull from sides of pan about ¼ inch, approximately 25 minutes.

FRUIT TORTE
(continued)

SIMPLE SYRUP

¼ cup kirschwasser
½ cup sugar
1 cup white wine

Mix ingredients, bring to a boil, and remove from heat.

**GLAZED
PINEAPPLE
MADAGASCAR**
YIELD: 25 servings

3 pineapples, peeled, cored, and cut into 25 ½″ rings
6 tablespoons green peppercorns, crushed
7 tablespoons sugar
1 quart orange juice
6 tablespoons honey
11 ounces light rum
St. Andrew's Glacé (see page 325)

1. Rub pineapple slices with green peppercorns and sprinkle one side with sugar.
2. Heat a sauté pan until very hot and add pineapple rings, sugared side down. Heat until caramelized.
3. Turn pineapple over and add orange juice, honey, and rum.
4. When pineapple is tender, remove, and place on a dessert plate.
5. Reduce sauce to syrup consistency. Pour over pineapple and garnish with a scoop of St. Andrew's Glacé.

**POACHED
GINGERED PEAR**
YIELD: 25 servings

25 firm pears
3 cinnamon sticks
1½ pounds ginger, peeled and sliced thin
9 cups sugar
2 gallons water
1 cup pine nuts, toasted

1. Peel pears and divide into 8 equal sections. Remove cores.
2. Sprinkle pears with sugar and let stand 20 minutes.
3. Combine cinnamon, ginger, and water and bring to a boil.
4. Add pears and sugar to the ginger syrup and simmer until tender, approximately 25 minutes.
5. Serve with some of the syrup and sprinkle with pine nuts.

POACHED PEARS WITH RICE FILLING

YIELD: 25 servings

2 teaspoons saffron
2 quarts white wine
1 quart water
8 cinnamon sticks
20 cloves
25 pears, cored, peeled, with stems on
Rice Filling (recipe follows)
Fruit Sauce, made with raspberries (see page 314)

1. Combine saffron, white wine, water, cinnamon sticks, and cloves and simmer 20 minutes.
2. Poach pears in wine mixture until tender. Remove and cool.
3. When ready for service, drain pears and slice vertically into about eight slices, starting 1½ inches from the stem.
4. Portion 1 ounce of Rice Filling in the center of a dessert plate and fan pear on top.
5. Carefully pour raspberry sauce around pear and tip the plate to let the sauce run into the pear.

RICE FILLING

1 quart milk
4 ounces long-grain rice
salt, to taste
2 ounces raisins
4 egg yolks
8 ounces sugar
1 teaspoon vanilla extract
4 ounces heavy cream, whipped
cinnamon, to taste (optional)

1. Combine milk, rice, and salt and simmer until rice is almost done, approximately 20 minutes.
2. Add raisins and cook until rice is soft.
3. Combine egg yolks, sugar, and vanilla. Add gradually to the rice mixture off the heat. Return to heat and cook until mixture thickens, stirring constantly. Do not allow mixture to boil.
4. Cool rice mixture and fold in whipped cream. Add cinnamon, if desired.

ALBERT KUMIN'S CHOCOLATE TRUFFLES
YIELD: 3 dozen

9 ounces semisweet chocolate, cut in ½″ pieces
8 ounces heavy cream
2 ounces butter
3 tablespoons sugar
3 tablespoons orange liqueur
¼ cup cocoa powder
⅛ cup instant coffee

1. Melt chocolate in the top of a double boiler.
2. Combine cream, butter, and sugar in a separate saucepan and bring to a boil.
3. Remove cream mixture from the heat and stir in chocolate. Add liqueur.
4. Cool mixture slightly and whip until mixture thickens, about 5 minutes.
5. Pipe into bite-size balls on parchment paper and chill.
6. Combine cocoa powder and coffee and roll truffles in this mixture just before serving.

CHOCOLATE BREAD PUDDING
YIELD: 25 servings

10 ounces brioche or other bread
12 ounces heavy cream
12 ounces semisweet chocolate
 8 ounces butter
12 egg yolks
1¼ cup almonds, finely ground
 1 pound sugar
12 egg whites
½ cup sugar
   Vanilla Sauce (recipe follows)

1. Soak bread in cream and purée in food processor.
2. Melt chocolate and butter together. Add bread mixture, egg yolks, almonds, and sugar and mix well.
3. Whip egg whites and sugar until soft peaks form and fold into chocolate mixture.
4. Pour into buttered molds. Bake in a water bath, in a 350°F oven for 20–25 minutes.
5. Cool to room temperature, unmold, and serve with Vanilla Sauce.

VANILLA SAUCE

1 quart half-and-half
16 egg yolks
8 ounces sugar
   dash of vanilla

1. Heat half-and-half in a stainless steel bowl or double boiler.
2. Combine egg yolks and sugar and temper into half-and-half by adding the hot mixture slowly to the cold so that the eggs don't cook too quickly. Heat, stirring constantly, until mixture thickens (do not boil). Strain and cool.
3. Add vanilla.

CHOCOLATE POLENTA SOUFFLÉ
YIELD: 25 servings

   cake crumbs, for dusting
52 ounces skim milk
   zest from 3 oranges
11 ounces sugar
1 ounce unsweetened cocoa
7 ounces cornmeal
4½ ounces unsweetened chocolate
14½ ounces egg whites
2 ounces sugar
   powdered sugar
1 quart Cappuccino Glacé (recipe follows)

1. Butter 25 individual soufflé molds and dust with cake crumbs.
2. Heat milk with orange zest and let sit for 10 minutes. Discard zest.
3. Combine 9 ounces sugar, cocoa, and cornmeal and mix together.
4. Bring milk to a simmer and sprinkle in sugar-cornmeal mixture, stirring constantly.
5. Simmer 20 minutes, stirring occasionally. Remove from heat.
6. Add chocolate, allow to melt, and cool to room temperature.
7. Combine egg whites and remaining sugar; whip until medium stiff peaks form.
8. Bake soufflés in a water bath in a 400°F oven until done, approximately 20 minutes. (Soufflés will increase in size; the center should still be creamy.)
9. Unmold on a 9-inch plate. Dust with powdered sugar and serve with 2 ounces of Cappuccino Glacé.

(continued)

**CHOCOLATE POLENTA
SOUFFLÉ**
(continued)

CAPPUCCINO GLACÉ
YIELD: 60 ounces

17 ounces skim milk
20 dark roast coffee beans
17 ounces nonfat yogurt
17 ounces low-fat ricotta cheese
 9 ounces maple syrup
      cinnamon, to taste

1. Bring milk to a simmer with 20 coffee beans, then remove from heat and let steep 20 minutes. Remove beans.
2. Combine all ingredients and purée in a food processor.
3. Place in an ice cream freezer and freeze according to manufacturer's instructions.

**CHOCOLATE
TERRINE WITH
MINT SAUCE**
YIELD: 25 servings

4 pounds semisweet chocolate
1 pound corn syrup
8 ounces butter
8 ounces water or liquor
2 quarts heavy cream
12 egg yolks
1 cup powdered sugar
2 teaspoons vanilla extract
    Mint Sauce (recipe follows)
25 mint sprigs

1. Melt together the chocolate, corn syrup, butter, and water.
2. Combine half the cream with the egg yolks.
3. Add the heavy cream and egg yolks to the chocolate mixture and cook 2–3 minutes. Cool to room temperature.
4. Combine the remaining heavy cream, sugar, and vanilla and whip until soft peaks form. Fold in the chocolate mixture.
5. Pour into two 10-inch terrine molds that are lined with plastic wrap. Chill overnight.
6. Unmold terrine and peel off plastic wrap. Slice ¾ inch thick and arrange on a plate. Serve with Mint Sauce and decorate with a mint sprig.

MINT SAUCE

- 1 quart half-and-half
- 12 egg yolks
- 8 ounces sugar
- 2 teaspoons vanilla extract
  few drops of mint extract

1. Heat half-and-half in a stainless steel bowl over a water bath.
2. Combine egg yolks and sugar and temper into half-and-half by adding the hot liquid slowly to the cold eggs. Heat, stirring constantly, until the mixture thickens (do not boil). Strain and cool.
3. Flavor with mint and vanilla.

FLAN DE MARANJA (ORANGE CUSTARD)

YIELD: 25 4-ounce servings

- 1½ pounds sugar (for caramel)
- 2 quarts milk
- 1½ pounds sugar
- 2 tablespoons vanilla extract
- 2 teaspoons grated orange zest
- 2 cinnamon sticks
- 16 eggs, beaten
- 4 egg yolks
- 6 oranges, peeled and segmented, for garnish

1. Caramelize the sugar by heating carefully in a heavy-bottomed pan and stirring until golden brown. Pour into the bottom of 25 custard cups.
2. Combine milk, sugar, vanilla, orange zest, and cinnamon and bring to a simmer.
3. Combine eggs and egg yolks and add some of the hot milk, stirring constantly.
4. Add the egg mixture back to the remaining milk, stirring constantly. Remove cinnamon sticks.
5. Pour custard into cups and bake in a water bath in a 325°F oven for 35–40 minutes.
6. Chill and unmold on a plate.
7. Garnish with orange segments.

GINGER CUSTARD
YIELD: 25 servings

2½ quarts milk
10 slices ginger root
1½ pounds sugar
15 eggs, beaten
 1 tablespoon vanilla extract

1. Scald milk. Add ginger and steep 20 minutes.
2. Combine sugar, eggs, and vanilla and temper into milk mixture by adding the hot liquid very slowly to the cold. Strain.
3. Pour into 25 buttered custard cups and bake in a water bath in a 325°F oven until set, approximately 30 minutes.

GINGER MOUSSE
YIELD: 25 servings

 4 ounces crystallized ginger, chopped
 1 cup water
 1 quart milk
12 egg yolks
 1 cup sugar
 1 ounce unflavored gelatin
10 ounces rum
12 egg whites
12 ounces heavy cream
 1 quart whipping or heavy cream (sweetened)
½ cup crystallized ginger, finely julienned
    chocolate shavings

1. Combine the ginger and water and bring to a boil. Remove from the heat and allow to steep for 20 minutes.
2. Heat the milk in a stainless steel bowl over a water bath.
3. Mix the egg yolks and sugar and temper by adding the hot liquid slowly and stirring. Heat until thickened, stirring constantly. Remove from heat.
4. Dissolve the gelatin in the ginger and water and add to the milk-egg yolk mixture. Allow to melt.
5. Flame the rum by heating in a sauté pan and allowing the alcohol to burn off. Add to the gelatin mixture. Chill until almost set.
6. Whip the egg whites to stiff peaks and fold into mousse.
7. Whip the heavy cream and fold into mousse. Pour mousse into champagne glasses and chill.
8. Decorate with whipped cream, chocolate shavings, and ginger.

ORANGE YOGURT CREAM

YIELD: 25 servings

1½ tablespoons grated orange zest
    juice from 12 oranges
  8 ounces sugar
  3 tablespoons unflavored gelatin
  4 ounces almond-flavored liqueur
  4 ounces water
1½ pints yogurt
  1 pint cream, whipped
 25 short dough bases (see Sweet Pie Dough, pages 312–313)
 25 orange slices, for garnish

1. Combine orange zest, orange juice, and sugar and heat to a boil.
2. Dissolve gelatin in liqueur and water and add to orange juice mixture.
3. Heat to dissolve gelatin and mix in yogurt. Allow to cool slightly at room temperature.
4. Fold in whipped cream and pour into 25 2½-ounce molds.
5. When set, unmold onto short dough bases cut just a little bigger than the individual molds. Decorate with orange slices.

ST. ANDREW'S GLACÉ (LOW-FAT ICE CREAM)

YIELD: 25 ½-cup servings

50 ounces nonfat yogurt
35 ounces low-fat ricotta cheese
20 ounces maple syrup
2½ tablespoons vanilla extract

1. Purée ricotta cheese in a food processor with a steel blade until very smooth.
2. Combine with remaining ingredients and mix thoroughly.
3. Pour mixture into an ice cream freezer and freeze according to manufacturer's directions.
4. Store in a tightly covered container in the freezer.

Note: Puréed fruit (1½ cups) may be added for variation.

VERMONT MAPLE MOUSSE
YIELD: 25 servings

12 egg yolks
6 ounces dark brown sugar
18 ounces maple syrup
3 tablespoons unflavored gelatin
6 ounces water
8 egg whites, whipped to soft peaks
36 ounces heavy cream, whipped
   Citrus Sauce (recipe follows)
1½ pints cream, whipped
   chocolate shavings, for garnish

1. Beat egg yolks and brown sugar until creamy. Add maple syrup.
2. Place mixture in a stainless steel bowl over a water bath. Heat until mixture thickens, stirring constantly. Remove from heat.
3. Add gelatin to water and allow to soften. Combine gelatin with maple syrup mixture and allow to melt. Chill mixture until almost set.
4. Fold in egg whites and then whipped cream.
5. Pipe into champagne glasses.
6. Pour sauce over top and garnish with whipped cream and chocolate shavings.

CITRUS SAUCE

juice and grated zest from 6 lemons
juice and grated zest from 6 oranges
6 ounces sugar
3 teaspoons arrowroot
6 ounces Grand Marnier

1. Combine lemon and orange zests and juices, sugar, and arrowroot.
2. Bring to a boil and simmer for 2–3 minutes.
3. Chill and add Grand Marnier.

ALMOND MACAROONS
YIELD: 350 ¾-inch cookies

2 pounds almond paste
2 pounds granulated sugar
10 ounces egg whites, approximately

1. Combine almond paste and sugar and mix with a paddle at medium speed until almond paste is completely combined with the sugar.
2. Add egg whites gradually and mix until it forms a medium stiff paste.
3. Press out with a plain tube on paper-lined sheet pans.
4. Dampen macaroons with a towel before baking. (Do not allow macaroons to dry before placing in the oven.)
5. Bake at 325°F until lightly browned.

BAKLAVA (GREEK FILO AND NUT PASTRY)
YIELD: 25 pieces

FILLING
8 ounces almonds, toasted
8 ounces walnuts, toasted
4 ounces sugar
4–6 ounces butter, clarified
1 box filo dough

SYRUP
zest from 1 lemon
1 cinnamon stick
3 cloves
¾ cup sugar
6 ounces water
8 ounces honey

1. Combine almonds, walnuts, and sugar and process until fine in a food processor.
2. Butter a 12″ × 16″ pan. Place one sheet of dough in the pan and brush with butter. Top with a second sheet of dough and repeat until you have six layers.
3. Spread half of the nut mixture over the dough.
4. Repeat this process until you have two layers of nuts and three layers of dough.
5. Score the filo into diamond shapes and bake in a 350°F oven until golden brown, approximately 35 minutes.
6. Combine all ingredients for syrup and bring to a boil. Strain.
7. Pour syrup over dough and bake an additional 10 minutes. Let the pastry rest one hour before cutting and serving.

DARK HARD GANACHE
YIELD: 3 pounds

1 pint heavy cream
3 ounces sugar
3 ounces butter
2 pounds sweet chocolate, chopped

1. Combine cream, sugar, and butter in a saucepan. Bring to a boil and remove from heat.
2. Stir in chocolate and refrigerate.
3. Cream lightly in mixer before using.

Note: This mixture is used for cake fillings, icing, and to form truffles.

FRANGIPANE (PETITS FOURS)
YIELD: approximately 100 pieces

CAKE
3½ pounds almond paste
3½ pounds sugar
3½ pounds butter
 35 eggs
1½ pounds cake flour

FILLING
    apricot jam, approximately 2 pounds
    fondant, approximately 4 pounds
    piping gelée, assorted colors

1. To make the frangipane cake, combine almond paste and sugar. Mix until almond paste is broken up very fine.
2. Add butter and mix until smooth.
3. Add eggs slowly and mix to completely incorporate.
4. Add flour. Pour into greased sheet pans and bake at 400°F for 15–20 minutes, until golden brown. Cool.
5. To assemble, cut each frangipane sheet into four pieces and split each piece in half. Fill with apricot jam and spread a thin layer of jam on top.
6. Cut cake into desired portions (approximately 1-inch squares or circles).
7. Dip squares in tempered fondant and set on glazing rack (do not coat bottoms with fondant).
8. Decorate petits fours with piping gelée.

Note: Bottoms of petits fours may be coated with chocolate.

LINZER DOUGH
YIELD: 8 10-inch cakes

2¼ pounds sugar
1½ pounds filberts (hazelnuts), ground
½ pound fine cake crumbs
3¾ pounds cake flour
1 ounce cinnamon
1 teaspoon vanilla
1 ounce baking powder
3 pounds butter
6 eggs, beaten

1. Combine all dry ingredients. Add butter and rub together until the mixture forms a fine crumb consistency.
2. Add eggs and mix until dough is formed. Chill.

PECAN DIAMONDS
YIELD: 300 1″ diamonds

COOKIE BASE
1 pound sugar
2 pounds butter
3 pounds cake flour
   zest of 1 lemon
3 eggs

FILLING
2 pounds butter
2 pounds light brown sugar
8 ounces sugar
1½ pounds honey
8 ounces heavy cream
4 pounds pecans, chopped

1. To make the base, combine sugar, butter, flour, and lemon zest and rub together until granular.
2. Add eggs and mix until ingredients form a dough. Chill.
3. Roll out and line an 18″ × 29″ sheet pan with dough. Bake until half cooked, approximately 15 minutes. Cool.
4. To make the filling, combine all filling ingredients except the heavy cream and pecans. Bring to a boil.
5. Cook 3–4 minutes, stirring constantly.
6. Add the pecans and heavy cream.
7. Pour pecan mixture into prebaked dough shell, and bake at 350°F until done, approximately 30 minutes.

PLÄTTAR (SWEDISH PANCAKES)
YIELD: 25 servings

24 eggs, separated
6 cups flour
2 tablespoons salt
⅓ cup sugar
1½ quarts milk
9 ounces sour cream
2 teaspoons grated lemon zest
4 tablespoons vanilla extract
4 ounces butter
   powdered sugar, for garnish
2 quarts lingonberries, fresh or canned
1 quart sour cream, for garnish

1. Beat egg yolks until thickened. Beat egg whites until medium stiff and reserve.
2. Combine flour, salt, sugar and sift.
3. Combine egg yolks, milk, and flour mixture.
4. Add sour cream and fold in egg whites.
5. Add batter to hot, lightly buttered plättar pan and cook until golden brown on both sides.
6. Dust with powdered sugar and serve with lingonberries and sour cream.

Note: A plättar pan is a cast iron pan that has 3-inch indentations for the pancakes.

WINE GELÉE WITH FRESH FRUIT
YIELD: 25 servings

2 quarts white wine
2 tablespoons Grand Marnier
10 ounces sugar
24 ounces water
1 ounce unflavored gelatin
4 pounds fresh fruit, cut into bite-size pieces (see note)

1. Combine wine, Grand Marnier, and sugar and heat until sugar melts.
2. Combine gelatin and water and allow gelatin to soften.
3. Add gelatin to wine mixture and heat until gelatin is melted.
4. Pour 1 ounce of wine gelée in a stem glass and chill until set.
5. Arrange fruit on top of gelée and fill with 1 ounce more of liquid wine gelée. Chill until set.
6. Repeat procedure until glass is full.

Note: Do not use papaya, kiwi, figs, or pineapple since these fruits contain an enzyme that dissolves gelatin.

Culinary Terminology

A la broche (ah-lah-broch). Cooked on a skewer

A la mode (ah-lah-mod). In the style of

A la vapeur (ah-lah-vahper). Steamed

A l'etuvée (ah-l'ay-tu-veh). Stewed

A l'huile d'olive (ah-l-weel d'oh-leev). In olive oil

A point (ah-pwah). Medium rare

Aspic (as-pik). Any jellied dish or a jellied glaze

Au gratin (o-gra-tehn). Sprinkled with crumbs and/or cheese and baked until brown

Au jus (o-zhu). Served with natural juice or gravy

Au lait (o-leh). With milk

Au naturel (o-na-tu-rehl). Plainly cooked

Aux champignons (o-shahm-peh-nohn). Cooked with mushrooms

Ballotine (bah-lo-teen). A rolled preparation of boned meat

Beurre (buhr). Butter; beurre fondu, melted butter; beurre noir, butter browned until it is almost black

Bien cuit (bian-kuee). Well done (meats)

Blanchi (blahn-shee). Blanched

Blanquette (blanh-ket). White meat in cream sauce

Bombe (bohmb). Fancy desserts made of ices, whipped cream, and fruit

Bouilli (bu-yeeh). Boiled

Braisé (breh-zeh). Braised: food well browned in a little hot fat, then simmered in a little liquid and cooked, covered, until tender

Brouille (broo-yeh). Scrambled

Café noir (kah-feh-nwar). Black coffee

Chaud (sho). Hot

Chiffonade (shee-foh-nad). Any dish served with shredded vegetables

Coeur (kur). Heart

Concasse (kohn-kass). Tomatoes, peeled, seeded, and coarsely chopped

Confit (kohn-fee). Medium-size pieces of

salted meat (goose, duck, turkey, or pork) simmered in and covered with their melted drippings
Congelée (kohn-je-leh). Frozen
Côtelette (kotlet'). Ground or chopped mixture fried in the shape of a cutlet
Coupe (koop). An ice cream dessert
Court bouillon (kur-bu-yohn). Liquid in which fish has been boiled
Croquante (kro-kant). Crisp
Croustillante (kroos-tee-yant). Crunchy
Cru (kruh). Uncooked, raw
Cuit (kuee). Cooked

Diable (dyah-bleh). Deviled
Duchesse (duh-shes). Potatoes mixed with egg and forced through a pastry tube
Dur (duhr). Hard, tough

En brochette (ahn-broh-shet). Broiled and served on a skewer
En coquille (ahn-ko-ki'ye). In the shell; in shell-shaped ramekins
En gelée (ahn-je-leh). In jelly
En papillote (ahn-pa-piyot). Baked in an oiled paper bag
Epice (e-pees). Spice

Farce (fars). Forcemeat. Stuffing with chopped meat, fish, poultry or nuts, well seasoned
Farci (fahr-see). Stuffed
Fines herbes (feenz-airb). Mixture of herbs, such as minced chives, parsley, and tarragon or thyme
Flambé (flahm-beh). A food served with lighted spirits poured over
Fluide (floo-eed). Fluid
Foie (fwah). Liver
Fond (fohn). Bottom
Fondue au fromage (fohn-duh-o-fro-mahzh). A melted cheese dish
Fournée (furh-neh). Baked
Frappé (fra-peh). Sweetened fruit juices frozen to a mush; iced drink
Fricassée (fri-ka-seh). Braised meats or poultry

Frit (fri). Fried
Froid (frwah). Cold
Fumé (fuh-meh). Smoked

Galantine (gahl-lenh-teen). Boned poultry, game, or meat stuffed and pressed into a symmetrical shape. Usually with truffles. Served cold.
Garni (garh-nee). Garnished
Garniture (garh-nee-tuhr). Garnish
Gateau (ga-toh). Cake
Gelée (je-leh). Jelled
Glace (glas). Ice, ice cream; extract
Glacé (gla-seh). Glazed
Gras (grah). Fat
Grillé (gree-yeh). Grilled or broiled

Haché (ah-sheh). Finely chopped or sliced
Huile (weel). Oil
Huile d'arachide (weel-d'ah-rak-eed). Peanut oil
Huile d'olive (weel-d'oh-leev). Olive oil

Jardinière (zhar-di-niehr). Diced, mixed vegetables
Julienne (zhu-li-en). Match-like strips of meat, vegetables, or cheese

Lyonnaise (lee-on-ez'). Cooked with onions

Macedoine (mah-se-dwahn). Mixture of vegetables or fruits
Miettes (mee-yet). Flakes, bits, or crumbs
Mousse (moos). Light, airy dish, usually containing beaten egg whites or whipped cream, for dessert or main dish; meat, fish, or poultry, finely ground, served in a mold
Moux, molle (moo, moll). Soft

Nappé (nap-pay). Coated thinly with sauce or jelly.

Oeufs (oef'). Eggs

Pain (pehn). Bread
Panaché (pah-nah-shay). Mixed (usually two vegetables)
Pané (pah-neh). Prepared with bread crumbs

Pelé (peh-leh). Peeled
Purée (pur-reh). Mashed

Quenelles (kuh-nell). Dumplings

Ragout (ra-gho). A stew with rich gravy
Raper (ra-peh). To shred or grate
Refroidi (reh-frwah-dee). Chilled
Revenir (reh-veh-nir). To fry lightly without actually cooking
Rillettes (ree-yet). Shredded meat and potted pork, "deviled"
Roti (ro-tee). Roast
Rouleau (ru-loh). Roll of
Roux (ru). A mixture of butter and flour used for thickening soups or sauces

Saignant (seh-nyahn). Rare
Saindoux (sahn-doo). Lard
Sans arêtes (sahnz-aret). Boneless

Sans peau (sahn-po). Skinless
Sauté (so-teh). Fried lightly in a little fat
Sec, seche (sek, sesh). Dry
Soufflé (su-fleh). A baked fluffy main dish or dessert made with milk and egg yolks into which stiffly beaten egg whites are folded
Sucre (soo-cruh). Sugar(ed)

Tarte (tart). Tart or pie
Temper. To increase the temperature of a cold mixture or liquid gradually by slowly stirring in a hot mixture or liquid
Tendre (tahn-druh). Tender
Terrine (teh-reen). Earthenware crock (usually used for foie gras)
Tiede (tyed). Warm
Trop cuit (tro-kuee). Overcooked

Vinaigrette (vee-neh-gret). A marinade or salad sauce of oil, vinegar, pepper, and herbs

Staff

La Brigade de la Cuisine	*The Kitchen Brigade*
Chef	Chef
Sous chef	Assistant head chef
Chefs de partie	Station chefs
Rotisseur	Roasting, frying, grilling
Entremetier	Eggs, vegetables, farinaceous
Potager	Soups
Poissonier	Fish
Saucier	Sauce, stewed, and sautéed
Garde manger	Larder
Chef de froid	Cold buffet
Tournant	Substitute
Communard	Staff canteen
Patissier	Pastry
Chef de glace	Ice cream
Commis	Assistant
Stagiaire	Work study cook
Apprenti	Apprentice
Mise en place	Prepreparation

Utensils

Coteau	Knife
Spatule	Spatula
Spatule en bois	Wooden spatula
Fourchette	Fork
Mandoline	Grater, cutter
Casserole	Pots and pans
Bain marie	Steam table wells
Chinois	Conical sieve (china cup)
Fouet	Whisk
Tamis	Sieve
Etamine	Cheesecloth

Size and shape

Morceau	Piece
Grand(e)	Big
Petit(e)	Small
Julienne	2″ × ¼″ × ¼″
Paysanne	½″ × ½″ × ⅛″
Brunoise	No larger than ⅛″ cube
Des	Dice
Batonnet	1¼″ × ¼″ × ¼″
Mince	Thin
Epais	Thick

RECIPE YIELD CONVERSION CHART

25 Servings	50 Servings	75 Servings	100 Servings	200 Servings
—	—	⅛ oz.	⅛ oz.	¼ oz.
—	—	⅙ oz.	⅙ oz.	⅓ oz.
—	—	⅕ oz.	⅕ oz.	⅖ oz.
—	—	¼ oz.	¼ oz.	½ oz.
—	—	⅓ oz.	⅓ oz.	⅔ oz.
—	¼ oz.	⅜ oz.	½ oz.	1 oz.
—	⅓ oz.	½ oz.	⅔ oz.	1⅓ oz.
—	⅜ oz.	⅝ oz.	¾ oz.	1½ oz.
¼ oz.	½ oz.	¾ oz.	1 oz.	2 oz.
½ oz.	1 oz.	1½ oz.	2 oz.	4 oz.
¾ oz.	1½ oz.	2¼ oz.	3 oz.	6 oz.
1 oz.	2 oz.	3 oz.	4 oz.	8 oz.
2 oz.	4 oz.	6 oz.	8 oz.	1 lb.
3 oz.	6 oz.	9 oz.	12 oz.	1 lb. 8 oz.
4 oz.	8 oz.	12 oz.	1 lb.	2 lb.
5 oz.	10 oz.	15 oz.	1 lb. 4 oz.	2 lb. 8 oz.
6 oz.	12 oz.	1 lb. 2 oz.	1 lb. 8 oz.	3 lb.
7 oz.	14 oz.	1 lb. 5 oz.	1 lb. 12 oz.	3 lb. 8 oz.
8 oz.	1 lb.	1 lb. 8 oz.	2 lb.	4 lb.
9 oz.	1 lb. 2 oz.	1 lb. 11 oz.	2 lb. 4 oz.	4 lb. 8 oz.
10 oz.	1 lb. 4 oz.	1 lb. 14 oz.	2 lb. 8 oz.	5 lb.
11 oz.	1 lb. 6 oz.	2 lb. 1 oz.	2 lb. 12 oz.	5 lb. 8 oz.
12 oz.	1 lb. 8 oz.	2 lb. 4 oz.	3 lb.	6 lb.
13 oz.	1 lb. 10 oz.	2 lb. 7 oz.	3 lb. 4 oz.	6 lb. 8 oz.
14 oz.	1 lb. 12 oz.	2 lb. 10 oz.	3 lb. 8 oz.	7 lb.
15 oz.	1 lb. 14 oz.	2 lb. 13 oz.	3 lb. 12 oz.	7 lb. 8 oz.
1 lb.	2 lb.	3 lb.	4 lb.	8 lb.

This chart can help you convert ingredient quantities when increasing or decreasing a recipe size from 25 to 200 servings. To convert, find the amount under the column for your recipe size, and then read across to the desired recipe size to find the new amount.

For serving yields not on this chart, use the following formula:

1. Divide the desired recipe yield by the original recipe yield. For example, suppose your recipe serves 8 and you wish to increase it to serve 20.

$$\frac{\text{Desired yield (20)}}{\text{Original yield (8)}} = \text{Conversion Factor (2.5)}$$

2. Multiply all original ingredient quantities by the conversion factor to get the new amounts. Original ingredient (8 oz.) × Conversion factor (2.5) = New ingredient amount (20 oz.)

Index